Hitch-hiker'

How to see the Empire before it all falls apart

This book is dedicated to the *Populi Romani;* during the exhaustive hours researching this book I got to know your temples, small towns, and home provinces. I am deeply sorry that the Christians, Muslims, medieval townsfolk (who were too lazy to quarry their own stone), and the mayor of Écija, Spain tore down your Amphitheaters, Temples, Fora and Monuments to hide your cultural identity and build Churches, Castles and most egregiously, a parking lot. You are not forgotten. And to the mayor who built the parking lot...

Espero que tu tumba quede bien pavimentada

[haec pagina meditate est pura]

Introduction

Welcome to Rome, dear traveler. We are not sure how you got here, whether by modified DeLorean, after dinner at a time traveling fine dining establishment, or perhaps dropped off by a friend in an old Police Box.

However, you may have arrived be assured that you are in the most fortunate position to be in possession of this guide. We at the Temporal Tourism Board have long been or perhaps, will have long been dedicated to providing much needed assistance to those who have found themselves out of time[1].

This volume has been compiled to guide you on how to succeed in Ancient Rome without really trying, or at the very least, help you figure out what may happen on the way to the forum.

This guide will cover the breadth of the Rome during the waning years of the Republic as well as the beginnings of the Roman Empire, from 100 B.C.E. until just around 300 C.E. before the capital city was changed from Roma to Byzantium, later named Constantinople. Why they changed it we can't say… people just liked it better that way[2].

Hopefully you are also fortunate enough to have wound up in Southern or Central Europe during this time-period. If your method of temporal displacement is finicky and you ended up in a different geographical location during the same time period, or the correct geographical location in a different time period, you may wish to consider consulting one of our other guides:

- *Hitch-Hiker's Guide to Ancient Mesoamerica: Mayan-dering from Teotihuacan to Tenochtitlán*
- *Hitch-Hiker's Guide to Pre-Columbian North America: Get a good pair of moccasins, no horses 'til 1519*
- *Hitch-Hiker's Guide to Dynastic Imperial China: Get your Hans off of my Qin and Xin*
- *Hitch-Hiker's Guide to Byzantine Rome: Roman through the streets of Byzantium.*

If you find that you are in possession of a guide for the wrong era or region of the world you happen to have found yourself, be sure to send a note to your past self in the future to be sure to purchase and pack the correct guide, so you will have had the correct one today.

We are here to help you get the most out of your temporal excursion.

---

[1] Or at the very least, out of sync with your own time.
[2] It's nobody's business but the Turks'.

You will find within this guide sections detailing everything you should need to know while traversing the many provinces we now know as Ancient Rome. Whether you need to what a reasonable price for a bed at a *tabernae[1]*, or getting directions to the *thermae[2]*, we've got you covered.

Through our visionary "Foresight through Hindsight™" program, we have been able to produce more accurate first editions than our competitors thanks to travelers such as you. If for whatever reason you find that some portion of this guide is inaccurate, unhelpful or would like to make an addendum before your untimely demise so you may avoid it later, we will be happy to investigate and rectify this in an earlier edition.

Your contributions will have been reviewed carefully after publishing, before the book has gone to print and may already appear in the copy you are currently holding. Verify that you have not already contributed in the back of the book before you consider contributing.

Please reach us in the following time periods:
Post 2260 AD:
Offices of the Temporal Tourism Board
P.O. Box ∞-8842
μnicipality of Nova Mediaurbs

Pre-79 AD:
Graffiti in Pompeii is astonishingly well-preserved. It is however, inadvisable to visit Pompeii during or after 79 AD. (See **Chapter VI** for directions to Pompeii)

Post 79 AD:
Caves on the shores of the Dead Sea have been shown to be excellent time capsules. (See **Chapter IX** for directions to Iudaea)

---

[1] *Tabernae,* from which we get the word Tavern. Like a restaurant where you can sleep, but they won't kick you out.
[2] Baths. Think hot, thermal baths.

We are required to give the following notice...

You should have received a copy of the pamphlet *A Responsible Temporal Holiday: Rules and Regulations to avoid existence failure* from the agent who booked your trip. This has been international law since a review of, to quote Supreme Court Justice Lloyd, "A number of shenanigans in the early days of time travel" referring to cases in 1885, 1955, 1985, and 2015[1].

If you, like us, didn't bother to read it either, or perhaps have arrived through a non-regulated method of travel, such as a temporal rift in a space storm. Here is an abbreviated version:

- *The space-time continuum is remarkably stable and self-correcting. Don't worry about it too much, but don't go mucking about willy-nilly.*
- *If you mess up your personal time stream with an existence paradox, you won't be around to be blamed.*
- *Don't tell anyone important about their destinies, as it will more than likely come about in the most cosmically ironic self-fulfilling sort of way. Besides, historical figures are notoriously not-genre-savvy, otherwise they would be here instead of being historical figures, a traveler named Spurinna[2] tried this with Caesar, and we all saw how well that turned out.*
- *Do not attempt to claim credit for inventing a style of music by playing a song for the cousin of the original lyricist.*

---

[1] Not to mention various other temporal hijinks featuring Dan Castellaneta, which may or may not be canon.

[2] Spurinna practiced a type of fortune-telling called *haruspex*, which involved trying to divine the future using animal organs, most importantly the liver. Far more useful than serving it with onions.

Gratias vobis agimus

We would also like to take this opportunity to thank all the hitch-hikers who will have had regaled us with tales of their temporal travels. We already will have stayed[1] up many nights diligently reading your input when we had published this edition.

---

[1] This is called the Future Perfect verb tense. We don't use it in English very often, but trust us, it already will have been a thing.

I When in Rome

Now, this is in fact the question, when in Rome are we? This guide is best suited for the waning years of the Roman Republic, and the early years of the Roman Empire. Approximately 100 B.C.E. to 300 C.E. or DCLVI A.U.C. to MLIII A.U.C. (*Ab urbe condita*, from the founding (of Roma), we feel that's the best time to really get a feel for Roman culture. During this period, you can be *romanced[1]* by the people of Hispania, the sights of Roma, and the history of Achaia.

Prior to that and you're limited mainly to Italia, parts of Africa, Hispania, Achaia and Gallia[2], travel is far more dangerous, and Latin is not nearly as widespread. After that the Roman Empire is divided into the east and west, new barbarian forces intrude into Roman territory with increasing regularity. Additionally, the religion of the Empire, and thus the culture, changes very rapidly and tumultuously with many of the places referenced in this guide being torn down by the new religious order. If you're more interested in these time periods, please see the relevant guides.

Roman territory is safe at various times, we point out many of the times where travel is unsafe in the relevant sections, if a province is going to be attacked by Goths, or a city destroyed by volcanic eruption, we try to give you a heads up. But it is entirely up to you whether you choose to heed or ignore such warnings. The general rule is the further away from Roma you are, the wilder it gets, and the longer a province has been under Roman control, the safer it is (with notable exceptions which have been... well... noted).

This guide is set up as follows: The first few chapters **I – V** give you the basic rules of travelling in the ancient world. After that, there are chapters on Italia, Europa, Africa, Asia and the Mediterranean islands: **VI – X**, the provinces within them are organized loosely by region with a vague path to and between them. For example, you're most likely going to enter Hispania Tarraconensis, then head south through Baetica, west to Lusitania then circling back round towards Gallia via northern Tarraconensis. Feel free to ignore this entirely and go wherever you please, it's your trip, not ours.

In the descriptions of some provinces, we'll get more detailed in explaining where you might things there, saving you from having to ask

---

[1] If you are reading this in an alternate timeline where the empire was named instead for Romulus's brother Remus, please substitute "Remantic" instead.
[2] What will become Italy, Northern Africa (excluding Egypt), Spain, Greece, and France, respectively.

directions to the amphitheater, or the baths. Keep in mind this guide is never complete, explore and talk to the locals, there will have been plenty we missed.

The next chapters **XI - XIII** include some practical knowledge for you, like how to find work, or don a toga. This is followed by some advice written in by ancient travelers.

The last chapters **XIV - XIX** are reference materials, who rules the Empire when, what days festivals are on, and some helpful phrases in Latin and Attic Greek[1]. While they're no substitution for years of language classes, they'll at least help you get around. Some words you will encounter will not be pronounced the way you are accustomed, so you will want to give this section a look.[2]

Each province, or in some cases, group of provinces, has a map where some of the major cities are labeled should you lose your bearings. There are also maps for the *regiones*[3] of Italia and Roma.

Throughout the guide, we'll mention many structures that are common in the Empire. An **amphitheater** is a place where games are held, these are less like backgammon and more like gladiators fighting and beasts being slain. **Theaters** hold performances of a Thespian nature, at some larger ones' playwrights will convene to compete with their tragedies and comedies. Greek theater is a tad more stuffy than Roman stuff.

You can hear musical performances at the local **Odeon**, as well as lyric poetry. The **circus**, or **hippodrome**[4] as they are called in Greek territory, is a place where you can watch horse racing of all sorts. No matter where you go in the world, races are popular and are run regularly.

There are thousands of temples you can visit, from an architectural standpoint you can gawk at the Doric, Corinthian or Ionic column styles, or examine the beautiful statues which adorn them. If you'd like to know which deity is which, then check out **Chapter XVIII**. In general, a **Capitolium** is a temple dedicated to the Capitoline triad, Jupiter, Minerva, and Juno. A **Mithraeum** is an underground temple dedicated to Mithras, who is much beloved by soldiers. A **Nymphaeum** is dedicated to… Nymphs, if you couldn't guess.

The **forum** or **agora** of a city is its primary meeting place, market, and center of everyday life. If you want to buy something, hear the latest rumors, or mingle with the locals, you must stop by here. The **bathhouses**, also known as **thermae**, are another frequent gathering

---

[1] Feel free to use the Greek on any floor of the home, if you like.
[2] Et Cetera, for example, is pronounced "Et Ketera".
[3] Regions. We aren't going to do all of these for you, so you better start thinking about cognates.
[4] They do not, however, ride the hippopotamus. It turns out "hippo" is Greek for horse. I know, we were disappointed too.

place. In addition to getting clean, you can meet with the locals and find out more about the area you're in. You can find a **stadium** (race-track), **palaestra** (workout area), or **gymnasium** (naked-place)[1] often attached to baths.

You will also travel around many of the natural wonders along the various **viae (**roads) which crisscross the empire. You can go for a swim in a freshwater **lacus** or may have to sail across a salty **mare.** Seek safe passage across any **flumen** you might encounter, swiftly flowing water can end with worse than soggy *subligaria.* The many **mons** can offer epic vistas, just stay away from ***Mons Vesuvius*** if it happens to be 79 AD.

A life filled with vagabondary and wandering should be an easy one. Don't forget to relax a little, take plenty of time to go sight-seeing, you're not in too much danger of missing anything until the Christians take over and start destroying anything pagan, make the most of your Roman holiday. Recline while eating, stop in and take quick dip at the baths, listen to some (hopefully good) lyric poetry, join a mystery cult, and don't forget that cardinal piece of advice: *When in Rome...*

---

[1] Would have made your 9th grade gym class more interesting.

II Catching a ride

Travelling is a sport. Much like the chariot races, except instead of speeding out of the gate for the win, your team meanders out, stops often to relieve themselves, and occasionally starts into a trot.

As in any case, travelling has its mythical heroes. Some travelers are fortunate enough to receive a flying wine cup, which carries them across the Mediterranean[1]. Others perhaps a bag of wind which will direct their journey homewards[2]. Still others still will have the opportunity to land upon an island populated only by women. Some guys get to have all the fun.[3]

With any good there is also bad, you may be shipwrecked, robbed, eaten by a sea monster, or turned into a pig. You may be lifted off the ground by a demigod and crushed or tied to trees and flung far off to the horizon. You may end up in a land populated not by women, but man-eating cyclopes, some guys never can catch a break.[4]

If you are in fact, not Aeneas, Jason, or Hercules, you're left with the problem of how to get to where you're going when you can't rely on the gods or fate to bail you out. One day might be a raging whirlpool and a rock dwelling sea monster, the next might be an island of beautiful women, but you cannot rely on luck to make it to where you're headed. All you've got on your side is your wits and the information in this guide. So, let's run down the do's and do not's of ancient travel.

HOW TO LOOK. While travelling through the Empire, there are a few things to bear in mind when it comes to your appearance. For men and women, a simple tunic will achieve the look of 'average Iulius or Iulia' without too much effort.

As a man within any civilized province, you cannot go wrong with a clean shave and trimmed hair. A short beard will give you the look of a working philosopher which may help or hinder you. But the longer and more unkempt your hair and beard are, the more likely you'll be considered the unfashionable fool, or worse, a barbarian[5]. Greek speakers

---

[1] The Sun God Helios gave Hercules this after being shot at by a hot and frustrated Herc in the African desert. Helios is apparently a pretty good sport. Some versions have it as a chariot instead, but we like the idea of a giant flying magic goblet.

[2] King Aeolus is not as genial as Helios. Expect it to contain all the winds except that which sends you straight home.

[3] Consider, however, what happened to all of the men of the Isle of Lemnos. You should be quite cautious should you happen upon such a place.

[4] These are mostly dangers of sailing the Mediterranean. Land is safer.

[5] You will also sound like a barbarian, which is anyone who doesn't speak Latin or Greek,

culturally wear beards, so you can grow out your stubble there with no issues. Also men should avoid wearing pants, it's seen as effeminate[1] unless you're in a colder northern climate.

For women, it's advisable to avoid the wearing of a toga, even if you're trying to *fit in* or *do as the Romans do* as it is a sign you might be a lady of the night. Also hair should be worn off the neck for the same reason. You might also want to forgo the use of make-up, since Roman make-up usually contained lead[2], but if against sound judgement you decide to, check **Chapter XII** for tips on how to apply Roman make-up.

WHAT TO HAVE WITH YOU. Pack light if you're wanting success. No one wants to hook their donkey up to your cart or sacrifice their precious hold space for most of your earthly possessions, your slaves, your wife, and your aged father. A military *sarcina* is the perfect travel pack, and you can probably forgo the packing of the entrenching tools, unless you're planning to participate in a military campaign on the side. If you really want to keep your pack light, you can rely on a good travel cloak and leave any tents at home, you may not stay as dry, but saving your back might be worth it. A full recommended list of what to bring can be found in **Chapter IV.**

WHERE TO STAND. Where one chooses to seek his ride will have a major impact on whether he will succeed in getting one. All of the points so far give one a certain curb appeal when it comes to catching a ride. A clean appearance, small amount of baggage and good road placement will make all the difference. Do not attempt to hitch on the edge of cliffs, or going up a steep surface, as they will be less inclined to help you out if it will be any major inconvenience.

HOW TO CONQUER BOREDOM. While travelling, even with a companion, you're guaranteed to spend a substantial amount of time being extremely bored. Do not despair, however, for there are numerous ways one can pass the time. If you have some papyrus you could try scratching out some poetry or list off all the cities to which you've travelled. You can also sing or talk to yourself if you're truly desperate. If you're not alone, you can always play *micatio,* Latin for flashing, which if you're unfamiliar is played thus:

---

because to them it sounds like "Bar bar bar bar. Bar bar bar bar bar."

[1] Real men wear tunics.

[2] They also used it as a sort of artificial sweetener. Think Sweet 'N' Low but with less damage to your internal organs. It's also in their pipes, in fact the Latin word for Lead, *plumbum,* is where we get the periodic symbol Pb and also the word "Plumbing". So watch out for that.

Both players face each other with one hand a fist, they say *micatio* aloud thrice and then then throw out a number between one and five with their hand, whomever calls out the total sum of both their hands wins the round.

Other travelers often swap stories (fantastic or ordinary) or compete in games like 'who knows the most lines of a poem.' [1]

HOW TO FLAG DOWN A RIDE. First things first, I'd recommend memorizing a few common phrases in Latin or Greek, such as *salve*[2] or χαῖρε[3] which are greetings, and may cause a fellow traveler to perk their ears. You can try waving your arms like a maddened orator, or if you're feeling bold simply leap in front of a donkey cart in hopes they will stop.

If you do get someone to stop for you do not approach them with a weapon drawn, this will only work against you as any well-meaning passerby will likely hurry on from you at this point. Also avoid running at them from the trees, yelling to get their attention, or brandishing a torch in their direction.

When it comes to bartering passage on a vessel, the most persuasive technique is of course using money, the thing that a captain usually wants. They can however, often be bribed with any number of items and may even be sympathetic to a sob story every once and a while.

WHERE YOU'RE HEADED. You can try to write out your destination on a piece of wood or papyrus. However, bear in mind many in this time period are illiterate, so you are simply trying your luck.

HOW TO SPEAK TO STRANGERS: It's unlikely anyone you encounter will know English[4], at the very least it will be quite surprising if they do. But fear not, all you must do is know Latin[5] and you can get by in just about any of the European provinces. For more or less anywhere else in the world you can use Greek, the Attic dialect is pretty common, and should get you started. Punic, Gaulish, and Sanskrit are also helpful, Egyptian isn't too bad once you figure those vowels out. A helpful list of phrases is found in the back of this guide.

If you do find yourself stranded in an area where you do not speak any of the languages, you can always try to communicate using written symbols or mimicry. The locals will either follow along or perhaps just

---

[1] There once was a man from *Lindinis*…
[2] Pronounced Sal-wey, or Sal-oo-eh if you're provincial. From this we get "Salutations"
[3] Pronounced "Khai-rey". Can also be used to say goodbye.
[4] Not any version of it you'd recognize, anyway. Anglo-Saxon used Runes at this time, good luck with that, Futhorc.
[5] Should only take a few months to get good and fluent.

have a good laugh, either way, if they don't kill or enslave you, then you'll be just fine.

WHERE TO STAY. This is a very easy question to answer if the weather is warm and your minimum standard of comfort is low. The areas outside of town are usually rife with available woodlands where you can camp out overnight. If you arrive in town early enough in the day, you can try your luck at the baths. For a *Dupondarius*[1] you'll have the opportunity to mingle with all manner of sweaty Romans who may offer you a free meal, and if properly plied, a bed for the evening.

Do be cautious with your potential hosts, especially if their wife is a known witch[2], which may result in unexpected animal metamorphoses. Or if they are an extravagantly flamboyant freedman, who might throw a dinner party and pre-death funeral for himself, and a party like that tends to drag[3]. Try to be the good guest, avoid bringing any misfortune upon the household, and if it is within your power, be sure to retrieve any spouses from the cold clutches of death[4]. Failing an opportunity to do that, a small token of appreciation will help you establish a reputation as a fine house-guest.

If your luck runs dry at the baths, you may be able to take advantage of an existing source of *hospitium* if you or your family are connected to any of the locals. If you are amongst Greeks, ζένια, *xenia* (guest-host relations), will get you a place to stay with no questions asked, you'll receive a parting gift, but be forewarned, you'll need to offer the same treatment should they ever come to your door in the future.

Sometimes though, you cannot find yourself a host to take you in and for some reason or another, you cannot rough it for the night outside of the town. This is when your turn to a *taberna* or *caupona*[5] to rent a room for the evening. If you're having trouble locating one, start by asking the casual wine drinkers around the nearest *vinaria*.

WHO TO TRAVEL WITH. Travelling alone has many benefits, it's cheaper, you can travel at your own pace, and your destinations are yours and yours alone. But solitude also has its drawbacks, it's more dangerous to travel alone, a partner could know another language, or be familiar with the area in which you're travelling or have family along the route.

---

[1] One-eighth of a *Denarius*, like slipping someone a fiver.
[2] You should also be cautious if she is an unknown witch.
[3] Trimalchio would fit right in with modern lottery winners who don't know what to do with sudden riches.
[4] You might have to fight Death incarnate, though. Don't expect games of chess or Battleship to cheat Thanatos.
[5] Another word for *taberna*.

A man can travel alone or in pairs, a man a woman can travel together, but women should not travel unaccompanied, especially in the provinces. Too many wolves on the lonely highways[1].

If you do have a travelling companion, ensure they are able to hold their own in a fight. Demigods are pretty good companions, they can fight scores of assailants, but they are uncannily drawn to trouble, often drink too much, and occasionally slaughter centaurs.[2]

Try to keep groups small, there should be only two, at the utmost three in any party. Any more than that and people are going to expect you to actually have your own money, and not rely on charity.

READING MILESTONES. A Roman milestone or *Miliarium* are emplaced every thousand Roman paces, hence a Roman mile. They contain a bit of information which varies from stone to stone. Some hold information about the person who placed it, typically an emperor and served to only let you know a mile had passed and how large someone's ego was[3], others inform you which portion of a road you were on, *Viam Aemiliam ab Arimino ad flumen Trebiam* (the Aemilian way from Ariminum to the river Trebia) and some just give you the distance to the next town or city, *a Lugduno milia passuum XVII* (17 miles from Lugdunum). It may benefit you to memorize the major route names between where you're starting and where you're headed.

DATING. Dating conventions in Roman times are unlike today's dates. Years were reckoned on a couple different factors. The Romans use the date based around 753 B.C.E. which was when Roma was founded. Every year is counted up from this, via *Ab urbe condita* (from the city's founding). Around Italia, they also reckoned individual years based on who was consul at the time, i.e. While Caesar and Pompey were consuls. The Greeks, specifically Athenians, reckoned years based on either who was serving as the Ἄρκων at the time, and also by tracking the Olympic Games, which began in the summer of 776 B.C.E. and repeated every four years hence.

TRAVELLING AT NIGHT. Night is the most dangerous time to travel, visibility is low, and the chance of encountering bandits is much higher. You will be unlikely to find anyone else willing to depart from mostly anywhere late in the evening, most people have better sense than to press

---

[1] But not the kindly ones that adopt twin babies who found cities.
[2] Don't let your wife listen to any lies a dying centaur tells you.
[3] Sort of like how the mayor of Chicago is listed on signs entering the city, except there is a lot more that needs to be updated every few years.

their luck as such. If you're outside of town, it's best to settle in somewhere off the beaten path and catch some sleep, keep a low fire if you must.

You should also know that leaving an inn during the middle of the night is considered rather suspicious, and the porter might suspect you of murdering your travelling companion, even if you have not in fact murdered your companion, but a pair of angry witches has done this instead.[1]

AVOIDING UNSAVORY CHARACTERS. On the road you'll encounter all manner of troublesome characters. Bandits, bears, barbarians all haunt the roads once you're far enough out of town. Some bandits will simply rob you and let you on your way, others might attempt to challenge you to a wrestling match or attempt to kick you off a sea cliff.[2] But thanks to the legions constantly on the march, banditry is not as common as it once was, but you still ought to beware.

Wild animals prove a threat as well, lions, tigers and even bears[3] stalk various parts of the Empire. Scores of venomous serpents lie in wait in the hotter regions of the world, scorpions may lurk beneath any stone or bush. And if you believe such tales, fantastic beasts may bring you to your end, such as the *Aeterna,* a beast with saw like horns which Alexander encountered on the plains of India.

The further away you are from Roma, the greater the barbarian presence will be.[4] The majority of the Mediterranean coastal regions have been long tamed, but there is a reason that Hadrian's wall is considered the end of the world.[5] Germania is another region which holds great perils; three legions were lost attempting to hold the province. You can try to avoid anyone who speaks using unfamiliar sounds out of fear, but where is the fun in that?

Just remember that traveling is about the experience, the memories gained by travel. Do not despair about the negatives highlighted here, you must persevere in order to reach the greatest rewards. Just heed the advice given in this guide and you'll be absolutely fine.

---

[1] Also, your friend is not dead yet, but his heart has been replaced by a sponge. He'll be fine so long as he doesn't bend over and let it fall out. He did kind of have it coming… Never bed a witch, if it can be at all avoided.

[2] Sciron: THIS. IS. ATTICA!!!

[3] Wizard of Oz references feel about as old as most of the rest of the literary references in this guide.

[4] You oughta know, Barbarbar.

[5] Because if you've already annexed 90% of Europe, but Scotland is just too cold.

III How much it's going to cost

Traveling during the Roman Empire requires a little money, especially if you're visiting the wealthier provinces. This chapter should provide you with a little context on how much you should be spending, and how to budget accordingly.

How much can you get for your dollar?

at the date of print

Aegyptus	1 Aegypta Drachma	42^{42}
Aethiopia	1 Endubis Coin	21^{26}
Bohaemum	1 Biatec	72^{00}
Carthago	1 Shekel	109^{66}
Gallia	1 Potin	49^{94}
Graeca	1 Drachma	45^{28}
India	1 Hemidrachma	24^{75}
Persia	1 Daric	$1,125^{01}$
Roma	1 Denarius	50^{24}

around DCCXXVII A.U.C. to MLIV A.U.C. (27 B.C.E. to 301 C.E.)

Denarius	1
Quinarius	$^1/_2$
Sestertius	$^1/_4$
Dupondius	$^1/_8$
As[1]	$^1/_{16}$

Please remember, gauging the value of ancient currency is a delightfully frustrating game. A denarius, being one day's wage will buy you plenty, or nothing, depending on what you're trying to buy and when you're trying to buy it.

What it costs
Some other guide books will make bold claims, "*See Rome for V denarii*

---

[1] *As* is pronounced as "Ass". Have fun saying things like "Save your As" or "Deposit your coin in the As hole."

a day," but not everyone is in that financial league or in a time-period where the denarius was nearly worthless. We've prepared example budgets so that you can decide on what sort of trip you want to take and how much money you'll need to bring. We'll cover each below.

UNDER THE STARS. This is the tightest imaginable budget for travelling. Either sleeping under the stars or in a kindly stranger's home or barn.[1] All your food must be purchased and prepared by you; luxuries such as dining out or fine wine are out of reach for one such as yourself. The daily budget is broken down thusly:

Nil	Nothing	Bed
I dup	(6^{30})	Dinner with leftovers for the next day
I dup	(6^{30})	per day or a *quinarius, sestertius* and a *dupondarius,* (44^{10}) a week

To round it off, maybe spend a second *dupondarius* on a flask of wine for when the week gets tough and you get lonely for a total of a single *denarius.* That's just (50^{40}) *a week!*

IN AN INN. If you have a decent amount of money to burn, then this might be the budget for you. In most towns you can find a cheap bed for an *as* or two if you know where to look, but if the weather is permitting, you should consider roughing it to save some cash. Approximately, your costs should be:

I dup	(6^{30})	Bed
I dup	(6^{30})	Dinner
I as	(3^{15})	Breakfast
I ses, I as	(15^{75})	per day or a denarius, dupondarius and an as, (110^{25}) a week

Perhaps splurge on a nicer bottle of wine with a *sestertius* and an *as* to bring your total to II ***denarii*** and I *quinarius* (126^{00}) *per week!*

ALL INN. So you're the one who could pay for whatever you like, but perhaps pretend you're broke. You like your beds soft, your wines fine, your meals prepared for you, and your water clear of any and all fecal matter. There is nothing at all wrong with that, and the following is a perfect budget for you.

---

[1] Or a mean stranger's barn, if he doesn't catch you.

I ses	($12^{60})	Bed
I ses	($12^{60})	Dinner
I dup	($6^{30})	Breakfast
I as	($3^{15})	Bath
I as	($3^{15})	Wine
III ses	($37^{80})	per day or five denarii and sestertius ($264^{60}) a week

Throw in three *sestertii* and do some shopping in the local forum, purchase some company, or commission a local poet to write you a song[1] and your total sits at six *denarii* ($302^{40}) *per week!*

How to get by cheaper
When you're on a tight budget, you're always looking for a way to save some coins. Here are a few tips for you to get your money's worth out of every last *as*.[2]

DIPLOMATA. The uncontested fasted way to get around is using the *cursus publicus,* but the *cursus* requires one to carry a *diploma.* These things are invaluable[3], they can get you a hot meal, a warm bed, and even a horse to get around on.

But the issue is getting one. Typically, you'd need the approval of the Senate, a Governor or an Emperor (After the first century, pretty much only from Emperors) to get one of these bad boys, but there are a couple loopholes in the system.

Now, if you're unwilling or unable to get a Senatorial decree to travel on the people's *dupondarius* or cannot convince the daughter of a governor to marry you so you can abuse the privileges of her father, you might be able to get one in a couple of other ways.

You could always dress as a centurion or equestrian (see Chapter XII), march into town, and demand the benefits of a *diploma* without producing one. Many provincials will provide you with such, and even though this is universally considered to be a *dick move*[4] it will likely work.

You could also try stealing a *diploma* from someone who actually was granted one, chances are, some random nobody in Hispania will not know you're not *Quintus Gaius Flaccus,* because who's he to know? As long as you're dressed well enough and can convince anyone you meet

---

[1] We'd recommend Τυβθυμπιν by Χυμβαϝυμβα.
[2] Don't lose your as, either.
[3] Worth considerably more than one from ITT Tech.
[4] From the Latin DICKVS MOVVS

that you're a different Quintus Gaius Flaccus, try *"scis quid, populi confundunt nos perpetuum!"* (You know what, people confuse us *all the time!*)

Another trick would be to attempt to forge a diploma, we'd recommend looking at a real one first to make sure you get it right. You'll need at least:

I.   The name of the individual issuing the diploma
II.   Your name as the recipient
III.   The act itself of granting rights
IV.   Further specifics
V.   The issued date
VI.   Witnesses

The punishment if caught abusing the system luckily is not too harsh. At worst you may be fined and be required to pay for your extravagant travel, or if the local governor is feeling generous, he may just issue an edict condemning such actions and basically saying "Don't *get caught* doing it *again*!"[1]

CAUPONAE ET TABERNAE. There are a few disadvantages of *cauponae*. First, they are esteemed by most to be only for the lowliest of classes, if this doesn't bother you in the slightest then it's no problem. Second, the conditions are generally considered to be poor, both water and wine are sometimes entirely undrinkable. Third, these motels were often off the beaten path or a ways away from the nearest settlement, and thus were safe-havens for all sorts of scum and villainy.[2]

On the other hand, though, apart from having to pay money, there is no other work required in securing lodgings. You don't need to hang around the baths hoping to catch someone in a generous mood, simply give money to the manager, and take whatever pitiful mattress they offer.

Tabernae are generally a bit nicer and cleaner. They tend to attract less disreputable customers than a *caupona*, but with that comes an obvious increase in expected price.

Guests typically have to pay up front at a *caupona* or *taberna*, but the services rendered are usually pretty cheap, typically not exceeding a *sestertius*, but on average being a *dupondarius* or an *as*.[3]

Any town in the guide listed as a *mansio* is a safe bet to stay. They are official stopping places for Romans on Senatorial or Imperial business.

---

[1] Consider also, many people you meet will also be illiterate. You could show them a takeout menu and if you are confident enough, probably pass it off as a genuine diploma.
[2] We must be cautious.
[3] Drop Your As at Quintus' Caupona!

You can find lodgings here guaranteed.

Warning! Guard your stuff well in a *caupona*. There are plenty of ne'er-do-wells who may try and make off with whatever they can carry. Be sure to bar the doors, Aristomenes, a travelling cheese merchant and frequenter of *cauponae* says pushing your bed in front of the door will not always stop an intruder from breaking in.

POPINAE, THERMOPOLIA, ET VINARIAE. When you're in town, you may have the desire to let someone else do the cooking for you. *Popinae* are small eateries that line the city streets, usually whatever is being served is held heated in jars dropped into the bar. A *thermopolium* is where one can go for a hot beverage, and a *vinaria* is a nice place to have a cup of wine. *Vinariae* often have bits of food available if you're feeling a bit peckish and want a little something to eat. All three establishments are frequented by slaves, sailors, soldiers and the lesser classes. They are a great place to get a feel for the city, ask around for places you may want to see, events that might be coming up, or directions if you're unsure of where to go next.

♦ Be cautious in choosing your dining location, some 'restaurants' known as *ganeae* are hotspots for illicit or immoral activities. Wandering into the wrong one could get some nasty rumors started about you, or if Fortuna does not smile upon you, a knife in your back.

WHERE TO BUY THINGS. While you're on your travels, you will undoubtedly have to acquire new items, which you may have had previously but have now worn through, lost, or had them stolen. You can save a *sestertius* or two by choosing where you make your purchases.

Caligae[1] are a must have if you're going to be doing a tremendous amount of walking, probably the cheapest place you could find them is next to any *castra*[2]. You may be able to convince a soldier or even a *caligarius*[3] to part with a pair for far less than you would from a shoe store in town. Veterans in general may have plenty of useful items to offer you, a military *sarcina* serves as a very fine hiking pack and there will be plenty of surplus at any camp.

Tunicae will be cheapest wherever sheep are shorn, but you can find a *centonarius* who can probably sell you some discount clothing he's patched together. Take note though, that shoddy clothes, while cheap and

---

[1] Sort of a cross between a boot and a sandal, with metal nails in the soles for traction.

[2] Military camp or fort.

[3] Military Shoemaker.

comfortable, will probably not get you any dinner invitations. Cotton clothing, while more expensive, is definitely worth the investment as it is lighter and cooler in the summer, if you're out east you should check the local prices.

There are plenty of ways to save *denarii* during your travels. *Cauponae* and *tabernae* will be full of travelers who may be willing to share a tip or two. But be sure to pass that information on to any others you meet on the road.

IV What to take

When you're travelling, you will surely need a good pack. No matter what you pack, it's going to be too heavy, it's going to hurt your shoulders, and a strap will always break at the most inopportune time. That being said, it's still an absolute necessity.

Some travelers will get by on the barest of necessities, only carrying the clothes on their back, a spare *tunica* and perhaps another pair of *subligaria[1]*. If we however, are travelling for any longer than a couple weeks, ensure we have enough to remain relatively clean and prepared for mostly any situation we might encounter.

We've included two suggested lists, one for men, and the other for women. As with everything else in the guide, it is only advice for you to follow at your own discretion.

The first and most important piece of gear is your pack, we carry, and recommend using a *sarcina,* the standard military pack of Marius' Mules. Now the standard issue pack is a simple *furca* T-frame which is held over the shoulder, typically attached is a *loculus* satchel, *patera* mess kit, *situla* cooking pot, net bag, and cloak bag.

One could do with only carrying a *loculus,* or use a different style of pack, but *sarcinae* are pretty light if you don't need the entrenching tools and are modular enough for any number of situations.

If you're the type to save money by always sleeping outside, you'll need to invest in a good bedroll. A *sagum* military cloak is usually pretty good, especially if it's been waterproofed with lanolin. Leather makes for a heavy and expensive, but durable bedroll which will help keep you separated from the cold ground. Straw serves as a decent form of bedding, but it's obviously unrealistic to carry around with you.

---

[1] Latin for "Under Ligaria"

Suggested list for men
Good pair of *caligae* with hobnails
A pair of *soleae*[1] (for when you're resting up or in town)
II *tunicae*
I *sagum* (doubles as a bedroll or blanket)
III pairs clean *subligaria*[2] (because your mother insists upon it)
  Remember *semper ubi sub ubi*[3]
I pair *udones* (for feet warmth)
III *sudaria* (for wiping the face, drying off, etc.)
I pair *bracae* (pantaloons, for keeping your legs warm in colder climates)
II *ligamenta* (in case you hurt yourself somehow)
A *xylospongium* (unless you'd rather share with everyone at the latrine)
An *ampulla* (for carrying water in)
A *situla* and *patera* (for cooking and eating)
A *funda* (sling for hunting)
Needle and thread
A knife (iron)
Wooden spoon
Wooden or clay cup
A torch
Flint for fire starting (used with your knife)
Reading material

---

[1] Sandals.

[2] We exclusively wear *fructus telae*

[3] *Ubi* means "where"

Suggested list for women
Good pair of *caligae* with hobnails
A pair of *soleae* (for when you're resting up or in town)
II long *tunicae*
I *peplos* shawl
I *sagum* (For use as a bedroll or blanket)
III pairs clean *subligaria*[1] (because your mother insists upon it)
II *strophia* (for under the *tunica*)
I pair *udones* (for feet warmth)
III *sudaria* (for wiping the face, drying off, etc.)
II *ligamenta* (in case you hurt yourself somehow)
A *xylospongium* (unless you'd rather share with everyone at the latrine)
Linen strips to line your *subligaria* (just in case, you know?)
An *ampulla* (for carrying water in)
A *situla* and *patera* (for cooking and eating)
A *funda* (sling for hunting)
Needle and thread
A knife (iron)
Wooden spoon
Wooden or clay cup
A torch
Flint for fire starting (used with your knife)
Reading material

---

[1] Try looking for some at *secretarium Victoriae*

These lists will either be lacking any number of items you'd consider essential or be entirely useless because you know exactly what you're bringing, and no one asked us for advice anyhow.

If you decide that our advice is mostly correct, but we're off somewhere, please feel free to adjust as much as you see fit. You won't hurt our feelings any, we're just trying to help. If you decide to add something you consider essential, perhaps consider something on the list of equal rate to maybe not be essential. When it comes to travel, every pound added equals more pain at the end of the day.

A good rule of thumb is to pack everything, and test the weight, if it's not comfortable, you're wrong. You must not forget during your travels you'll want to pick up a souvenir or ten, and if your pack is nearly full or already heavy at the start of the trip, you'll be in a world of woe once you try and cinch shut your *loculus* over that bust of Cicero you simply couldn't pass up.

V How to *not* die

FOOD. Obviously, your primary concern when it comes to not dying is not starving. The cheapest way to eat is cooking food for yourself. The food is usually pretty cheap if you visit any number of stands in the local forum, keep in mind that the further something has to travel, the less fresh and probably more expensive it will be, so maybe skip the sea-fish you can buy in southern Germania.

If you can hunt, trap, fish or forage, gathering food while you're on the road is a bit easier. But since you'll likely not be lugging around a bow or spears for hunting, maybe just stick to setting up a snare when you go to sleep and maybe you'll have a rabbit for breakfast.[1]

Bread is often the cheapest food you can buy at the market, in a lot of cities it's usually subsidized. Pulses can be soaked overnight and boiled in the morning for a hot and hearty breakfast worthy of any Roman farmer. Some fruits and vegetables are fine to be eaten raw but be sure to wash off any fertilizer that may be left on them. You might want to consider skipping *garum* or salt in favor of much cheaper herbs. Olive oil is the main staple when it comes to cooking, it's not too pricey in small quantities, and available farm fresh.

Do not eat *colocasia* (taro root) raw, as they are slightly toxic uncooked, and you don't want to spend your day with your *xylospongium* in your hand.

If you are truly desperate, you could ask locals if you could work for some food, spending a morning hauling in nets or digging out a boulder so a farmer can plough isn't the worst thing that can happen, so you don't starve to death.

Here are a few meal ideas that will make you feel like Apicius himself.

Boiled asparagus (simply boil with a bit of olive oil)
Bread (dip in olive oil seasoned with herbs if you're feeling fancy)
Chick-peas (soak overnight and then boil with olive oil)
Colocasia (Taro root, par-boil, then roast on a stick[2])
Quail, snake, rabbit, fish (or anything else you can catch, roast on a spit)
Fresh fruit
Salted or dried meats and *buccellatum* (hardtack, shelf stable and travels

---

[1] Nothing like a coney and taters. Boil 'em mash 'em stick 'em in a stew.

[2] Be sure to cook well to break down the needle-like calcium oxilate fibers imbued in the root, which is like eating fiberglass insulation as though it were cotton candy. This stuff really doesn't want to be food.

well)

WATER. Dehydration is a viable threat to your health, as well as water-borne diseases you may contract from unsafe water. The cleanest water for drinking would be rainwater you collect yourself. After that it will come from the aqueducts, which often have sediment filtering to catch most of the water-borne debris.

In smaller villages you can ask around to find the nearest spring, Romans have pretty high standards for sanitation, and wouldn't go drinking from a tainted water source, they are quite weary of stagnant water.

Avoid drinking any water which has been moved through a metal pipe. Roman pipes are often made of lead, and so the water is just on the wrong side of toxic.

Baths, while a great place to socialize are not often cleaned. *Caldaria* in particular breed plenty of bacteria due to their increased temperature. The sick are encouraged to bathe and there is no stigma against bathing with an ill person. They tend to visit the baths in the afternoon, so the best time to visit would be the morning, but that's no guarantee of safety. Bathing etiquette will be covered in **Chapter XII.**

Latrines are another place for both socializing, and contracting illnesses. While the process of using the latrine itself is quite sanitary, and truly genius, the cleaning of oneself leaves much to be desired. Using a *xylospongium,* a simple sponge on a stick, you clean your backside. After use, it's usually 'washed' in a bucket of brine and vinegar before going to the next person. Hence our recommendation to bring your own, and maybe clean it yourself.

SLEEPING. If you're carrying a *sagum* than you can plop down mostly anywhere and get a good night's rest underneath it. The issue comes when the weather is not cooperating. If you're committed to staying outside you probably brought some water-proofed pelts to set up a single man tent. You could either hang it on a line, prop it with some makeshift poles, or if you're truly desperate, just wrap yourself up in it so you stay dry on both your over and undersides.

But if you're caught in a storm and your lack of planning has brought you to be tent-less, then there are a few ways you can stay *somewhat* dry. Somewhat ironically, under an aqueduct is an excellent place to keep the water off you (but probably not the best place to sleep), barns and stables are usually dry, but it's not a good idea to be caught in one if you haven't asked the owner for permission to stay there.

Trees, depending on the type, will block rain fairly well unless it's a torrential downpour. All in all, that can be a pretty miserable night, but if you can pull through it, nothing will stop you. But maybe that will teach you to short Jupiter on a sacrifice.

In a city, you will have no problem getting out of the rain, even if you can't find anywhere to safely sleep. Temples, arches, theaters, pretty much any structure with an overhang will protect you from the rain at least.

GETTING ATTACKED. When you're traveling on your own, there is no denying that you may become the target of a band of brigands. Whether they are highwaymen on the road to Narbo, or a pair of muggers late at night in Roma you've got three basic options: fight, run, or call for help.

Unless you've bothered to bring a sword, you're more than likely outmatched and beaten to a pulp. Even if you're armed, many brigands are former soldiers who will likely have plenty of combat experience. Running is an excellent option, and the one we'd recommend most, try to avoid as little contact with the assailant as possible and get as far away as you can.

If you're cornered and there is nowhere to run, calling for help may yield results; try *Aliquis adiuva me! Adpugnor!* (Somebody help me! I'm being attacked!). Your cries may attract nearby soldiers, the roads are pretty well patrolled, and cities usually have watchmen on the lookout for fire or disorder. You can also just hand over everything you have without a fight. Sometimes it's better to do that and walk away with your life, rather than try and be Hercules.[1]

SHIPWRECKS. It's seemingly unavoidable for any frequenters of the Mediterranean, that you may be shipwrecked, lost at sea, or otherwise marooned. If you wash up on an island and there only seems to be one woman about, she's a witch, and you may be turned into a pig if you haven't been already. (If you have been turned into a pig, see **Chapter XII** for potential methods of breaking curses). If you land somewhere with a flock or herd of animals, they're probably sacred to a god, or owned by a cyclops, don't mess with them.[2] If you're thinking of sailing towards an inexplicably alluring call of some maiden-bird monsters, don't.

ILLNESS. Perhaps an inevitability when you're on the road is that you'll get sick. Luckily, medicine is practiced regularly throughout the Empire, somewhat unluckily, is for every form of medicine ahead of its time,

---

[1] It's usually better to do anything than be Hercules, unless you like mucking out immortal cow stables and holding up the sky, all while your stepmom tries to have you killed.

[2] It is a good idea to shear a sheep and wear its wool if their owner is blind, and also pretty stupid. Also, a good joke alias can help you outwit them. Suggestions: Οὖτις (Owtis, *Nobody*) or ἡ μήτηρ σή (Hey Mayter Sey, *Your Mother*).

there will be a salve[1] made of human breastmilk and flower petals. Some of their herbal treatments are pretty good, some of them are in fact a load of bovine excrement, literally.[2]

Bad doctors will tell you to go make an offering to Aesculapius. A decent doctor will probably offer a couple of treatment options, then recommend you make an offering for good measure afterwards. A great doctor will be well known, and far too expensive for you to afford. Doctors expect money for their services and are unlikely to provide charity work.

♦ If you are anywhere in the Empire between CMXVII-CMXXXIII A.U.C. (165-180 C.E.) or MIV-MXIX A.U.C. (251-266 C.E.) there are Empire spanning plagues of probably smallpox[3], wiping out thousands of people a day. Take extreme precautions. It's best to avoid major cities during this time, maybe sit tight in the rural areas of the Empire, where ever they may be.

---

[1] Strangely, not pronounced Sal-way, they would call it *ungentum*.

[2] Helpful phrase: Does this contain cow crap? *Estne plenum merdae bovis?*

[3] You'd hope that if you had a variola vaccine after the 1800s that you'd probably be safe. You might, but who's to know how much the virus mutated in 60 or so generations of humanity before we learned to kill it. Probably best to play it safe.

VI Italia

What better place is there to start or finish your trek through the Roman empire than in Italia? A land of coasts filled with the fresh sea breeze, hillside vineyards, sprawling cities, robust rivers, and the seat of all things Roman. This chapter divides Italia into the eleven *regiones* set by Augustus and Roma gets a section to herself.

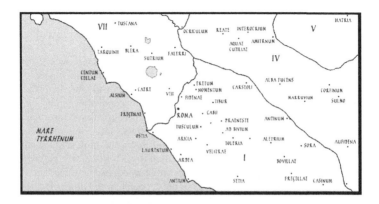

Regio I: Latium et Campania

Latium et Campania is the region Roma occupies, the surrounding area is filled with Latin cities, most of which having histories ancient even during the time of the Romans. Roma herself is included at the end of this chapter in a special section.

The port city of **Ostia** is the primary way of entering or leaving Roma by sea. As the port for the busiest city in the world you can find ships going far and wide here, hitching shouldn't be much of a problem. If prices are too steep or the crew seems unsavory, another will be along in a matter of no time. There are several *horrea*[1] around if you're looking for work, the warehouses are constantly moving goods and looking for strong backs.

In addition to the economic and traveling reasons to visit, the city has several temples including a nice Capitolium in the forum, two temples to Bona Dea, a temple to Hercules, a temple to Vulcan[2], and another to Serapis. The theater is small for such a large city, 3,000 seats, but it is later expanded to 4,000. Beast fights and gladiatorial bouts are also held here. There are over a dozen baths here, the nicest being the Imperial baths off the forum. The city is connected to Roma via the *Via Ostiensis.*

Fidenae is north of Roma on the *Via Salaria.* Do not attend the gladiatorial games here in DCCLXXX A.U.C. (27 C.E.), the shoddy wooden amphitheater collapses and causes the deaths and injuries of thousands. The Sabine city of **Eretum**, was one of those who fought against Aeneas

[1] Not the type of establishment you might think. Those are called *lupanarium* and are concentrated in Regio II of Rome.
[2] Live long and prosper.

when he first settled in Italia. Here the *Via Nomentana* which runs from
Roma through **Nomentum**[1] joins the *Salaria*. The Sabine-Latin city was
captured during the battle of *lacus Regillus* and is praised for the fertility
of its fields.

The city of **Tibur**[2] is found on the thusly named *Via Tiburtina*, which
heads east out of Roma and into Samnium. There are several temples
here, dedicated to Hercules, Sibyl, Vesta and Tosse[3]. **Carseoli**, like Alba
Fucens in Samnium, occasionally hosts state political prisoners.
Columella holds an estate here while he writes his agricultural musings.[4]
The *Tiburtina* also called the *Valeria* here continues into Samnium.

On the *Via Praenestina* to the southeast of Roma is **Gabii**, situated on
lacus Gabinus. The twins Romulus and Remus were raised here before
one of them went on to found Roma. Sextus Tarquinius once lead the
army here in a ruse to gain the trust of the people, before killing their
leadership and causing the city to submit to Roman control. He then fled
there after his attack on Lucretia and was killed for his prior actions. The
city during the Republican era is largely depopulated and used in
metaphors for a place that has fallen from its old heights. Its temple to
Juno sees continual use into the Empire though.

Praeneste at the end of the *Via Praenestina* is a favorite resort town
due to its cool breezes. It's surrounded by the villas of wealthy Romans
who make fun of the locals' accents in line with typical Roman
snobbery. There is a temple to Fortuna Primigena in the forum as well as
a Nymphaeum. There was a battle fought here at the end of the Social
War[5], Marius the Younger was besieged by Sulla and committed suicide
to avoid falling into enemy hands.

On the *Via Latina* south of Roma is **Tusculum**, the first *municipium
cum suffragio* established by Roma. The city is popular amongst the
Roman elite, Cicero has a villa below the city, as well as seventeen other
prominent Romans. The theater is found in town.

The postal station of **Ad Bivium** sits at a departure from the *Via
Latina,* the *Via Labicana*. The town primarily deals in the production of
coal. **Toleria** is a small farming community further down the *Latina*. The
city of **Anagnia**, is used by several Emperors as a vacation spot to avoid
the summer heat in Roma, notably Marcus Aurelius, Septimius Severus,
Commodus[6] and Caracalla. The city also has a rare collection of linen

---

[1] Name TBD.
[2] Part of the infamous Latin League, along with Nomentum. Standings of the XXIV season:
Tibur Tigers, 8 wins, 2 losses, Nomentum Nymphs, 7-2 with one tie.
[3] Tosse worshipers are not known as Tossers.
[4] Real scroll rollers, I tell you what. Couldn't put it down.
[5] And you think that your TwitBookInstaFacePage blows up, you've got nothing on the Social
War.

codices, which contain sacred Etruscan writings.

Aletrium is east of **Anagnia** off of the *Latina,* in thick olive-growing country. There are a few Etruscan era temples here. **Bovillae** is one of the ancestral homes of the *gens Iulia* and after the fall of Alba Longa, the cult of Vesta was transferred here. The city has a few things to do, there is a circus built in honor of Augustus, a temple to Veiovis, a theater and attached acting school.[1]

On the banks of the *Liris flumen,* is the town of **Fregellae**, a place so loyal to Roma, they once burnt the bridges over the river, trapping Hannibal and his army on their side. They did rebel in the late second century B.C.E. and felt the wrath of Roma. If you're feeling under the weather, there is a large temple of Aesculapius here.[2]

The olive oil of **Casinum** is supposed to be of highest quality, we'll let you judge. The city has a nice amphitheater, built using reticulated brickwork, the theater on the hill above it follows the same style. Ummidia Quadratilla, the woman who built the amphitheater and theater has a major passion for theater and the arts, after dying she is honored with an impressive mausoleum. Nearby is Varro's villa, where Mark Antony hosts the occasional orgy.

Much further along the *Via Latina* is **Teanum Sidicinum**, which is noted for its massive theater, one of the largest in Italia, extensive baths and a well-renowned amphitheater. There is a branch road here, which connects the town to **Sinuessa**[3] on the coast.

Capua is most famous for its massive amphitheater, the second largest in the entire Empire, only surpassed by the *Amphitheatrum Flavium* of Roma. There is also one of the first schools of gladiatorial combat here.[4] The city's theater is found on the south side of the *Via Appia,* the primary baths are across the road to the north. The forum has a Capitolium and there is also a temple to Mithras. East of the amphitheater is a temple of Diana on *Mons Tifata,* well known throughout the region.

On the *Via Popilia* south of **Capua** is **Nola**, which is where Augustus died in the same room as his father 72 years prior, thus he is honored here with a splendid temple. There is a spacious amphitheater as well. The road continues around the base of *Mons Vesuvius* to the town of **Nuceria Alfaterna**. It is the chief city of the valley surrounding the *flumen Sarnus,* with the god of the river being especially honored here on

---

[6] From whom we get the Commode.
[1] The student plays here, as student plays always have been, are all about being needlessly rebellious against their parents who pay their way to acting school. No one understands me!
[2] If you are not feeling ill, the temple is still there. It doesn't have a conditional existence.
[3] The salty sea air does wonders for the nasal passages.
[4] They do not do angsty plays here.

their coins.

The city of **Salernum** was originally a military colony, but now is an extensive trading center. The port is quite busy, and you may be able to catch a ride from there. The road continues south in Lucania et Bruttium.

The city of **Aricia** is found on the *Via Appia* south of Roma. The leeks and cabbages here are reputed to be of the highest quality. The woods nearby are sacred to Virbius, and the *lacus Nemorensis* has a temple dedicated to Diana which is shared by many cities in the area. **Velitrae** to the south is where Augustus grew up, you can check out a small pantry like room that is claimed to be his nursery on his grandfather's country estate, and the locals swear he was born here, despite the conflicting reports that we was in fact, born in Roma.[1] There is a small amphitheater here, and temples to Apollo, Sancus, Hercules, Mars, Sol, and Luna.

Setia was supposedly founded by Hercules after he killed a race of giant cannibals there.[2] **Terracina** is where the *Via Appia* and the western coastal road meet. The city has a few things to see and do, the theater is found at the bottom of the hill near the port, the nicer baths are in this vicinity. The theater is north of the Capitolium which is in the forum built by Sulla. A sanctuary to Feronia is found to the northwest.

After Cicero is assassinated near **Formiae** in December of DCCXI A.U.C. (43 B.C.E.), he his buried in a tomb there. **Minturnae** to the east has a nice temple and amphitheater, both built using reticulated brickwork[3], as well as a Capitolium. Nearby, at the mouth of the *Liris* is a grove sacred to the nymph Marica[4]. At **Sinuessa** the *Appia* turns eastwards away from the coast. *Mons Massicus* nearby the city grows grapes and produces wine of great quality. The baths at **Aquae Sinuessanae** are said to treat infertility in women and insanity in men. The *Via Domitiana* begins here, extending as far as **Neapolis.**

Volturnum is where the *Domitiana* crosses the *flumen Vulturnus.* The city regularly tries to shirk its military responsibilities. **Puteoli Cumae** is a busy port, handling all of the imports and exports for the region. There is the third largest amphitheater in all of Italia here. There are a couple markets as well as the forum, a stadium and large baths. Nearby at *lacus Avernus* is a supposed entry to the Underworld. If you're in the area in DCCXC A.U.C. (37 C.E.) you might be able to catch Caligula riding his horse across the gulf of **Baiae**, he'd previously been told that he'd have a better chance of riding across the bay on his horse than he would of being Emperor. So of course, as anyone would, he ordered a massive

---

[1] Still in a closet, just in Roma instead.

[2] Just where you want to found your city. Ancient cannibal grounds.

[3] What is reticulated brickwork? We're not telling. You'll have to see for yourself.

[4] You must say her name three times to honor her properly.

pontoon built and trotted across.[1]

Baiae has several temples to Diana, Mercury and Venus, and is a popular resort town. Nearby **Misenum**, is the base of the *Classis Misenensis,* the most important Roman fleet which protects western Italia and polices the *mare Tyrrhenum.*

The city of **Neapolis** is one of the more popular resorts in Italia. It retains the Greek language and customs for a very long time. The surrounding countryside is filled with private villas. The city itself has a theater and several baths, a temple dedicated to the Dioscuri as well as numerous travel amenities. Claudius and Tiberius often vacation here.

The cities of **Herculaneum** and **Pompeii** are must sees before DCCCXXXII A.U.C. (79 C.E.) as in, you must see them before the streets are flowing with lava. The baths of the former are supposed to be better than those in **Neapolis**.[2] **Pompeii** has an amphitheater and palaestra in the southeastern corner of town, its two theaters are next to the Cardo Maximus on the south end of town. On the west side of town are temples to Venus, Apollo and Jupiter, with the forum east adjacent. There are a few baths around the city, two of the larger ones are found in the center of town.

On the coastal road south of Ostia is **Laurentum**, which is named after the laurel tree. The town of **Ardea** is found further south. Far enough from Roma to avoid the activity of the city is **Antium**, where numerous Romans build villas to get away from Roma and relax.

---

[1] If you can organize that kind of public works project on a dare, you probably deserve to be emperor.

[2] Whether you are talking about Neapolis, Greece or Neapolis, Ohio, this is still true.

Regio II: Apulia et Calabria

Apulia et Calabria is the region occupying the southeast of Italia and its heel. It is bordered by Lucania et Bruttium to the southwest, Latium et Campania to the west, and Samnium to the north. It is a rich region, with fertile fields producing wheat and olives.

Aequum Tuticum is not far from the border of Samnium on a crossroads of the *Via Traiana* and *Via Herculeia.* It was supposedly founded by the Greek hero Diomedes after the fall of Ilium. The *Traiana* turns south at **Aecae** running mostly parallel to the coast. The town turned against the Romans in favor of the Carthagineans during the Second Punic War.[1]

Luceria to the north has a monumental amphitheater, capable of seating 18,000. The city did not fare well during the civil war between Augustus and Marc Antony, but Augustus settled it with a few thousand veterans and began some public works projects. Not too far north is **Larinum**, which has a 12,000 seat amphitheater. During the wars with

---

[1] And you thought your Punic blows up…

Carthago, the Romans defeated Hannibal here; afterwards the city was incorporated into Roman territory.[1]

The city of **Canusium** is a major center for Apulia. It was also founded by Diomedes and named after his dogs. It is situated near the *flumen Aufidus.* There are temples here dedicated to Jupiter and Minerva, and an amphitheater sits at the base of the acropolis. The area surrounding is blanketed by fields if you're looking to stay for the season and make some money as a farmhand.

Caelia and **Barium**, are found near the coast on the *Via Traiana,* the latter is one of the more important ports in the entire region. The fishing industry is strong here, and you can find some work if you need it. The coastal road also joins the *Traiana* here.

Brundisium sits at the end of both the *Traiana* and the *Appia.* A city of over 100,000 people, you'll find it's quite crowded. Near the port are two pillars marking the end of the *Via Appia.* The city has a fine selection of cheeses made from the local flocks that live in the countryside.[2] If you're looking to meet the poet Vergil, do so before DCCXXXV A.U.C. (19 B.C.E.) as he dies here. The port here is renowned, you can easily hitch a ride over to Dyrrhacium in Macedonia or Apollonia in Epirus and the *Via Egnatia* is considered an extension of the *Appia* with the quick jaunt across the *Hadriaticum mare,* being of little difficulty or expense.

To the south, in the heel is **Lupiae**, a major exporter of soft limestone,[3] there is a theater and a 25,000 seat amphitheater here. **Hydruntum**, further south is an important port and technically closer to Apollonia than **Brundisium**, but you'd have to walk further to get here... so it's up to you.[4]

Uxentum and **Callipolis** are found on the west side of the heel, they're nice enough places but there isn't much touristy stuff to do there. They do have plenty of fishing, shepherding, and farming to do though. **Manduria** has a curiosity at its well, its water level never seems to decrease, no matter how much water is drawn from it. Oh, also there is an almond tree growing out of the middle of it.

The town of **Sipontum** has a port and mostly deals in grain, it's found on the coastal road just south of the spur that comes off the eastern coast of Italia.

Further south, the salt marshes around **Salapia** provide much of the salt for the region. Salt mining is fairly lucrative, and is the origin of the word salary, from *salarium* which is the amount of money deducted from

---

[1] Just what you want, a city built on ancient Hannibal grounds.
[2] Well, made from the milk of the local flocks. Cheese isn't *usually* made from entire flocks.
[3] It's like buddah.
[4] Uphill, both ways, mumble grumble.

your paycheck in advance to purchase salt. You'll pass through
Barulum, which was known to the Phoenicians who settled it as the
"land of wine," Not far after **Barulum** the coastal road joins with the
Traiana at **Barium.**

Taking the *Via Appia* from Roma, you can stop at **Aquilonia**, where a
fierce battle once took place between the Romans and the Samnites. The
Samnites, needing men, conscripted all the locals, and any who refused
were executed on the spot, the pile didn't get large before they caught on.
On the Roman side, the soldier responsible for the sacred chicken augury
falsified a good omen and was put forward of the front line to test his
reading of the fates. A spear to the chest determined his outlook had not
been good.[1]

Tarentum sits on the western side of the heel, on the coast of the *mare
Ionium.* Originally a colony founded by virgin-borne Spartan exiles.[2] The
city had two Greek theaters, one to the southwest and another near the
agora. The larger of the two is demolished and replaced with an
amphitheater. There are a couple baths in the city, and temples to
Poseidon, Aphrodite and Pax.

---

[1] To be fair, they would have put him on the front lines if his fortune telling was true. It's kind
of like burning a witch. If she burns, she's a witch. If not... She still burns. Moral: don't run
afowl of bird augury.

[2]. The really confusing ones are the Spartans born of virgin *men.*

Regio III: Lucania et Bruttium

Lucania et Bruttium are found in the southwestern portion of Italia, Lucania in the north and Bruttium occupying the toe. It is bordered by Apulia et Calabria to the northeast, and Latium et Campania to the northwest.

Eburum is a Lucanian city not far from the border of Campania, above the *Via Popilia*. Down on the coast is **Paestum**, a former Greek colony with great temples to Hera, Athena and Poseidon. The city's forum is built over the agora, and a Capitolium is found here. There is also an amphitheater to the northeast of town. Near the temple to Athena is a Heroum dedicated to a local hero, who's heroics will surely be preserved for all time, and needn't be mentioned here.[1]

Grumentum to the east of the village of **Consilinum** off the *Popilia* has one of the few amphitheaters in Lucania. There is also a theater here and a couple small temples. The town of **Buxentum** is one of the few ports on the *sinus Terinaeus,* despite repeated colonization efforts, it struggles to be of any note.

The ancient city of **Consentia** was the capital of the Bruttii, who once defeated Alexander the Great's uncle at the nearby town of **Pandosia**. Under Augustus, **Consentia** becomes an important stopover, so you'll have an easy time finding somewhere to stay here. On the northern coast of the toe is **Vibo Valentia**, it was originally called **Hipponion**[2] by the Greeks who founded it. While the city has a couple temples, it is mostly known for its timber exports and shipwrights. If you're in the market for a boat in Italia, this is the place to go.

Rhegium is a former Greek colony at the tip of the *paeninsula,* it is the cheapest place for you to catch a ride over to Sicilia with sailors crossing regularly. The baths are found near the sea, and the salt air does wonders for the bathers. There is a small odeon[3] in the northeast of town, and a temple to Isis and Serapis.

Not far from **Rhegium** is **Locri** on the southern coast. There are temples here to Zeus, Aphrodite and Persephone. The city's theater is built into a hill and the *cavea* is cut out of the rocks at the hill' base.

On the southern coast east of **Consentia** is the former Greek city of **Crotona**, which is renowned for its school of physicians.[4] The city also boasts two defensible ports and a beautiful marble temple of Hera. The port of **Roscianum**, to the north is capable of accommodating 300 ships

---

[1] This is a tribute to a guy who did a thing…
[2] Literally "Horse Onion", hence the change.
[3] Great kids shows for only 5 asses.
[4] Expect cheap, low quality medical care, like getting your hair cut at the cosmetology school, but an increased risk of being worse off than when you arrived, also like cosmetology school.

at a time, so it may be a good place to look for a ride.

Thurii and **Heraclea** have an interesting history. **Thurii** was originally a colony of Panhellenic nature, when the colonists, many of whom were Athenian, began growing crops in an area where Athens had laid claim to, they started a war, so an exiled Spartan general lead the people of **Thurii** to victory and **Heraclea** was founded as a compromise between the two parties.[1] **Thurii** is called **Copia** for a short while after their defection to Carthage, but that doesn't last for long.

The city of **Metapontum** sits on the coast not far from the border with Apulia et Calabria. The city's period of chief importance was during the Greek occupation of southern Italia, but it has since lost vigor. It does have a theater, built on the remains of its old *ekklesiasterion,* Greek for "old men meeting place." **Potentia** is a ways to the northwest but fails to live up to its potential.[2]

---

[1] Now they just have a bitter basketball rivalry, but the locals REALLY care about it.
[2] Hey, that's my job!

Regio IV: Samnium

Samnium[1] occupies a portion of the eastern coast of Italia and a wide swath of its interior. It is bordered to the south by Apulia et Calabria, to the west by Latium et Campania and to the north by Picenum and Umbria. The *Viae Salaria* and *Tiburtina* run from Roma to the coast through the region. In the early Empire, the *Tiburtina* becomes the *Valeria*. The *Via Appia* crosses the region in its southernmost portion. A coastal road connects it to its northern and southern neighbors, as does its main interior road which follows the base of the *Apenninus Mons.*

Reate is the ancient home of the Sabine people, from which the first men of Roma kidnapped their wives. After the war was settled, the city joined with the Romans. In addition to its rich culture and history, the city has nice public baths. **Aquae Cutiliae** to the east has mineral hot springs providing the water for its baths, the nearby lake also has an interesting phenomenon of floating islands.

The road splits at **Interocrium**, the *Salaria* continuing towards the coast, and the *Via Caecilia*[2] cuts a ways south then runs parallel to the sea. **Amiternum** sits on the *Via Claudia Nova* which connects the *Caecilia* to the *Valeria* in the south. There is a theater and amphitheater for your entertainment needs.

The city of **Alba Fucens** is on the *Via Valeria* not far from when it enters the region. Important state prisoners are often held here, so you should feel secure when within its walls due to increased security. There is a small amphitheater built into the terrain.

Marruvium to the south has been reviewed as most splendid by Pliny and Strabo. Stop by to see what all the fuss is about. The city of **Corfinium** is further along the *Valeria.* It sits near a bridge over the *Aternus flumen,* which gives it great strategic importance if you're planning defenses for an impending invasion. The regions internal southeast running road starts here and runs to **Beneventum.**

The town of **Sulmo** is south off the road a little ways, in addition to its baths, theater and amphitheater, Ovid chose here as the location of his villa, so it must be pretty nice. **Theate** or **Teate** sits on the *Valeria* much further down the road. It's a large city, with several temples, a theater, and amphitheater. It was supposedly founded by Achilles in honor of his mother, Thetis. Because we know that's what every mom wants for Mother's Day, a city.[3] **Aternum** sits on the coast, its most impressive

---

[1] I amnium.

[2] You're breaking my heart/you're shaking my confidence daily…

[3] All six of Achilles's brothers died as infants, but if they'd lived they would only ever hear about how Achilles gave me a town, why can't you be more like Achilles…

building is its temple to Jupiter Aternium. The port is active in trade with provinces to the east, so you may be able to hitch a ride from here.

Anxanum is to the south on the coastal road, it's a busy commercial center, said to have been founded by Solimus, a Trojan refugee.[1] The opulent town of **Histonium** has a nice bath and theater if you're looking to relax. It was reportedly founded by the hero Diomedes.

Aufidena, Aeserina and **Bovianum** are all found along the interior road headed southeast through the province. Each exhibits examples of cyclopean walls if you're an architecture nerd passing through. If you didn't know, this means gigantic boulders of limestone fitted together with minimal spacing and no mortar in between, which obviously could only have been done by cyclopes, and no one else. **Venafrum** is west of **Aeserina**, and boasts a 15,000 seat amphitheater, 3,500 seat theater and odeon. Its olive oil is hands down the best in Italia, and their iron and brickworks are always needing a hand if you're stuck in down.

South of **Bovianum** is **Saepinum**, which has nice temples dedicated to Jupiter and Apollo and a theater. The locals are forbidden from harming shepherds passing through, so if someone menacing approaches, try telling them you're just looking for a lost sheep.

Ligures Baebani was originally founded by a tribe of Gallia from Etruria who were forcibly deported here, but the city became normal Roman city and past hostilities were forgotten with time. The city hosts a large orphanage which serves over a hundred children funded by interest on government loans.

The city of **Caudium** is a popular stopping point on the *Via Appia.* **Beneventum** is a sprawling city, roads span out in all directions from the city. Its main attraction is the 10,000 seat theater, but the main baths are also quite splendid. Trajan also builds a triumphal arch here probably due to his repeated visits.

The city of **Aeclanum** is further south along the *Appia,* the amphitheater here is excellent, and the baths aren't too crowded if you get there earlier in the day. Just south of the city is the *lacus Ampsanctus*, where the primary shrine to Mephitis is found. Travelers often sacrifice animals to her by dropping them into the sulfuric fissures found here.[2]

---

[1] A great place to go if you need *protection*.
[2] Because everyone knows that the best way to improve the smell of sulfur is with animal carcasses.

Regio V: Picenum

Picenum is a region of Italia on the eastern coast, it is surrounded by Umbria et Ager Gallicus to the north and west, and Samnium to the south and west. It is entered either by the *Via Salaria* which comes from Roma to the west, or along the coastal road running roughly north to south.

Entering the province along the coastal road from Umbria brings you to **Ancona**, the main port city of the region. It was originally founded by the Greeks and still has a thriving Greek populace. The most impressive thing here is the triumphal arch erected by Trajan at the entrance to his expansion of the port. Further along the coast is the city of **Potentia**, which has a small theater on the east side of town and baths south of that.

Much to the south and forked off of the coastal road is **Firmum Picenum**. It is the local seat of Roman power having been originally founded as a Latin colony, it has a theater and amphitheater. **Cupra Maritima** is the location of a temple to Cupra, a fertility goddess. **Castrum Truentinum** is a fort-town on the coast and serves as the termination point of the *Via Salaria.* West of **Truentinum** is the city of **Asculum**, which has a Capitolium, theater, amphitheater and temple of Vesta. The city was the site of Pyrrhus of Epirus' epic pyrrhic victory against the Roman forces.[1]

In the far south of the region is the city of **Hatria,** also known as **Atria, Hadria** or **Adria**. Whatever you want to call it, you can find a theater here in town. The city shares its namesake with the Emperor Hadrian, whose family is originally from here.

---

[1] If we win one more battle against the Romans, we will be ruined. -Plutarch

Regio VI: Umbria et Ager Gallicus

Umbria et Ager Gallicus is the region between Picenum and Aemilia, bordered by Etruria to the west. The *Via Flaminia* comes into the region from Roma in the south, crosses the entire southern portion of the province to the coast, and then ends in **Ariminum** before the *Via Aemilia* begins.

The first city in the region on the *Flaminia* is **Ocriculum**, while it is so close to Roma you might as well just go there instead, it does have a small theater and amphitheater, as well as finely decorated baths in which you can relax. **Narnia** is rumored to be ruled over by a talking lion and was once frozen in an unending winter before some children defeat the witch and restore the area.[1]

Further east along the road is **Interamna**, which has a 10,000 seat amphitheater as well as a theater and several temples. The historian Tacitus is born here. Northwest on a branch of the *Via Flaminia* is **Carsulae**, which has a theater and amphitheater as well as mineralized hot baths and the twin temples; it does have a touristy air to it though.

Spoletum is northeast of **Interamna** on the main branch of the *Flaminia,* sporting an amphitheater, theater, Capitolium, and a small temple to Drusus and Germanicus.[2] Martial says the wine here is quite fine, and the Emperor Aemilianus is murdered here while on his way to Roma. **Tuder** lies on the far western side of the region from **Spoletum**, like many other cities it has a theater and amphitheater which are worth checking out if you're passing through. The city-folk claim that the monster Cacus[3] was killed here by Hercules as he was passing through with Geryon's cattle.

Mevania sits on the western branch of the *Via Flaminia* not far from where it rejoins the main route. It has a few temples, a theater and an amphitheater not far outside of town. If you're looking for work as a shepherd, try the pastures near the *flumen Tania,* for cattle rearing, there are herds of white oxen near the *flumen Clitumnus.* **Nuceria Camellana** is nestled on the slopes of the *Mons Apenninus.* The primary export here is wooden barrels used for various purposes.

The road here splits again, heading to Ancona on the coast of Picenum, or continuing through the region. If you take the northeastern fork, you'll pass through the *forulum,* a tunnel dug by the Romans to allow the *Via*

---

[1] It's actually an ancient city in almost the true geographic center if Italy. Wait, why am I doing the facts now?

[2] One of the dozen or so emperors named Julius Caesar, because why be Julius Caesar the IXth when you could be Julius Caesar, victor of the Germanic tribes?

[3] Fire breathing giant son of Vulcan. He did not live long or prosper.

Flaminia to pass through the mountains uninhibited. **Forum Sempronii** with its impressive statue of Vertumnus, the god of seasons.

On the coast is the town of **Fanum Fortunae**, so named for its temple to Fortuna. Just north up the coast, the *Via Flaminia* ends at **Ariminum**, a large port city with an impressive amphitheater in the northeast corner of the city, capable of holding 15,000 spectators. The theater is in the center of town, just off the forum. In this form, Caesar makes his appeal to his legions after crossing the *Rubico* and marching on Roma. As he is crossing the river, he allegedly says: *Alea iacta est,* the die is cast.

Regio VII: Etruria

Etruria is one of the larger *regiones* in Italia, originally the land of the Etruscans, the Romans over time overcame their ancient rival and subsumed them. It is bordered by Latium and Campania to the south, Umbria et Ager Gallicus to the east, Aemilia and Liguria to the north. The *Via Aurelia* runs along the coast through the region, the *Viae Clodia* and *Cassia* through its interior.

During the rules of the Emperors Claudius and Trajan, the **Portus Augusti** is built on the coast at the mouth of the *Tiberis.* You're guaranteed to find a ride out of here. The harbor is massive and artificial, wide arms protrude out from the mainland coming in towards the *pharos* which has a unique origin. Its foundation is made from the hull of the ship used to transport the obelisk from Aegyptus to the Circus Neronis in Roma. The giant vessel is sunk in order to build the lighthouse atop it.[1]

Fregenae is a Roman *colonia* just west of Roma on the coast on the *Via Aurelia.* We'd recommend skipping it, due to its surrounding marshes causing prevalence for disease. The resort town of **Alsium** is found further north, celebrities such as Julius Caesar and Pompey Magnus have vacation homes here. **Caere** is one of the larger cities in southern Etruria. It has six temples, including one to Hera. The last king of Roma was exiled here after the expulsion of the Roman monarchy.

The city of **Centum Cellae** is another resort town, its name comes from the hundred halls of the Imperial villa found here. **Tarquinii** is an ancient city from which the last two kings of Roma came. The city was a center of the Etruscan religion, and its monumental temple can still be seen, the *Ara Reginae.*

Cosa is much further north and sits of the *Aurelia* near where it meets with *Clodia* at **Rusellae.** It has numerous temples, including a Capitolium, Mithraeum under the Curia, and temples to Jupiter, Liber, Concordia and Mater Matuta. There is an odeon here as well, and the port is filled with fishermen if you're looking for work. The locals also produce *garum* here, so beware the smell. The city wanes during the 1st century and is revitalized by Emperor Caracalla.

Rusellae sits on the shores of the *lacus Prelius.* There is an amphitheater, baths and a temple to the Imperial cult here. The city's main exports are timber and grain. There is a port on the *flumen Umbro,* with a temple dedicated to Diana nearby. **Populonium** near the coast is a robust mining and ore processing town dealing mainly in iron and copper. It is one of the few Etruscan cities actually founded on the coast.

---

[1] It's like taking the box a lamp comes in and using it as the endtable to put the lamp on.

The coastal city of **Pisae** is found not far from where the *Viae Aurelia* and *Cassia* meet. It has an amphitheater, theater, baths, and temples to the Imperial cult and Vesta, not one of these structures however, has any sort of tilt to them.[1] **Luna** is another coastal city located a ways after the two *Viae* meet, it has an amphitheater, theater, Capitolium and temple to Diana. The port is busy with the export of fine marble quarried nearby, ships sail frequently to Roma if you're heading south. The road continues northwest along the coast into Liguria.

Veii sits on the *Via Cassia* near Roma and is where the *Via Clodia* begins. It has a celebrated temple dedicated to Juno, with additional sanctuaries to Minerva, Mars and Apollo. There is a theater as well and grand baths built by Augustus. After the loss of the battle of Allia in the 4th century B.C.E., some of the Roman soldiers considered abandoning Roma in favor of **Veii**. Thankfully, 5-time dictator Camillus successfully opposed that plan.[2] **Blera** is a small town, but its people are friendly and it's a nice place to stop and rest.

The city of **Tuscana** further north is busy due to its crossroad locations on the trade route between **Tarquinii** and **Volsinii** and the *Via Clodia*. It was supposedly founded by Ascanius, the son of Aeneas, after he found a litter of twelve puppies there. The road continues to **Rusellae** where it joins with the *Aurelia*.

Sutrium is northeast of **Veii** on the *Via Cassia*. An Etruscan tomb here was converted into a Mithraeum, and the rock-hewn amphitheater is quite striking. The city of **Falerri** is found to the northeast of **Sutrium**. There is an amphitheater and theater, and Juno is chiefly praised. Emperor Gallienus is possibly born here around CMLXXI A.U.C. (218 C.E.) if you'd like to verify and get back to us.

The Roman city of **Volsinii** is on the shores of *lacus Volsiniensis*, the originally Etruscan city was razed by the Romans and relocated to its current position. Voltumna was the chief god of Etruscan **Volsinii**, with the new city favoring Nursia. There is an amphitheater and baths here.

Clusium hosts the remains of the tomb of Lars Porsena, but the tomb was destroyed, along with much of the city by Sulla. **Perusia** to the northeast off the *Via Cassia* has temples to Vulcan and Juno.

To the north on the *Cassia* is **Arretium**, an industrial powerhouse during the early Empire, you can buy bronze and iron tools and weapons here pretty cheap. The wares of the city are exported all across the Empire making way as far as India and Britannia, so you know they're of good quality. The city itself has an amphitheater, theater, several baths, and a few temples.

---

[1] Rimshot.
[2] Good thing, too, or we'd have the Weeian Catholic Church and say lovely things were Weeantic.

Florentia has a beautiful marble paved forum, which is dominated by its Capitolium. There are numerous amenities here, including an amphitheater, theater, two bath complexes, and a temple of Isis. It is surrounded by rich agricultural land, thanks to the *Arnus* river valley.

Pistoriae is near the site where traitor Cataline and his conspirators were slain, the field makes a fine place for a picnic. **Luca**, like **Pisae** is found near where the *Viae Aurelia* and *Cassia* meet, you can find an amphitheater, theater and circus here. This city is where Caesar, Pompey, and Crassus reaffirmed their Triumvirate.

Regio VIII: Aemilia

Aemilia is the region formally known as Gallia Cispadana, it takes its name from the *Via Aemilia* upon which are the majority of its cities. It is bordered by Umbria et Ager Gallicus and Etruria to the south, Venetia et Histria and Transpadana to the north, and Liguria to the west.

Heading northwest along the *Via Aemilia* from Umbria brings you to **Caesena** which has a bathhouse and a few smaller cult centers. You'll pass through the town of **Faventia** before reaching **Bononia**, which has baths, and sanctuaries to all your favorite Egyptian deities. **Mutina** is the best place in the area for anything ceramic you may need, the oil lamps here are of the finest quality. There is also an amphitheater here if you find yourself staying for a little while. In addition to the *Via Aemilia,* a second road intersects here, heading on to Verona in the north.

At the forum in **Regium Lepidi**, you can find fine gold jewelry made by the mixing of Roman and Gallic styles. **Parma** boasts a theater and amphitheater to meet your entertainment needs if you're stuck in town.[1]

The city of **Placentia** sits upon the *flumen Padus,* it has a nice Emporium built when the city was first founded due inaccessibility caused by rampaging Carthaginians. The *Via Aemilia* terminates here. If you come early enough, you can still see the vestiges of the Etruscan religion, especially in the discipline of augury using animal bladders.[2]

---

[1] Great powdered cheese, too.
[2] Better than what the Celts do with them, stuffing them with sausage or turning them into musical instruments. Perverts.

Northeast of **Parma**, also on the *Padus* is **Brixellum**. Just up the coast from Ariminum is the port-city **Ravenna** which, in addition to being a busy port, has its own pharos, a circus, amphitheater, theater, and temples to Apollo, Jupiter, and Neptune.

Regio IX: Liguria

Liguria is found along the northwestern coast of Italia, bordered by Etruria, Transpadana, and Alpes Maritimae to the east, north and west respectively. The main roads going through are the *Via Aurelia* and *Via Postumia,* which later form the principle portions of the *Via Iulia Augusta.*

Entering the region on the *Via Aurelia* brings you to the small fishing and merchant town of **Segesta Tigulliorum**. The city was once an island, but later connected to the mainland, if you're disappointed by this **Segesta**, you probably meant to visit the one in Sicilia, which is much better.

After this is the port-city of **Genua**. There is an amphitheater on the outskirts of town. The city is either named after *genu* (the knee) or Janus, the two faced god of doors.[1] Westwards is **Vada Sabatia**, yet another port. It is difficult to reach as it is found nestled at the meeting points of the *Alpes* and *Mons Apenninus.* The *Via Iulia Augusta* descends from Aemilia and passes through the town before heading westwards.

Album Ingaunum just down the way has an amphitheater and fine baths. This area is safe to travel during the late days of the Republic, as the local tribe signed an agreement to be fully romanced by the Romans.[2] **Album Intemelium** has a theater. The city is probably your last stopping point before entering Alpes Maritimae and continuing west towards Gallia.

North of **Genua** on the *Via Postumia* is **Libarna**, a city located on important crossroads leading into the mountains. In addition to being well fortified and a commercial center, it is well entertained by its theater and amphitheater. There is a large bath complex as well.

Dertona is a fortified river town on the edge of the region. It is one of the more considerable towns in the region with plenty to see and do, during the Imperial era there is usually a garrison here. The road here continues through Aemilia towards Placentia. West of **Libarna** are the renowned hot spring baths of **Aquae Statiellae**, be sure to stop in for a quick dip if you're passing through.

Pollentia,[3] sits near the northwestern edge of the region, it has an amphitheater, theater and temple to Diana. It is well known for its pottery and the quality of its brown wool. A road connects it with Transpadana to the north, and the coast to the south. To the southwest is **Augusta Bagiennorum**, is the capital of the Bagienni tribe. It has an

---

[1] Or Gene, the two-kneed guy from Poughkeepsie.
[2] If you catch our drift. Which is to be incorporated into Roman society.
[3] It's murder on the seasonal allergies.

amphitheater, theater and baths. Both cities are found on the banks of the *flumen Tanarus*. **Ceva** is a town to the south, renowned for its goat's cheese.

Regio X: Venetia et Histria

Venetia et Histria comprise the northeaster portion of Italia. It is bordered by Transpadana to the west, Aemilia to the south, Raetia and Noricum to the north, and Pannonia and Dalmatia to the east.

Cremona is the sister city of Placentia, founded around the same time. The poet Virgil[1] sometimes owns an ancestral farm here when its not confiscated by the Roman state. **Brixia** sits to the far north of **Cremona** at the base of the mountains, there is a Capitolium in the forum, baths and a theater here.

The city of **Bedriacum** lies east of **Cremona** on the *Via Postumia.* Be careful if you're passing through in DCCCXXII A.U.C. (69 C.E.) as the city is the site of two battles between the four claimants to the Imperial throne. (See **Chapter XVII**). The small city of **Mantua** is to the east, off the road, and is the hometown of Vergilius.[2] Further east is the trade hub of **Hostilia** on the *Padus.*

Further along the *Postumia* is **Verona**, which boasts the fourth largest amphitheater in all of Italia behind Capua and Roma seating 25,000 spectators. The city also has a nice theater, and several spas and baths, and a Capitolium. The baths of Iuno in **Calidarium** are well worth a visit for the relaxing dip you'll take.

Just around the curve of the mountain range's base is the city of **Vicentia**, which has a strong wool industry and local marble quarry which attracts lesser known artists and buyers if you're wanting to pick up a bust cheaply before you head home. The road splits here, with the *Postumia* continuing northeast and another road heading north into Raetia. **Patavium** is found to the southeast of **Vicentia** on the banks of the *flumen Medoacus*. It claims to be the oldest city in all of northern Italia founded by the Trojan Antenor. The city has an amphitheater, theater, Capitolium, baths, Mithraeum and is famous for its shrew taming.

The port city of **Atria** is south of **Patavium.** It has a series of lagoons and marshes interlinked by canals known as the *septem maria,* the seven seas, where sailors could test their nautical skills by successfully navigating them. The *Via Annia* begins here, heading through **Patavium** and **Altinum** before ending at **Aquileia**. **Altinum** is an important port city which has baths, the *Via Annia* has high embankments to prevent flooding of the road along this section.

Northeast of **Vicentia** is **Acelum**, which has an amphitheater, theater and baths. The road heads into Raetia just to the north of here. Further

---

[1] Yeah, we spelled it Vergil earlier, what of it?
[2] Maniacal laugh.

south along the *Via* is **Tarvisium**, there is a Quadrivium there.
Opitergium is an important city which, after the completion of the *Via Postumia* swells to over 50,000 residents, but alas fate is cruel and the city is sacked in CMXX A.U.D. (167 C.E.) by the barbarians.

   Iulia Concordia is the place where the *Viae Annia* and *Postumia* meet. At the end of the *Postumia* is **Aquileia**, a bustling city. It has an amphitheater, theater, circus, three bath houses, several temples including a Mithraeum, and synagogues. The metal and glass working shops are great to browse and compare prices. Just like **Opitergium** it is besieged by barbarians in the second century but weathers the attack. It is also held under siege for several months by the Emperor Maximinus Thrax until Thrax gets axed by his own troops.

   Emona sits on the far eastern side of the region, near Pannonia Superior. It was founded long ago by the Argonauts while they were passing through.[1] Currently it is mostly a town of traders and craftsmen.

   Ad Tricesimum is to the north of **Aquileia**. It is an important *mansio* on the road north to Noricum, you shouldn't have any trouble finding lodgings. There is a temple to the Celtic deity Beleno on the hill near the center of town. **Iulium Carnicum** sits just below the entrance to Noricum. It is considered to be the northernmost city in Italia.

   Tergeste sits on the western coast of the *paeninsula Histria* and has its own theater. Further down the coast is **Parentium**, which has temples to Poseidon and Mars on the western side of its forum.

   The city of **Pola** is found on the southern coast of *Histria* and boasts the sixth largest amphitheater in the whole Empire. There are also two theaters here, a large temple dedicated to Roma and Augustus, and a smaller one to Hercules. The villas here have beautiful mosaics, you might be able to sneak a peek if you can convince a wealthy patron to host you for the evening.

---

[1] That's what the Argonauts did, towns springing up behind them like fertile patches of grass behind a cow.

Regio XI: Transpadana

Transpadana is the region beyond the *Padus* in the northwestern corner of the province. It is surrounded to the north and west by the *Alpes* mountains, bordered on the west by the Alpes provinces, and Raetia to the north.

The city of **Ticinum** in the southeastern corner of the region has some of the finest bow makers in all Italia, so it's a must stop for archery enthusiasts. The *Via Regia* starts here heading into the mountains. **Laumellum** is a *mansio* if you're looking for a place to stop and rest. You'll pass through the village of **Cuttiae**, sadly it's only a *mutatio* (horse-changing station) and not a *mansio*, so you're better off moving along. The city of **Industria** lives up to its name. Its craftsmen make fine bronze statues, some of which adorn the sanctuary of Isis just outside of town. The city of **Augustus Taurinorum** sits at the base of the mountains. Inside the city walls you can find a theater. It was originally a Celtic village but was destroyed by the very cold elephants of Hannibal. The current city is built around the *castrum* placed by Caesar. The road continues west from here into the Alpes Cottiae.

To the north of **Cuttiae** is **Vercellae**, which is a nice place to rest and has an amphitheater, theater and circus[1] for your entertainment. Nearby Gaius Marius once defeated a Germanic horde and pushed them from the area. **Eporedia** is a city originally built to help defend Italia from Gallic invasion and probably your last stop before entering Alpes Poeninae, it has an amphitheater and theater. Its name comes from the combination of Epona,[2] the Gallic goddess of horses and *reda,* a kind of wagon. You may be able to hitch a ride on a cart out of here if you're lucky.

The small town of **Novaria** is found east of **Vercellae**, which has finely decorated baths. **Mediolanum** acts as the main road hub for the region, and much of northern Italia in general. The city is renowned for its schools, and has an amphitheater, theater, circus and the famous Baths of Hercules. It will eventually become the capital of the Western Roman Empire. **Comum** is nestled at the foot of the mountains beneath Raetia, it has baths and a library and is the birthplace of both Pliny the Elder and Younger.

---

[1] Now featuring Hannibal's magnificent elephants!

[2] The horses here come when you call if you play an ocarina.

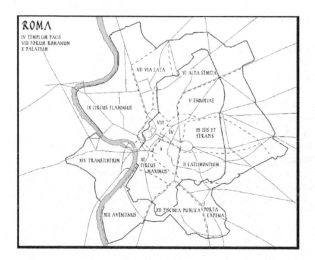

Roma

Roma, the *Urbs Aeterna[1]*, the capital of the world, the city of the seven hills, the place to which all roads lead, the city not built in a day. Roma is divided into XIV *regiones* which start in the southeastern corner of the city and move in a semi-counter-clockwise pattern, with occasional forays into the center of the city.

The Servian Wall was built originally during the last days of the Roman monarchy and maintained throughout the Republican era. By the third century, the Servian Wall had fallen into disuse, prompting the construction of the Aurelian Wall at the end of the 3rd century. Many of the landmarks listed here are destroyed and rebuilt at various times. When visiting, keep in mind that the places given may exist at the time you're present, may have already been destroyed, or may not in fact exist yet.

The periods with the most construction for the city would be during the last few years of the Republic, then under the Emperors Augustus, Trajan and Hadrian, Nero built several things which were toppled by later Emperors out of spite.[2]

---

[1] Latin for Urbs Eternal.

[2] Or were maybe burned by Nero himself. Little man loved fire.

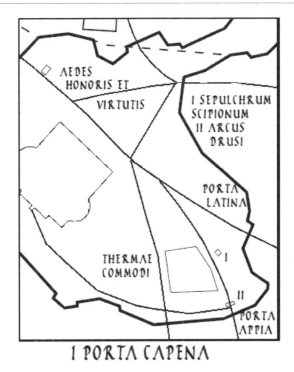

I PORTA CAPENA

Regio I: Porta Capena

Regio I takes its name from the **Porta Capena**[1], where the *Via Appia* runs from the Circus Maximus down to the **Porta Appia**, the road forks into the *Via Latina,* which exits through the **Porta Latina**, and the *Via Ardeatina* which exits through the **Porta Ardeatina**. The region is filled with working class people who frequent the baths beneath the Aventine.

The **Porta Capena** itself is often surrounded by beggars hoping to make a coin off the hard working people who may have a soft spot for those down on their luck. On the north side of the *Appia* is the **Aedes Honoris et Virtutis**, originally honoring Honos alone, Marcellus added the section dedicated to Virtus after his victory in Syracusae. In front of the temple is the **Ara Fortunae Reducis** dedicated to Fortuna Redux after Augustus returns from Asia.

---

[1] In all these instances, Porta means "Gate" or "Doorway", Ancient Rome was not filled with canals. New Rome will not be flooded until 2147.

The **Thermae Commodi** or **Cleandri** serve the people of the region and are just south of the nearby Thermae Caracallae. The baths include a gymnasium. Across the *Appia* from the baths is the **Sepulcrum Scipionum,** where the members of the Scipio family are interred. The **Arcus Drusi** straddles the *Via Appia* south of the baths not far from the **Porta Appia**.

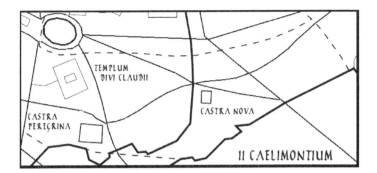

Regio II: Caelimontium

Regio II takes its name from Collis Caelius, the Caelian Hill. It is an area for the fashionable affluent community in Roma. It encompasses the entire hill and stretches eastward stopping just before the Sessorium.

On the hill, just south of the Amphitheatrum Flavium is the **Templum Divi Claudii** it has an entrance on the southside, facing the Palatine Hill. It is damaged during the Great Fire, and partially demolished by Nero before being restored by Vespasian.

If you're looking for a good time, or well, perhaps an o.k. time, there are many *lupanaria* in the region. They are of… questionable cleanliness, the nicer ones can be found in the Subura.[1]

South of the temple is the **Castra Peregrina** where the *frumentarii* are stationed. There is a shrine to Jupiter Redux here. Just off the northern corner is the **Arcus Dolabellae et Silani** built by the two consuls by senatorial decree. To the east, outside of the Servian Wall is the **Castra Nova equitum singularium**, the Imperial cavalry bodyguard is stationed here.

---

[1] There are also some bakeries nearby if you're hungry after.

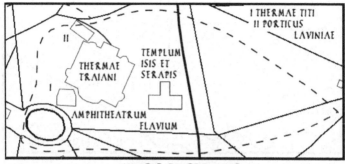

III ISIS ET SERAPIS

Regio III: Isis et Serapis

Regio III is named for its temple of Isis and Serapis. The *Via Labicana* runs along the southern edge of the region, passing through the ancient **Porta Querquetulana** before reaching the Porta Praenestina.

The **Templum Isis et Serapis** is found on the south side of *Oppius Mons,* the Oppian hill. It overlooks the valley between the Oppian and Caelian Hills. During the reign of Nero, much of his Domus Aurea[1] is built here, only to be destroyed and built over by those who followed him. The **Thermae Titi** was one of the earlier of these, with the much larger and grander **Thermae Traiani** helping cover the rubble further. Trajan's baths have a peculiar orientation, designed to reduce wind and increase total sun exposure, the Nymphaeum inside has beautifully decorated mosaics and the gymnasium is quite spacious.

On the northeastern corner of Trajan's baths is the **Porticus Laviniae** which helps served the shopping needs of the people crammed into the Subura at the northwestern base of the hill.

In the southwestern part of the region is the **Amphitheatrum Flavium**,[2] the largest amphitheater ever built by Roman hands.[3] It holds over 50,000 spectators, with regular games, beast fights, and even the occasional naumachia.

Just west of the amphitheater is the **Colossus Neronis** which depicts the Emperor as the sun-god Helios or Apollo and lends to the

---

[1] Nero's Golden House, a lavish palace built over the ruins burned by the Great Fire of Rome. No wonder he was suspected of arson.
[2] This is *the* Colosseum that you think of when you think of Roman colosseums. If you ask about the Colosseum at the time, however, you'll be directed to the Colossus at Rhodes.
[3] Or the hands of people involuntarily employed by the Romans.

amphitheater's later nickname.

To the east of the amphitheater is the **Ludus Magnus** where gladiators are trained in the arts of combat. There is room for a few spectators here and you can watch the men train. The **Ludus Matutinus** nearby is where the beast fighters train, the **Ludus Dacicus** and **Ludus Gallicus** trained gladiators following those particular styles.

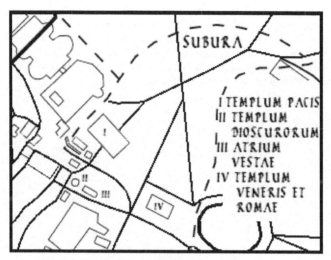

IV TEMPLUM PACIS

Regio IV: Templum Pacis

Regio IV gets its name from the Temple dedicated to Pax just of the Forum. On the wall of the **Templum Pacis** hangs the great *Forma Urbis* which shows the city in much greater detail than we ever will, so be sure to check it out.[1]

Directly southwest of the **Templum Pacis** is the **Forum Piscarium**, if you're craving some fish, just pass the fish markets is the row of **Tabernae Novae** to meet your shopping needs. To the southeast is the **Templum Antonini et Faustinae**. The temple was originally built for the deified wife of Antoninus but was rededicated after his death to the both of them. Across the *Via Sacra* is the **Regia**, which was originally the residence of the Roman kings, but now serves as the residence and office of the Pontifex Maximus. West of the **Regia** is the **Templum Divi Iulii**. The temple was built by Augustus in honor of Caesar after a comet, the *Sidus Iulium,* passed overhead for seven days, conveying that the assassinated dictator was in fact deified.[2]

---

[1] And send us some pictures, preferably not selfies. No offense, but we'd rather see the intact map than 30% Map/70% your vapid duck face.

[2] Rulers being declared living/posthumous gods is sort of a hallmark of polytheism. Since practically everything has a god, it isn't so much a stretch to say emperors become them; it's pretty difficult to contradict. Just be careful not to declare yourself a (or THE) God if you are

Across the *Via Sacra* from the **Templum Divi Iulii** is the circular **Aedes Vestae**, the sacred fire of Vesta burns here and is attended day and night by the Vestal Virgins. Nearby to the east is the **Atrium Vestae** where the Vestal Virgins take residence. West of the Temple is the **Templum Castoris** dedicated to Castor and Pollux, erected out of gratitude for Roman victory at *lacus Regilius*. Between the Temples of Caesar and the Dioscuri is the **Arcus Augustus**, built in honor of his victory over Marcus Antonius and Cleopatra.

On the eastern side of the region, at the end of the *Via Sacra* in front of the Amphitheatrum Flavium is the **Templum Veneris et Romae** dedicated to Venus Felix and the goddess of Roma Aeterna. Be sure not to mock the temple's design in front of Hadrian, it's a good way to get yourself exiled and executed, just ask the architect Apollodorus who finds himself exiled and executed.[1] Just south of the temple is the **Arcus Titi**, built in celebration of his victories in Iudaea.

On the northern side of the region is the **Subura**, a district known for its prostitutes, and extremely cramped living. The slums houses have incredibly cheap rooms to rent if you're ok with the potential threat of being robbed, assaulted or murdered. Also, as previously mentioned the *cleaner*[2] brothels in the city can be found here.

---

not a Roman King, you don't have enough spears to back that up and you might get the cross for that sort of thing.

[1] Well, I guess now you can't.

[2] Whatever that means…

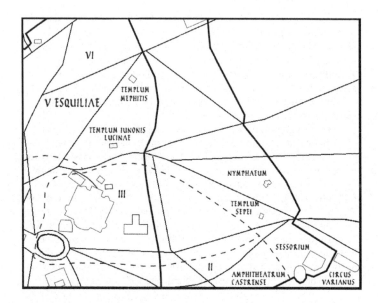

Regio V: Esquiliae

Regio V is named for the *Collis Esquilinus,* around which the region is situated. The *Vicus Longus* acts as the western boundary for the region. It is a fashionable residential district and has several luxury amenities. The **Templum Mephitis** is just south of the *Vicus Patricius.* South of that, on the *Mons Cespius* is the **Aedes Iunonis Lucinae**, where Juno is worshipped as the goddess of women and childbirth.[1]

The Esquiline region is home to several gardens, the **Horti Lolliani**[2] was created from property seized from a witch. Partially inside and outside of the Servian Wall are the **Horti Maecenatiani**, which sprawl out around the **Porta Esquilina**, the gate is also restructured and renamed the **Arcus Gallienus**, the *Viae Tiburtina* and *Labicana* begin here.

---

[1] Elsewhere she is worshipped as the Goddess of getting to a municipal office before it closes, which is helpful but not really one of her primary epithets.
[2] Lollia Paulina was accused of meeting with astrologers and therefore exiled. Witch!

Adjoining the gardens of Maecenas is the **Horti Lamiani** where you can see many fine statues of gods and Emperors and god-Emperors. On the eastern side of the region are the **Horti Liciniani** which has a nymphaeum and definitely does not have the Templum Minervae Medicae but does have a beautiful **Nymphaeum.**

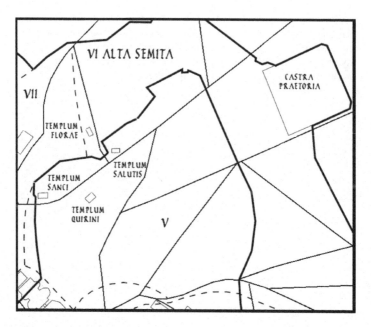

Regio VI: Alta Semita

Regio VI is named for the *Alta Semita* which runs from Campus Martius[1] in the southwest and becoming the *Via Nomentana* as it heads northeast out of the city. The region encompasses much of the *Collis Quirinalis.*

Just inside of the Servian Wall, north of the *Alta Semita* is the **Templum Semonis Sanci Divi Fidii** originally introduced to Roma by the Sabines. On the south side of the street is the **Templum Quirini**, the deified Romulus. The **Templum Salutis** dedicated to Salus is found near the **Porta Salutaris** north of the *Alta Semita.* The road from that porta leads to *Via Salaria Vetera* at the **Porta Turata**.

The northern area is covered with gardens, including the **Horti Sallustiani**, which has a fantastic collection of marble statues. The **Castra Praetoria** where the Imperial bodyguard is garrisoned is at the region's eastern end.

---

[1] The modern city of Detroit, Michigan has a park named after this one, and they pronounce it "Campus Marshes." They are wrong.

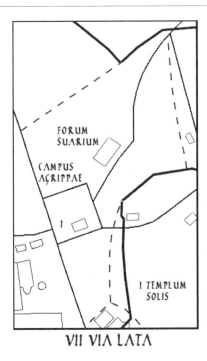

VII VIA LATA

Regio VII: Via Lata

Regio VII takes its name from the *Via Lata,* which is the urban section of the *Via Flaminia.* It encompasses the area of the Campus Martius east of the *Via Lata,* and west of the Quirinal Hill.

The **Campus Agrippae** was built by Agrippa and finished by Augustus. On the western edge there is the **Porticus Vipsania** built by Agrippa's sister. Inside is a map of the Roman world carved in marble, similar to the *Forma Urbis* found at the Templum Pacis. On the southern edge of the campus is the **Templum Solis** dedicated to the sun.

Just northeast of the campus is the **Forum Suarium**, where some little piggies find themselves going to market, while other little piggies stay home. To the north of the forum are the **Horti Lucullani**, which, like many other gardens in the area is filled with marvelous marble men.[1]

---

[1] Great name for a rock band.

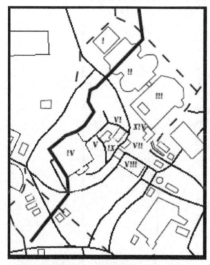

I TEMPLUM TRAIANI
II FORUM TRAIANI
III FORUM AUGUSTI
IV TEMPLUM IOVIS OPTIMI
   MAXIMI
V TABULARIUM
VI TEMPLUM CONCORDIAE
VII ROSTRA NOVA
VIII BASILICA IULIA
IX TEMPLUM SATURNI

VIII FORUM ROMANUM

Regio VIII: Forum Romanum

Regio VIII is named for the **Forum Romanum** which is one of the earliest locations one can find in Roma. Its northern boundary is the **Templum Traiani,** where the deified Emperor is worshipped. Just below that is the **Forum Traiani** which he built. Inside you'll find the **Columna Traiani**[1] as well as is equine statue and a library. The column is covered with images portraying his two successful military campaigns against the Dacians. Alongside the forum to the northeast is a shrine of Libertas.

Southeast of Trajan's Forum is the **Forum Augusti**, where you can find the **Templum Martis Ultoris** built by Augustus. He vowed to build the temple during the battle of Philippi where he brought Brutus to justice. To the south is the **Forum Iulium,** which contains the **Templum Veneris Gentricis**. The temple is built by Caesar and Augustus in honor of the goddess. It burns in the first century but is quickly restored by Domitian. Adjoining the **Forum Augusti**, between it and the Templum

---

[1] Trajan liked to name every banal object after himself. Here are the *vestes Traiani*, and the *xylospongium Traiani*, and the *lectulus Traiani*, and the *Canis Traiani*, and the other *Canis Traiani*, and the other other *Canis Traiani*…

Pacis is the **Forum Nervae**, which contains the **Templum Minervae** due to Nerva's[1] particular fascination with the goddess.

At the base of the *Mons Capitolinus* is the **Rostra Augusta** or **Nova**, replacing the **Rostra Vetera** which was found to the north. The **Curia Iulia** is where the senate meets for official proceedings having replaced the older **Curia Hostilia**.

The **Rostra** is a great place to drop in if you're looking to hear orations of any kind. South of the **Rostra** is the **Templum Saturni**, which holds the treasury during the time of the Republic. Inside is a statue of the god bearing a scythe, his legs are wrapped with strips of wool only removed during Saturnalia.[2]

To the east is the **Basilica Iulia**, the basilica is a popular meeting place for Romans, and you can rub elbows with potential hosts here if it's too late in the day for bath.[3] Between the basilica and Saturn's temple is the **Arcus Tiberi**, built to honor his recovery of lost standards. Southeast of the Basilica is the **Templum Divi Augusti** where the deified First Citizen is worshipped.

At the base of the Capitoline Hill is the **Arcus Septimii Severi**, commemorating his Parthian victories. Just west of the **Rostra** is the **Aedes Concordia**, which acts as the temple for other temples to the goddess throughout the Empire, it sits just below the **Tabularium** where all official records are kept. The **Scalae Gemoniae** are the stairs leading up the Capitoline hill. At the summit of the hill you can find the **Arx** as well as the **Templum Iovis Optimi Maximi**, and the **Saxum Tarpeium**, which you'd do well to avoid being thrown from.[4]

The **Arx** has sentries posted who watch for signal fires from Transtiberim warning of potential attack. The *auguraculum* is found here, where priests conduct the auguries,[5] as well as several temples to Iuno Moneta, Honos and Virtus, and Vediovis. For a short time on the summit you can find the **Arcus Neronis**, but it is demolished shortly after his death by some of the many who hated him.

---

[1] Sort of how W.P. Kinsella, author of the book that *Field of Dreams* was based on, is obsessed with J.D. Salinger's Catcher in the Rye because there is a character named Kinsella in it. For further reading, please don't see Shoeless Joe. That book sucks.

[2] Leg warmers were all the rage in the 0080s.

[3] Dirty Elbows.

[4] *Arx tarpeia Capitoli proxima,* The Tarpean Rock is near the Capitol, a classic reminder that a fall from grace ends with your head being bashed in.

[5] But are *they* witches? Nooooooo!

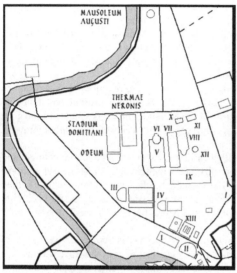

I CIRCUS FLAMINIUS
II THEATRUM MARCELLI
III THEATRUM POMPEII
IV THEATRUM BALBI
V THERMAE AGRIPPAE
VI PANTHEON
VII SAEPTA IULIA
VIII TEMPLUM ISIS ET
    SERAPIS
IX DIRIBITORIUM
X TEMPLUM MATILIDAE
XI TEMPLUM HADRIANI
XII TEMPLUM MINERVA
XIII TEMPLA

IX CIRCUS FLAMINIUS
Regio IX: Circus Flaminius

Regio IX is named for the circus found near its southern edge, which was used for games before the city had a need for a permanent structure for such activities. It encompasses the area of the Campus Martius west of the *Via Lata*. Much of this area is ravaged during the Great Fire but is largely rebuilt by Titus and Domitian.

The **Circus Flaminius** is found near the *flumen Tiberis*. It isn't a circus like many of the others found in Roma or around the Empire, but holds games nonetheless. Just east of the circus is the **Theatrum Marcelli**, to the north are the **Theatra Pompeii** and **Balbi**, both of which have adjoining Portici which serve refreshments between plays.[1]

The **Stadium et Odeum Domitiani** are found north of Pompey's theater. Just to the east of the stadium are the **Thermae Neronis**. Across the street to the east are the **Thermae Agrippae** and the **Pantheum**. These baths were the first public baths constructed in Roma, they include a gymnasium and some of the most groundbreaking artwork at the time of their construction. The temple is dedicated the "all" the gods, but more

---

[1] Just like during the intermissions at my high school plays. Rome has significantly fewer Rice Crispie bars and snickerdoodles loosely wrapped in cellophane and sold by Mrs. Heckenberg.

like "several" gods, but the Romans got a little hyperbolic with their nicknaming. In the courtyard in front of the **Pantheum** is the **Arcus Pietatis**, dedicated to the goddess.

Next to the baths of Agrippa is the **Saepta Iulia** where citizen men can cast their votes, Portici line both sides of the structure. The **Porticus Argonautarum** on the west and the **Porticus Meleagri** on the east. On the eastern side there is an entrance to the **Templum Isis et Serapis** where the Egyptian deities are worshipped.[1]

To the north are the **Templa Hadriani et Matilidae** to the deified Emperor and his also deified wife.[2] South east of Isis and Serapis' temple is the much smaller **Templum Minervae Chalcidicae.** South of the **Saepta Iulia** is the **Diribitorium** which is another voting hall. On the *Via Lata,* not far south of the **Saepta** is the **Arcus Claudius** commissioned after his victories in Britannia.

North of the **Theatrum Marcelli** is the **Porticus Octaviae**, named after the sister of the Emperor Augustus. Inside are the **Templa Iovis Statoris** and **Iunonis Reginae.** Next to the Porticus is the **Templum Apollonis Sosiani**. Directly south, between the circus and the theater is the **Porticus Octavia**, which was rebuilt by Augustus and dedicated to his military victories in Dalmatia.[3] It has been described as the most beautiful off all the Portici.

---

[1] "All" the Egyptian gods.
[2] Goddess of moving things with the mind and getting revenge on evil primary school principals.
[3] Word is he took care of CI Dalmatians.

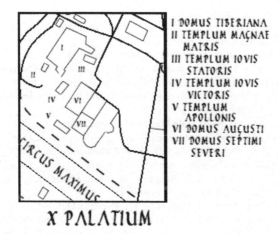

I DOMUS TIBERIANA
II TEMPLUM MAGNAE
   MATRIS
III TEMPLUM IOVIS
    STATORIS
IV TEMPLUM IOVIS
   VICTORIS
V TEMPLUM
  APOLLONIS
VI DOMUS AUGUSTI
VII DOMUS SEPTIMI
    SEVERI

X PALATIUM

Regio X: Palatium

Regio X is named for the *Collis Palatium.* It has long served as the home
of the Emperors.[1] The **Domus Tiberiana** sits on the northwest corner of
the hill, overlooking the Forum Romanum. Southwest of the palace is the
Templum Magnae Matris, dedicated to the foreign goddess Cybele.
East of the **Tiberiana** is the ancient **Templum Iovis Statoris**, not far
from the **Templum Iovis Victoris.**

The **Domus Augusti** is just east of the Jupiter Victor, which is a
neighboring home to the **Domus Septimi Severi**, which undersees much
expansion under later Emperors. On the southern slope of the hill is the
Templum Apollonis built by Augustus, overlooking the Circus
Maximus. At the head of the temple is the **Arcus Octavii** built in honor
of Augustus' father.

---

[1] You need to burn down part of the city to not live here.

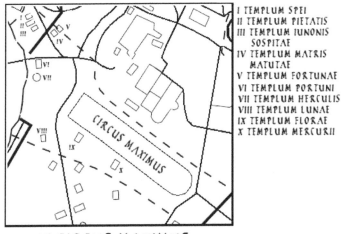

I TEMPLUM SPEI
II TEMPLUM PIETATIS
III TEMPLUM IUNONIS
   SOSPITAE
IV TEMPLUM MATRIS
   MATUTAE
V TEMPLUM FORTUNAE
VI TEMPLUM PORTUNI
VII TEMPLUM HERCULIS
VIII TEMPLUM LUNAE
IX TEMPLUM FLORAE
X TEMPLUM MERCURII

XI CIRCUS MAXIMUS

Regio XI: Circus Maximus

Regio XI takes its name from that greatest of all the circuses, the **Circus Maximus**. The gargantuan hippodrome fits over 150,000 spectators, the circus is packed with shops of every imaginable design[1] and is an incredible fire hazard until refurbished in stone by Trajan. At the eastern end of the circus is the **Arcus Titi**, built in celebration of more of his victories in Iudaea.

The region also includes the **Fora Boarium** and **Holitorium**. The **Templa Spei, Pietatis** and **Iunonis Sospitae** are found at in the **Holitorium**, just south of the Theatrum Marcelli. The **Templa Matris Matutae** and **Fortunae** are found on the northern side of the street, on the other side of the Servian Wall.

---

[1] Seriously, there was a Best Buy kiosk. It sold Papyrus scrolls and Abacai and wanted you to buy their extended service plan (one denarius for one year) in case any of the beads fall off. "I don't want to buy it if it is junk and the beads will fall off." "It's not junk, sir, very high quality, finest Egyptian beads." "Then why do I need the warranty?" "In case they do." "If that's likely, I don't want it." "It won't." "Then why do I need the service plan?"- Ionus Pinnetus.

In the **Forum Boarium**[1] are the **Templa Portuni** and **Herculis**, with the **Templum Lunae** at the south end on the slope of the Aventine. East of the forum is the **Arcus Argentariorum**, which is where the money changers congregate if you're looking to exchange some currency. The **Templum Florae** and **Templum Mercurii** are found just south of the circus, at the bottom of the hill.

---

[1] MooMoo Market

Regio XII: Piscina Publica

Regio XII is named for the **Piscina Publica**[1], a public swimming area found in the southern portion of the region. The boundaries are the *Via Appia* to the north, the *Via Ostiensis* to the west, and the *Via Ardeatina* to the east.

The **Thermae Caracallae** are built over the **Piscina**. Underneath the baths is a **Mithraeum.** The **Templum Bonae Deae**[2] is found on the Aventine Hill, in the part of the region found inside the Servian Wall.

---

[1] Looks like it is called "Public Fish", doesn't it?

[2] Good gods, y'all!

Regio XIII: Aventinus

Regio XIII is named for the *Collis Aventinus,* which is the southernmost of the seven hills. It is a working class area with numerous temples to foreign deities, far too many to list here.[1]

There is a **Templum Iunonis Reginae** on the northern slope, not far from the Forum Boarium,[2] the **Templum Summani** is found nearby to the east. The **Templa Minervae** and **Dianae** sit on opposite sides of the street near the top of the hill.

Near Diana's temple are two **Thermae**, one of Sura and the other of Decius, which serve clientele too wealthy to be bothered with the baths of Caracalla at the bottom of the hill. South of Minerva's temple is the

---

[1] Okay, here's some, since you asked.

[2] A forum for cows, by cows.

Templum Voltumni, which is across from the **Aedes Cereris, Liberi et Liberae**.

Also found on the Aventine is the **Forum Pistorium**, where bakers sell their wares. The constant presence of fresh-baked goods makes the forum smell quite pleasant as opposed to the *Fora Suarium* or *Boarium*.

Just south of the Porta Trigemina is the **Arcus Lentuli et Crispini** built by the consuls as part of a planned restoration project of Augustus. The **Emporium** is the city's main river port, many wares can be bought and sold here cheaply, and you can most definitely find work here if you need it.

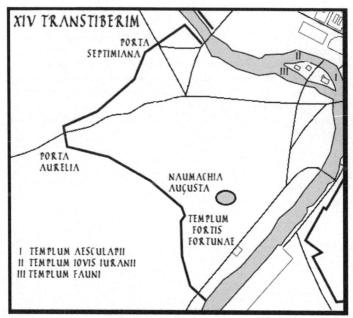

Regio XIV: Transtiberim

Regio XIV is named for the fact that is, well, across the *Tiberis*. It
includes the *insula Tiberina*, and everything west of the river. Most of
the area included in the Aurelian Wall is occupied by villas owned by
some of Roma's wealthier citizens and a few gardens.

On the island are the **Templa Fauni, Sanci** and **Aesculapii,**[1] as well as
numerous other shrines dedicated to various deities.

In the south of the region you'll find the **Naumachia**[2] built by
Augustus, which is sparingly used. And the **Templum Fortis Fortunae**
which is near the **Porta Portuensis.**

---

[1] It's there if you are under the weather, or if you are healthy. It doesn't care.

[2] A place to stage naval battle recreations, which is pretty impractical no matter what your
level of civilization. Augustus surely promised it'd get used all the time, like a pair of roller
blades, too cold to use on Christmas morning and too small to wear by spring.

VII Europa

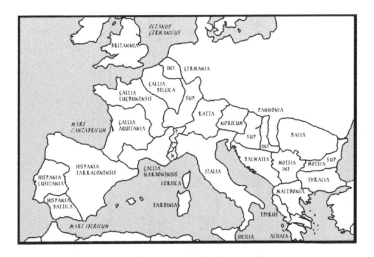

Europa, excluding the former Greek territories entrenched in their Grecian ways, is truly the example of what it means to be in Roman territory. All throughout Gallia and Hispania, roads are maintained, aqueducts flow, and Latin flows off the tongues of provincials, even if they amusingly get it wrong on occasion.[1]

There is something that will appeal to any sort of traveler in Europa. If you like history, the old cities of Achaia, Hispania, and southern Gallia will appeal most to you. Perhaps you'd rather sip an excellent wine from Narbo or try fresh oysters from Britannia; there are plenty of excellent food options anywhere you go. Playwrights, musicians, and mimes[2] can be found in any of the cultural centers across the continent, and amphitheaters and circuses dot the landscape if the games and races are more your interest.

---

[1] Ironically, it is the Catholic Italian monks who probably ruin it the most during the middle ages with their lousy Ecclesiastical pronunciations, giving us gems like "Pachem" and "Etsettera" Ptooey.

[2] We're sorry.

Alpes Maritimae

Size: 3,338 square Roman miles
Capital: Cemenelum
Government: Imperial Province
Religion: Roman, Grecian, Celtic Polytheism
Language: Latin, Gaulish, Greek
Established: DCCXL A.U.C.) (14 B.C.E.)
De-established: MCCXXIX A.U.C. (476 C.E.)

The southern most of the Alpine provinces, Maritimae has one major
route through it, the *Via Iulia Augusta* which follows the coast. The
province only has a handful of cities. During the winter, you'll want to
use this province to bypass the *Alpes,* as the mountain passes are rather
impassable.

   Portus Herculis Monoeci is situated closest to Italia. An ancient town
first used by the Greeks. The only temple in the area is that of Hercules,
thus the name. Caesar stops here on his way to Achaia after subduing
Gallia.

   Cemenelum is the provincial capital and has an amphitheater and baths are on the south side of town. The city is a military garrison securing the pass between Italia and Gallia. So be on your best behavior to avoid trouble with the soldiers.

Nicea is adjacent to **Cemenelum,** but it hasn't much to offer, and you're better off staying in the capital. **Antipolis**[1] is further down the coast and, being well fortified, acts as a gate into Gallia. It is a wealthy town with an amphitheater and theater. There is a thriving port here, trading with its former parent-city, Massalia.

[1] The Un-city.

Alpes Cottiae

Size: 1,898 square Roman miles
Capital: Segusio
Government: Imperial Province
Religion: Roman, Celtic Polytheism
Language: Latin, Gaulish
Established: DCCXXXIX A.U.C.) (15 B.C.E.)
De-established: MCCXXIX A.U.C. (476 C.E.)

The middle of the three Alpine provinces, most of the cities in the province follow a pass through the *Alpes*. Following the *Via Domitia* from Augustus Taurinorum, you'll enter the province and hit the small Celtic village of **Ocelum**, then the town of **Ad Duodecimum**. Eventually you'll reach the city of **Segusio.**

  Segusio is the oldest city in the Alpine region. It has baths, an amphitheater, and a triumphal arch dedicated to Augustus. Travel through the pass is guaranteed thanks to an agreement made by Caesar with the local king. West of **Segusio** you pass through the *mansio* of **Scingomagus**, which is considered the boundary between the Italian and Gaulish sides of the *Alpes*. The castra **Ad Martes Ultor,** which has a temple dedicated to Mars Ultor, is found further west. Next is the castra of **Caesao** and the town of **Durantium**, which is considered the border marker between the Italia and Gallia. *Mons Matronae* is a hill at the end of the pass, the *Via Domitia* begins here. **Brigantium**[1] sits on the edge of the domain of the province. It was originally founded by the Greeks, you can find an amphitheater and a bathhouse here, as well as a place to rest for the evening before heading down out of the mountains.

---

[1] There are about a half-dozen Brigantiums across the empire. It's kind of the Burlington of the Roman World.

Alpes Poeninae

Size: 4,303 square Roman miles
Capital: Octodurum
Government: Imperial Province
Religion: Roman, Celtic Polytheism
Language: Latin, Gaulish
Established: DCCXXXIX A.U.C.) (15 B.C.E.)
De-established: MCCXXIX A.U.C. (476 C.E.)

The province of Alpes Poeninae is the northernmost of the three Alpine provinces, it straddles the strategically important pass of Poeninus. The people living in the region are no strangers to travelers, as they see merchants pass through constantly during the summer months. South of **Octodurum** is a temple to Jupiter Poeninus for whom the region is named. Be cautious if you're here in DCXCVIII A.U.C. (56 B.C.E.) as Galba is busy fighting with the locals here.[1]

You can either enter the region from the north or south of the Poeninus pass, the southern-most city near the pass is **Augusta Praetoria Salassorum,** which is a nice Roman city. It has an amphitheater, forum, baths, a roofed odeon and some temples. There is an arch dedicated to Augustus east of the Porta Praetoria. It may be wise to purchase some cold weather clothing here if you plan to continue north, otherwise you'll be frozen faster than Hannibal's elephants.

Octodurum has a few things to offer other than the obvious rest needed before or after braving the pass. The city has a 6,000 seat amphitheater, mostly for local use. Hot baths (important given how stupidly cold it is), a couple temples and the forum. From here you can head east of the city through the town of **Sedunum** toward Raetia, or north to *lacus Lemannus* in Germania Superior. **Sedunum** and surrounding area is filled with the suburban villas of prominent Roman Gaulish families, the city itself has heated baths.

---

[1] The Romans win, and end up burning the village and leaving town because they were short on supplies and didn't want to keep battling with Gallic raiding parties who didn't want to give up.

Gallia Narbonensis

Size: 36,900 square Roman miles
Capital: Narbo Martius
Government: Senatorial Province
Religion: Roman, Grecian and Celtic Polytheism
Language: Latin, Greek and Gaulish
Established: DCXXXIII A.U.C. (121 B.C.E.)
De-established: MCCXXIII A.U.C. (470 C.E.)

Gallia Narbonensis has a couple of options for entering the province, depending on when you visit. The oldest route is the *Via Domitia,* which crosses the *Alpes,* passes through **Arelate**, **Nemausus,** and **Narbo** before crossing the Pyrenees and joining the *Via Heraclea.*
Augustus commissions the *Via Iulia Augusta* which follows the coast from Italia across the *Alpes,* it forks south, and the spur brings you to

Massalia, the main road continues through **Aquae Sexitae** then ends at
Arelate. The *Via Agrippa* starts north from Arelate and passes through
Avenio, Arausio, Acumum, and **Valentia** on its way to Lugdunum.

If you're coming from Alpes Cottiae, you'll reach the castra
Vapincum. At first the economy is mostly sheep-based, but over time
more settlers arrive from Italia and the town steadily expands. The first
major town you'll run across on the *Domitia* is **Arelate**, the city rises to
prominence after siding with Caesar during the civil war, gaining all the
possessions from nearby **Massalia**, which sided with Pompey. **Arelate** is
a major crossroad town, the *Domitia* continues west from here, the
Agrippa starts here, and later the *Iulia Augusta* connects Placentia to
along the coast. There is a decent sized port, allowing you to hitch a ride
to **Narbo** or towards Italia. The city has an amphitheater, theater, and
circus to visit if you're stuck in town for a couple days. The city also has
an impressive set of water-works including a truly massive water-mill
which is worth a look.

Continuing west on the *Domitia* you'll come to **Nemausus,** which has
the 7th largest amphitheater in the entire Empire.[1] It has a large
Corinthian temple in forum, another temple dedicated to Augustus, a
circus, and a theater. A spring in the north-west corner of the city feeds
the baths and a little pool with a neat nymphaeum set up.

Narbo Martius is the capital and namesake of Narbonensis, it's almost
impossible not to end up here if you're moving through Gallia or
Hispania. **Narbo** is renowned for its rosemary flavored honey, it's worth
the *dupondarius* to get a small taste.

The amphitheater sits on the east side of town, it's surrounded by the
baths, and a market. The forum is located in the middle of town, the *Via
Domitia* acts as the Cardo Maximus for Narbo. There is a triumphal arch
sitting just at the top of the forum. Also in the forum is a Capitolium and
an altar to the Imperial Cult. The provincial seat for the Imperial Cult is
on the east side of town near the amphitheater. Due to its status as a busy
port, the city has a large horreum for storing goods. It's not hard to find a
day or two of work here if you're strapped for *denarii.* The river port of
Narbo has frequent barges heading down the *flumen Atax* to port. Ships
constantly set sail to all parts of the Mediterranean.

If you take the *Via Aquitania* from **Narbo** you'll wind up in **Tolosa**, it
acts as the crossroads between the *flumen Garumna* and the *Aquitania.* It
has baths, theaters, a forum and a small circus. Continue up the road and
you'll enter Gallia Aquitania.

♦ FYI, not a place you want to be speaking Latin[2] in around DCXLV

---

[1] It's on signs on the road into town and everything!

[2] Assuming you've picked it up by now. Or keep barbaring on in English, eventually (in like

A.U.C. (109 B.C.E.), the locals rebel against Roma and kill the local garrison. Try *"ne edhiai mi Ithalia"* (I'm not from Italy).

The second route leading west from Italia is the *Via Iulia Augusta,* which is the primary route to bring you to **Massalia**. Originally a Greek settlement, Massalia is a major trade exchange between Gallia and Italia, slaves come from the north, goods come from the south. The city has large markets, temples to Artemis, Apollo, Leucothea and Cybele. Two of the temples are on the acropolis, and another by the behind the theater on the west side of town. The agora is located just north of the theater. The city loses a tremendous amount of prominence in DCCV A.U.C. (49 B.C.E.) to **Arelate** after siding with Pompey against Caesar.[1] It's a good place to celebrate *Anthesteria* to Dionysus or *Thargelia* to Apollo.

Continue west on the *Iulia Augusta* and you'll reach **Aquae Sexitae**, probably the oldest Roman town in all Transalpina. Sitting right in between **Arelate** and **Massalia**, it's a rather traveler-friendly town. It's got a small amphitheater and natural hot spring baths.

The last major route in Narbonensis is the *Via Agrippa* heading north from **Arelate**. **Avenio** is a former colony of Massalia, which came under Roman rule when Massalia did. There isn't much to do here unless you're just staying the night. **Arausio** is a small town, it has a Triumphal Arch dedicated to Tiberius, a small theater with a very distinct *Scaenae Frons*[2]. **Acumum** is just north of **Arausio** and is a pretty standard town with a small bath house and a forum.

Valentia is fairly close to the border of Lugdunensis. It sits on a crossroads of sorts between the *Agrippa* and the *flumen Rhodanus*. It as a few amenities, including an amphitheater and theater near the river, an odeon, circus, forum, temple to Cybele and a Mithraeum. You can find work at the busy river port.

1300 years) someone will understand you.
[1] Which is why it's no longer around. Just kidding, it's now called Marseille.
[2] This means they have a better backdrop in their theater than a painted bedsheet.

Gallia Aquitania

Size: 66,723 square Roman miles
Capital: Mediolanum Santonum
Government: Imperial Province
Religion: Latin and Celtic Polytheism
Language: Latin, Aquitanian, Gaulish, Celtiberian
Established: DCCXXVII A.U.C. (27 B.C.E.)
De-established: MCCXXIX A.U.C. (476 C.E.)

Aquitania comprises the bulk of western Gallia, there are three primary routes entering the province. The *Via Aquitania* comes from Narbonensis from Narbo and ends at **Burgidala**,[1] the *Via Asturica Burdigalam* from Hispania which also leads to Burdigala, and the *Via Agrippa* west from Lugdunensis, which passes through **Augustoritum** and terminates at **Mediolanum Santonum.** In general, Aquitania is lacking in Roman cultural development, it holds some harsh opposition to Roman ideals and may be best to avoid for the casual hitcher.

Heading up the *Aquitania* from Tolosa you'll pass through a number of small Gallic towns, making your way up the *flumen Garumna* towards **Burdigala.** The locals will be hostile, or ambivalent depending on when you ask. The route faces some instability until the rule of Augustus, and then things become considerably safer. The city of **Burdigala** is important if you're looking to catch a ride into Hispania, up the coast to Lugdunensis or Belgica, or across the sea to Britannia, there is always work to be found, and plenty of places to stay.

West from Lugdunum brings you to **Augustonemetum** also called **Nemausus,** a small city which is rich agriculturally, but not so much culturally. Heading further west, you'll reach **Augustoritum.** The city has a spacious bath with lovely decorations. The theater is south facing, near the river, east of the Cardo Maximus. The city's amphitheater is located on the west side of the city. It is decently sized and has regular games for entertainment. The forum is partially surrounded by a portico, and as per the usual, found in the center of town. Near the river is the temple complex, with sanctuaries to Diana, Venus, Jupiter, and Minerva.

The *Agrippa*'s western branch ends in **Mediolanum Santonum**, the capital of Aquitania. Like **Burdigala**, its importance is linked to its trade. Goods move in and out, and therefore so do travelers. There of course is a forum, amphitheater, baths, temples, and a large arch dedicated to Tiberius.

---

[1] Bring back some wine from this region. People will pay good money for a couple thousand-year-old Bordeaux.

Following the coastal road up from **Mediolanum** leads to **Lemonum,** a flourishing city in the early empire. It has an amphitheater that rivals the one in Nemausus, as well a couple baths, one of which is exquisitely decorated, a temple to Mercury and a couple altars dedicated to multiple deities, a theater and forum.

Next is **Argentomagus,** which has a theater, amphitheater, baths, numerous temples to Venus, Apollo and chiefly Mercury. After this you'll pass through **Avaricum,** the site of an intense siege by Caesar during the Gallic Wars, out of 40,000 inhabitants total, 39,200 were slain under Caesar's wrath.[1] During the Imperial period, it does quite well under Roman rule. After which you'll enter Gallia Lugdunensis.

---

[1] Leaving only 2% of the previous population. They were duodecentimated.

Gallia Lugdunensis

Size: 72,247 square Roman miles
Capital: Lugdunum
Government: Imperial Province
Religion: Latin and Celtic Polytheism
Language: Latin and Gaulish
Established: DCCXXVII A.U.C. (27 B.C.E.)
De-established: MCCXXXIX A.U.C. (486 C.E.)

There are two main routes from the south to enter the province. One is the *Via Agrippa* from Narbonensis, and the other is the road north from Mediolanum Santorum. A few smaller routes approach from the east and north from Germania and Belgica.

Coming north on the *Agrippa* you enter **Vienna.**[1] A small city with a circus and temple to Augusta and Livia. Unless you're too tired to move on, just proceed to **Lugdunum**.

Lugdunum[2] is the provincial capital and a major crossroads for the entire region. Lugdunum has both a theater which seats 4,500 (later 10,070) and an odeon which seats 3,000. They are located close to each other on the west side of town, the odeon situated to the north of the theater. The city has a circus on the west side, a little ways behind the theater and odeon.

There is an impressive amphitheater, but during the early Empire, seats are reserved for Gallic delegates by name. It is found on the tongue[3] of land between the *flumina Arar* and *Rhodanus.* The city has two forums, the old forum is found on the west side, up on the hill overlooking the rivers. The new forum is behind the odeon a little ways to the south.[4] There is a Capitolium and temple to Augustus in the old forum.

There is a temple to Jupiter in the new forum. Behind the theater is a temple to Cybele. There is a temple of Mercury near the new forum, a temple to Diana down near the *Arar,* and a temple to Mars south of the old forum. To the south is Gallia Narbonensis, the west is Gallia Aquitania, and a ways to the north is Germania.

Heading north you'll enter **Cabillonum,** a former Celtic trade hub that has been Romanized. It has an amphitheater, baths, and plenty of places to stay. From here you can head northeast into Germania Inferior, north to **Andematunnum** or northwest to **Augustodunum.**

---

[1] You know it today as… Shoot. What was the joke? …um… Little tinned sausages!
[2] It gets the Lyon's share of the attention.
[3] The theater, not the delegates.
[4] Just like any town with two of the same chain of grocery stores, one is the good one and the other is the "ghetto" one.

Andematunnum has a temple, baths, and theater. It serves as a crossroads for several rivers as well as many of the Celtic villages in the area. The road continues to the northeast into Germania. It might be best to avoid the area around the DCCCXX's A.U.C. (Late 60's C.E.), as there is some turmoil caused by the Imperial turnover between Nero, Galba, Vitellius and Vespasian.

Augustodunum boasts the sixth largest amphitheater in the Empire, and an impressively sized theater as well. It has baths, temples to Janus, Berecyntia, Apollo, Diana, as well as a Capitolium. Augustus built the city out of gratitude for the local tribes who had long supported Roma. He builds a grand city in Gallia and fills it with the many monuments you'll see upon visiting. Heading north you'll come to **Augustobona Tricassium,** strangely enough it's one of the few *Augusto*-anythings that isn't named for the Emperor, it's actually a pretty nice area once the swamps south of the city are drained. It is the last town you'll hit before entering Gallia Belgica.

From the **Augustodunum**, you can proceed southwest, which will turn north bringing you to the river town of **Decetia**, here Caesar one settled a dispute between the local tribes. To the west is Gallia Aquitania and **Cenabum** is found to the north.

The city of **Cenabum**[1] is a typical Roman town, rebuilt after being razed due to a Celtic uprising. It has a theater, forum, and decent port where you may be able to find a ride down the river *Liger* down to the next few towns or walk it if you'd rather save some coin.

The next city west is **Caesarodunum**, which has the fourth largest amphitheater in the Empire.[2] The city also has an expansive Gallic temple and a couple bathhouses.

To the west is the town of **Iuliomagus.** It has an amphitheater, baths and a Mithraeum. You should also check out the local pottery workshops or the bronze-smiths. The road here forks, the southern fork heads to **Condivincum** which has a bath and temple to Mars but lacks any form of major entertainment. From here road turns south and heads into Gallia Aquitania.

The northern fork goes to **Condate Redonum, Fanum Martis, Vorgium** and **Darioritum.** Each town is nice enough; however, they aren't exactly known for their popular attractions. No matter which way you go, you'll have to come back the way you came anyway so it may not be worth the trip.

Heading north from **Cenabum** leads you to **Lutetia,**[3] which has public

---

[1] Cenabum translates roughly to "Hobo Dinner", that thing when you cook potatoes, carrots, and meat in foil on a fire.
[2] Maybe the province is compensating for something?

baths, an amphitheater, and temple to Mars. The city is located on an island in the *flumen Sequana* and has an important river port with a monumental pillar dedicated to Tiberius and several other deities. To the north from here is Gallia Belgica.

Westward is **Rotomagus**, a city of great prominence in the province. It has a large amphitheater, temples to Roth and Venus, and baths. Closer to the coast is **Iuliobona,** which has a 3,000 seat theater, baths, Mithraeum and temple to Apollo. Near the theater you can spot a marvelous gold and bronze statue of Apollo, and the villas surrounding the city are lovely if you can convince the owner to show off and give you a tour.

---

[3] If you have a date in old Lutetia she'll be waiting in Paris, France.

Gallia Belgica

Size: 43,672 square Roman miles
Capital: Durocortorum
Government: Imperial Province
Religion: Roman and Celtic Polytheism
Language: Latin and Gaulish
Established: DCCXXVII A.U.C. (27 B.C.E.)
Conquered: MCCV A.U.C. (452 C.E.)

There are several roads that cross in and out of Gallia Belgica from
neighboring provinces. There are two roads west from Germania
Superior, one west from Germania Inferior, and three north from Gallia
Lugdunensis.

The furthest east route from Lugdunensis and the southern-most route
from Germania both come to **Divodurum Mediomatricorum**, the city
was originally a Gallic town before being conquered by Caesar. Apart
from sitting on crossroads, the city has splendid baths and an
amphitheater. To the north is **Augusta Treverorum** which is a large
city, supporting baths, an amphitheater, theater, circus, and a temple to
Mars and a sanctuary for the local Treveri. North from here leads toward
the province of Germania Superior.

West from **Divodorum** is **Durocortorum**, which is probably too rich
for you. There are numerous temples here, scattered around the forum to
Bacchus, Mars, Ceres and Venus. West of the city center is a large
amphitheater with regular gladiatorial bouts and beast fights. It has
exquisite baths right off the forum. The forum is large and partially
surrounded by a stoa. The citizens are rather wealthy in the area, so price
of goods may be a bit high. The road splits here, going north or west.

You'll pass through **Augusta Suessionum** before reaching
Samarobriva. A large city with baths, a forum and large amphitheater.
The city is frequently raided by local Celtic tribes, to be careful while
traveling in the area. The road here forks again, a route south leads into
Lugdunensis, and a route west to **Gesoriacum.**

Gesoriacum is the base of naval operations in the area, with the
Britannic fleet stationed there. It is the cheapest and safest place to cross
to Britannia, and you should definitely go if you can.[1]

---

[1] Nowadays it's just plain Boulogne.

The road loops back east and hits **Nemetacum** and then **Bagacum.**
According to legend, **Bagacum** was founded by Bavo, cousin of Priam,
after he fled from Ilium, much like Aeneas to Roma.[1] The city has a
double forum,[2] and spacious baths. The road forks again here, one leads
back to **Durocortorum** and the other into Germania Inferior.

---

[1] And when I ran away from home it was just to a cardboard box in the back yard. I could
have founded a city.
[2] Like a super-Wal*Mart.

Britannia

Size: 61,817 square Roman miles
Capital: Camulodunum, Londinium
Government: Imperial Province
Religion: Latin, Celtic Polytheism
Language: Latin, Brittonic
Established: DCCXCVI A.U.C. (43 C.E.)
De-established: MCLXIII A.U.C. (410 C.E.)

Britannia is an island off the northern shores of Gallia. It's a largely wild
and untamed province, short-lived in Roman control and resistant to
much of Roman culture.

   Caledonia, the region north of Hadrian's wall can be written off, the
wall is and should be very well considered to be the end of the world,
stray north at your own risk.[1] The southern coast of the island has several
major ports, two major roads run parallel to the shores north-south.

   The ports of **Rutupiae** and **Portus Dubris** are found along the

---

[1] Have you seen the plaid skirts they wear up there for Heracles's sake?

southeastern shore of the island. **Rutupiae** is the grander of the two, renowned for its quality oysters throughout the Empire. The city also has an amphitheater, baths, *mansio* and several temples. **Dubris** harbored the Classis Britannica and has a couple lighthouses to forewarn sailors. Just up the road inland is **Durovernum Canticorum**, which has a theater, baths, and a brothel.

The **Londinium** is the later capital of the province, it is razed by Boudica in DCCCXIV A.U.C. (61 C.E.) So you may wish to avoid the city at that time unless you're on pretty fantastic terms with the local Icenii. The city bounces back within a decade, growing more rapidly than any other city in Britannia. The city sits on the *flumen Tamesis*. The amphitheater can be found little ways northwest of the forum. The basilica and adjoining forum here, is one of the largest structures built by the Romans north of the Alps. The city has numerous temples dedicated to Jupiter, Isis, Diana, as well as a Mithraeum.

There are a couple bath houses along the river, with another just south of the amphitheater. The city is known for its numerous, clean brothels.[1] Check in at a local taberna for directions. The river port allows for easy boat access to save you some walking if you can afford to book passage.

Camulodunum is the original capital of the province. It is also sacked and razed by Boudica. The city (when not burnt to the ground) has a couple theaters, several Celtic and Roman temples, and the island's only Circus.

The city of **Venta Icenorum**[2] sits northeast of **Camulodunum** on the flatlands, it is the capital of the Icenii tribe and does not fare well after Boudica's rebellion is crushed.

North of **Londinium** is the town of **Verulamium**, the city likewise is razed by Boudica, here there is a bath complex and theater. Much further to the north is the small town of **Venonis**, which is built around the local castra. **Lindum**, named for a nearby pool is located to the northeast. Before it becomes a colonia it is mostly just a small fort town, but after it gains considerable size. It has a forum, baths, and temples to Apollo and Mercury.

There is a ferry crossing across the estuary *Abus* at **Petuaria**. The settlement itself is abandoned not long after its founding, but the ferry continues to operate. Northwest of the estuary is **Eboracum**,[3] a strong military fort in the early days of the province. Over time it expands considerably and eventually will be the capital of the northern of the latter two Britannia provinces. It has baths, a theater, amphitheater, and

---

[1] How many times have you gone to a restaurant or brothel and left just because of the state of their bathrooms?

[2] You can order one of those at Starbucks now.

[3] Even Old, Old York, was once Eboracum.

most importantly in this part of the Empire, fortifications.

On the northeastern edge of the province is **Segedunum.** The eastern most of the fortresses along Hadrian's wall. There is a civilian town surrounding the fortifications. **Coria** is originally a military outpost until the Roman forces fall back from north of the wall. After which, the fort is partially converted to a civilian town with numerous temples and a forum, which is never quite finished.

West of **Coria** is the fort of **Vindolonda**. Here there are reports that a commander named Flavius and his family stationed at the fort have encountered a talking mouse named Minimus. On the western side of the island, along the wall is **Luguvalium.** The city has a Mithraeum and temple to Mars, identified with the local god Belatucadros.[1] There are rumors that a Roman veteran, known as Marcus Aquila travelled north of the wall with a Britannic slave to retrieve the lost standard of the 9th legion. Their success in this endeavor has not yet been confirmed, so if you see them out and about in Caledonia or Britannia let us know.

Heading back south, you pass a *castra* known as **Galacum** before reaching **Deva Victrix**, a fort-town with an amphitheater and baths. Further south is **Viroconium**, a decommissioned fort where you can find a nice forum and baths. **Glevum** is mostly occupied by retired veterans and is heavily Romanized. If you find yourself missing Italia then you'll feel a little more at home here.[2]

Southwest of **Glevum**, you will find the absolute, indisputably finest baths in Britannia at **Aquae Sulis**. If you're in southern Britannia and don't stop in for a dip here, you're genuinely missing out. The road south forms a loop heading back towards **Londinium**, you'll first pass through **Durnovaria**. The road here heads northeast into **Venta Belgarum**, which has a Capitolium and temple to Epona in the forum. **Calleva Atrebatum** sits on the intersection of a couple roads, one heading back towards **Glevum** and the other to **Londinium.** The city has a Capitolium, baths and amphitheater.

---

[1] If you can't beat 'em... say their gods are the same as yours.
[2] Sort of how if you miss old people from the Midwestern United States, you can visit Florida.

Hispania Tarraconensis

Size: 163,398 square Roman miles
Capital: Tarraco
Government: Imperial Province
Religion: Roman, Greek, Celtic, and Phoenician Polytheism
Language: Latin, Greek, Punic, Celtiberian
Established: DCCXXVII A.U.C. (27 B.C.E.)
Conquered: MCCXII A.U.C. (459 C.E.)

The most common land route for entering Hispania Tarraconensis is the
Via Domitia, which generally follows the southern coast of Gaul, through
Narbo Martius and across the Pyrenees. Once across the mountains, the
Via Heraclea, later the *Via Augusta,* which goes through **Tarraco,
Valentia, Carthago Nova,** and then north and west to Corduba. The *Via
ab Asturica Burdigalam* connects the *Via Aquitania* in Gaul to **Asturica
Augusta** in Hispania. The *Via Lusitanorum* heads south from Asturica
into Hispania Lusitania. For what it's worth, some superb olive oil is
manufactured in the region.
    Tarraco is the provincial capital of Hispania Citerior and later
Tarraconensis, captured by the Romans during the Second Punic War by
the Scipiones. It was fortified as a military port and the walls built up.
Augustus, who recuperates here during the Cantabrian and Asturian
Wars.

During this time he makes major improvements to the city, which expands and gains considerable importance. In celebration of Augustus, who is much beloved in the city, a local cult is established to him, first an altar and then an entire temple to *Divus Augustus*. A beautiful temple shared between Jupiter and Europa sits at the top of the city. There are temples to Minerva and Tutela in the city as well. Local cults to Jupiter-Amon and Isis are also found here.

There is truly massive circus in the middle city, just below the temples. With a capacity of 30,000 you'll have no problem getting a seat to watch a few races. There are two forums in the city. The older Colonial Forum in the lower city and newer Provincial in the middle. The theater sits in the lower city, not far from the docks. If the weather is fair you should try and catch a play. The amphitheater of **Tarraco** is equally as impressive as the Circus, holding at least 15,000 entertainers. Stop in if there are games going on and you'll be surely entertained. The town has a large bathing complex, complete with all amenities. In upper city is the Palace of Augustus, used while he was recovering during the Cantabrian and Asturian campaigns.

West of **Tarraco** is the city of **Ilerda** where you can cross the *flumen Sicoris*. The silver mining town of **Osca** is further along the road, there is a school here founded by Sertorius meant to teach the local Iberians about Latin and Roman culture, so stop in if your Latin is a little rusty.

Caesaraugusta is not far south of **Osca** on the *flumen Iber,* it is a military veteran colony founded by Augustus and has a theater that's quite nice.[1] **Clunia** sits to the west of **Caesaraugusta** it has a theater, baths and large forum. The road continues westward towards **Asturica** through **Pallantia**.

In the middle of all of Hispania is the town of **Toletum**, it's a small but well-fortified town. It has one of the largest Circuses in Hispania despite its relatively small size as a town.[2]

A ways south of Tarraco is **Saguntum,** a booming commercial city with a temple to Diana just off the forum, a large circus, amphitheater, tower dedicated to Hercules and a theater. The city is historically relevant due to its role in the beginning of the second Punic War where it sided with the Romans.

Further south is **Valentia** a colony established in DCXVI A.U.C. (138 B.C.E.) It is basically a veteran retirement community at this point, which means if you're a veteran yourself you'll find no shortage of wine or beds to stay in. It's a fine town to spend a day or two getting lost in, hang out with the locals, hear their stories.

---

[1] It mostly performs repeat showings of M*E*C*H (*mobilis exercitus chirurgicus hospitalis)*
[2] Earliest hallmarks of Spaniards doing stupid stunts with animals.

♦ It's best to avoid **Valentia** in DCLXXIX A.U.C. (75 B.C.E.) Pompey razes the city to the ground so it's not a place you'll want to be if you like not being dead.[1]

One of the largest cities in all Iberia, with a population of about 30,000, **Carthago Nova** is known for its wealth, trade and splendor. The city's wealth stems from its natural lead, silver and iron deposits, as well as a large harbor. You might be able to catch a ride to Africa, Corsica, or even back to Italy. The voyage to Africa should only be about a day and a half long.

The city boasts plenty of opportunities for sight-seeing. Carthago Nova boasts both an amphitheater and theater within the city walls. The theater lies just west of the hill of Aesculapius.[2] The amphitheater sits between the hill of Aesculapius and the hill of Hephaestus. Entertainment should include gladiatorial displays, plays and dancing. There are a few temples throughout the city, a prominent one stands to Aesculapius atop his hill. You can find some baths on the west side of town, you should stop in and rub elbows with whomever you can. You might be able to talk your way into someone's house rather than risk renting a room at a *caupona*. The public latrines are a similar place to meet up with locals who may be willing to put you up for the night.[3] Against the western wall, atop the *Arx Hasdrubalis* is the Punic Palace, which was the last bastion of resistance to fall in the city while it was under siege by Scipio. This is an excellent opportunity to see Carthaginian architecture, especially contrasted against the newer Roman structures. The city's forum is located near the center, a little ways east of the *Arx Hasdrubalis.*
♦Be forewarned, the city is renowned for its production of *garum,* which as a finished sauce adds a delightfully salty, not too fishy flavor to food, but while it's being made it's a bucket filled with fermenting fish guts that smells a tad like a sweaty boot filled with dog vomit.

Heading west along the *Ab Asturica Burdigalam* will land you in a series of nothing towns, **Iturissa, Pompaelo, Veleia, Vindeleia** and **Pallantia**, the locals are friendly enough, but the culture is heavily Celtiberian, so it wouldn't hurt to brush up on the language before breezing through.

At the end of the *Ab Asturica Burdigalam* is **Asturica Augusta,** a small city built up from a *castra* established by the Victorious 6th and the Twin 10th legions. Serves primarily as a military and mining administration center. Bad news is that there is next to nothing to do here, good news is with baggage trains going all over from the mining operations you have an excellent chance of keeping your time here short.

---

[1] What is it with Pompey and destroying cities?

[2] The hill exists no matter how you feel about it.

[3] Who hasn't taken home a transient from a rest stop bathroom?

Lucus Augusti to the northwest is very well defended, the walls are tall and you can rest assured you'll be safe here. The port city of **Brigantium**[1] sits in the northeastern corner of Hispania. The port here brings trade from Hispania Lusitania and Gallia, the lighthouse known as the tower of Hercules shines down around the harbor.

---

[1] Yes, another Brigantium.

Hispania Baetica

Size: 28,927 square Roman miles
Capital: Corduba
Government: Senatorial Province
Religion: Roman, Greek, Celtic, and Phoenician Polytheism
Language: Latin, Greek, Punic, Celtiberian
Established: DCCXXVII A.U.C. (27 B.C.E.)

Following the *Via Heraclea* west from Carthago Nova will bring a
traveler into the province and on to **Corduba,** the capital of Hispania
Baetica, to the west is **Hispalis** heading south will bring you to the city
of **Gades**, one of the most ancient cities in all Western Europe. The *Via
Heraclea* is later expanded and renamed the *Via Augusta.* The region is
well known for its production and export of fine olive oil.

The *Via Augusta* enters the province from Gallia Tarraconensis to the
east, near the border of the provinces is **Iliturgi**, a city which was
punished with total genocide during the second Punic War for their
betrayal of Roman forces.

Corduba, like Tarraco, flourishes under Augustus, until the Imperial
period it's a town like most others. It is sacked by Caesar in DCCIX A.U.C.
(45 B.C.E.) for supporting Pompey. It's worth noting that the city produced
both the Elder and Younger Seneca, as well as the poet Lucan. Perhaps
the most splendid temple to the Imperial Cult is found here Corduba.
Under the order of Claudius and finished by Domitian, it was built by
some of the most skilled craftsmen out of marble of remarkable quality.
Its position of prominence in the city allows it to be viewed from some
distance on the *Via Augusta.* The theater is in the new city and rests
against the wall of the old city. Sadly, even though he was born in the
city, it's unlikely you'll see any of Seneca's tragedies here.

The amphitheater stands just south-east of the theater, on the east side
of the new city. The circus lies east of the temple of the Imperial Cult, it
runs east to west, so the best viewing are on the stretch to avoid having
the sun in your eyes or burning down on your neck. If you're there late
enough, you can get a look at the Palace of Maximian situated northwest
of the old city. The city's forum doubles in size during the Imperial era,
it's a good place to meet up with locals, find a deal or two and ask for
directions. You also might be able to hop a barge on the *Baetis* and take
it down to **Gades**.

♦ If you're feeling up to a bit of adventure, there is supposedly a large
treasure buried near Corduba, maybe grab a shovel and you poke around,
you may strike silver! It would be unethical for us to tell you where.

Colonia Iulia Firma Astigitana, also known as **Astigi** stands firm at

Caesar's side during the civil war and rises to prominence under the Empire. Here you can find a nice forum, gymnasium, heated baths, and many fine homes if you can convince someone to take you in for the evening. The city of **Carmo** lies in between **Agisti** and **Hispalis**, it's a growing city under the Empire and has its own amphitheater.

Hispalis grows as an economic powerhouse throughout the late Republic and early empire, anything you need to buy in all of Hispania can be bought here in the markets. Make sure not to take the first offer you come across though, here you can afford to ask around and get competitive prices. The stall vendors sometimes like to take advantage of tourists, but are ultra-competitive for a sale, if you talk to a couple, you may be able to convince them to drive down the prices by telling them the other guy is selling it cheaper. While the city has a few temples if you're interested, all the entertainment is located in nearby Italica.

The city of **Italica** has prospered since its founding during the Republic. Even with a population of only 8,000 the city has several amenities including the third largest amphitheater in the entire Empire, (25,000 seat capacity) to the north of town. A circus and theater on the east side of town, near where the new and old cities meet. The east side of town hosts a lovely temple dedicated to Isis. A temple of Trajan built by Hadrian (both come from here) has beautiful columns with marble lugged all the way from Euboea. It's recommended you try and take your way into the home of one of the wealthier citizens if you can catch them in the right mood. Their houses are fantastically decorated and worth a look if you can get one. You can also try sneaking in during *salutatio,* unless the steward is paying close enough attention and tosses you out.[1]

South of **Hispalis** are the cities of **Orippo**[2] and **Ugia** on the *Via Augusta* towards **Gades.** The city of **Rotae** is a resort town, just north of the island city. **Portus Gaditanus** acts as the port for the island. You can hitch a ride across the bay easily here.

A city with more ties to Hercules is **Gades**, which sits on a small island a couple hundred meters off shore near the mouth of the *Baetis.* It's filled with wealthy *equites.* While not technically true, it was often (rather incorrectly) referred to as the 'most western city' under the dominion of Roma. During the reign of Augustus and beyond, the city has only grown wealthier as time has gone on. Most of the citizens hold multiple estates in the area. There is a small theater in the middle of the island, near the western shore. Since population of Gades tends to be on the wealthier side the plays are usually of better quality, but a seat may cost you a couple *dupondarii.*

---

[1] Just don't go thieving or you'll get what you deserve.

[2] Tourism slogan: Get Ogripp'!

On the southern end of the island is a temple to Melqart, identified as the Tyrian Hercules. The temple hosts an oracle, but only priests are allowed inside. A second temple to Moloch stands on the island, and even held human sacrifices until that nonsense was abolished by Caesar. On the south-eastern shore stand two pillars built by the original Phoenician settlers. Some who visit there and sacrifice to Hercules at the temple refer to them as the real 'Pillars of Hercules,' Strabo writes in from Pontus that the claim is utter rubbish.[1] Near the city the *tumulus* of Geryon after Hercules killed the monster. Ask a local to show you around, if they aren't too busy they usually don't mind. They love showing off their connection to Hercules. The dancing girls of Gades are infamous throughout the empire, if you can make it into one of the local's extravagant parties to see them, you should.

---

[1] The pillars of Hercules are metaphorically the opposite banks of the strait of Gibraltar, the channel between the Mediterranean and the Atlantic, through which he travelled on one of his labors. Anyone who claims mere columns are his pillars is surely trying to lure you into an ancient tourist trap.

Hispania Lusitania

Size: 52,383 square Roman miles
Capital: Emerita Augusta
Government: Imperial Province
Religion: Roman, Greek, Celtic, and Phoenician Polytheism
Language: Latin, Greek, Punic, Celtiberian
Established: DCCXXVII A.U.C. (27 B.C.E.)

There are two primary routes into Hispania Lusitania, there is a fork in
the road headed west on the *Via Augusta,* the southern route takes you to
Gades, the northern route leads you to the capital of Lusitania, **Emerita
Augusta**. The other way into the province is following the *Via
Lusitanorum* south from **Asturica Augusta.**

Heading northwest from **Corduba** you'll arrive in **Emerita Augusta**.
A 15,000 seat amphitheater sits along the eastern wall near the southern
aqueduct.[1] Be sure to stop in to see the games if you have time. The
theater is right next to the amphitheater and produces some excellent
Roman comedies. The city has a large circus that greatly resembles the
Circus Maximus in Roma, if a bit scaled down, it seats up to 30,000. It's
located just east of the city's outer walls. The city has two forums, the
Municipal Forum is at the intersection of the Decumanus Maximus and
the Cardo Maximus. The Provincial Forum is farther up from the *Cardo*
and marked by an arch. There are four major temples, one dedicated to
the Imperial Cult and another to Mars just off the Municipal Forum, one
is next to the theater is dedicated to Mithras, Serapis and some other
exotic gods, and the fourth is off the Provincial Forum. Emerita has a
nice selection of baths, including one with a snow pit.

North of **Emerita Augusta** is the city of **Norba Caesarina** which is
known for its numerous stork nests. In the northeast corner of the
province, further up the road, is the commercial hub of **Salamantica**
which was taken from the Carthaginians. The road continues north into
Hispania Tarraconensis towards **Asturica**.

In the southern portion of the province, you'll come to **Pax Iulia,** it's a
nice town to rest up in before continuing down the road. Further south
you'll come upon **Myrtilis Iulia**, which is at the northern-most navigable
part of the *flumen Anas,* you can catch a barge from here down to the
gulf of Gades for a couple *as* or free if the pilot is feeling generous.[2] The
city of **Lacobriga** is on the southwestern coast, it has a small port, you

---

[1] 47th largest in the empire!

[2] Better show him your *as* just to be safe.

can probably catch a ride to Gades or up to **Olisipo.**

If you're heading south on the *Via Lusitanorum,* you'll hit **Bracara Augusta,** a standard Roman town, you shouldn't have any trouble finding somewhere to stay here. Moving on you'll reach **Aeminium** and **Conimbriga,** the former is a small town in the shadow of the later. Unless you absolutely must stay in **Aeminium,** we'd recommend **Conimbriga,** which boasts an amphitheater, three heated baths, two fora, and plenty of *tabernae.*

At the end of the *Via Lusitanorum* is **Felicitas Julia Olisipo** on the west coast of Hispania, a large city with plenty to do no matter your interests. Numerous temples fill the city, ones to Jupiter, Concordia, Livia, Diana, Minerva, Cybele, Tethys, and even Idae Phyrgiae. There is also a theater, circus, forum, and of course the port which can get you has far as Britannia for the right price.

♦ Olisipo is also a major producer of *garum[1],* so maybe don't hang out too long if you don't care for the smell of rotting fish. The city is also prone to periodic earthquakes, due to some sort of bad business with Neptune, so an offering to the sea couldn't hurt.

---

[1] Worchester sauce is made pretty much the same way as garum, so if you have had that, don't be too scared of ancient Roman condiments.

Germania Superior

Size: 36,938 square Roman miles
Capital: Mogontiacum
Government: Imperial Province
Religion: Roman, Celtic and Germanic Polytheism
Language: Latin, Gaulish and Germanic
Established: DCCCXXXVI A.U.C. (83 C.E.)
De-established: MXIII A.U.C. (260 C.E.)

Germania Superior occupies the area east of Gallia and west of Raetia.
Numerous roads enter the province from all directions, with a couple

major entry points in the south, central and northern regions each.

Entering the province from Alpes Poeninae brings you to **Aventicum.**
It is the capital of the Helvetii[1] people and a colony of Augustus. It has
an amphitheater, theater, baths and a few temples including one to
Mercurius Cissonius. To the north, further up the road is **Augusta
Raurica,** which has a theater, forum, temple to Jupiter and amphitheater.
It also has any travel amenity you might need on your way through the
province.[2] The road also forks here, either meeting with the western of
the two north-south running roads or continuing northeast.

Arae Flaviae lies a ways northeast from **Raurica,** it has baths and a
nice temple district. The road continues to **Sumelocenna,** a well-fortified
town. The road runs east into Raetia, west towards **Argentoratum** or
north towards **Alisinensium.**

If you are coming from Lugdunensis in the west, you'll soon reach
Vesontio, which is a fortified town. It has a triumphal arch dedicated to
Marcus Aurelius, a Capitolium, as well as temples and local cults to
Cissonius, Cybele, Apollo, and Mars. There is an amphitheater not too
far outside the city walls.

The road pushes east before turning north to **Cambete,** the road here
either continues north or heads southeast to **Augusta Raurica.** At
Argentoratum you can either head eastwards to **Sumelocenna** or north
to **Aquae.** The baths there are reputedly excellent for the treatment of
arthritis.[3]

Closer to the frontier is **Noviomagus Nemetum,** a fair sized city with
numerous temples, a forum, and a theater. Further up the road is
Borbetomagus, it's technically been re-named **Augusta Vangionum**,
but the name refuses to stick.[4] It has a forum, Capitolium and temple to
Mars.

North of **Borbetomagus** is **Mogontiacum,** the provincial capital of
Germania Superior, and base of various legions and the local Roman
river fleet. There are temples to Cybele and Isis just off the forum. There
is also a pillar to Jupiter found north of town. The capital has the largest
amphitheater in Germania; it is found south of town and also doubles as
a Circus.[5] The city also boasts the largest theater in Germania, and
probably north of the Alpes, it is located just south of town.

♦ If you're into that sort of thing, the assassination of Severus Alexander
occurs here in CMLXXXVIII A.U.C. (235 C.E.). We do feel we have to
remind you to *not* attempt to stop the assassination, it will only result in

---

[1] Makers of fine fonts.

[2] Flying wine cups, even.

[3] Best relief until the invention of Tylenoleoum, which is also a type of flooring.

[4] The modern one is so much better. This is true: the city is now Worms, Germany.

[5] Agustus probably wanted to flood this for naval battles, too.

either your erasure from the time-line or the near immediate correction of the timeline by fate, usually in a cruelly and comically ironic way.

Northwest of **Mogontiacum**, up on the river, proximal to the border of Germania Inferior is **Confluentes.** Which is found where the *flumina Musalla* and *Rhenus* meet. Just north of here is a temple of Mercury and Rosmerta.

To the direct north of the capital is **Aquae Mattiacorum**, which is famous for its recreational pools, not just for people mind you, but for horses too! Also, if you do happen to be a lady, the town is a great place to get your hair dyed a fashionable shade of red as all the popular women about town do as you've surely noticed. The dye used is naturally harvested here.

East of **Mogontiacum** is **Nida**, a nice town with a temple to Jupiter, several *Mithraea,* a theater, forum and baths. The road here turns sharply to the south, passes through **Alisinensium** then curves east and enters Raetia.

Germania Inferior

Size: 13,540 square Roman miles
Capital: Colonia Claudia Ara Agrippiensium
Government: Imperial Province
Religion: Roman, Celtic and Germanic Polytheism
Language: Latin, Gaulish and Germanic
Established: DCCCXXXVI A.U.C. (83 C.E.)
De-established: MXIII A.U.C. (260 C.E.)

Germania Inferior occupies the area north of Gallia Belgica but south of the *Rhenus*, the main road runs from Superior along the river to the coast, another comes up from Belgica to meet the first at **Colonia Claudia Ara Agrippiensium**.

Bona[1] is the first town you'll come across on your way up from Germania Superior. It's a fine place to rest, but there isn't much to do here. **Colonia Claudia Ara Agrippiensium (CCAA)** is the provincial capital, but there isn't much here when it comes to entertainment. The city has a Capitolium and Mithraeum, temples to Mercury-Augustus, and shrines to the local female deities called Matrones, the city has rather fine baths near the river's edge.

Entering the province from Belgica, you'll come up the road to **Atuatuca Tungrorum** then to **Coriovallum**, which has a bathhouse (they're less common up here than in Gallia).

Northwest of **Agrippiensium** is the fort-town of **Ulpia Noviomagus Batavorum**, which springs up while the 10th legion is stationed here, after their redeployment, the town suffers a bit economically. Past **Noviomagus** are a couple forts called **Traiectum** and **Albaniana**.

Close to the coast is the city known locally as the **Forum Hadriani**, officially **Municipium Aelium Cananefatium (MAC)** and **Lugdunum Batavorum**. There is a canal dug at **MAC** between the *flumina Rhenus* and *Mosa*. Suetonius writes that Emperor Caligula declared war on Neptune at **Lugdunum Batavorum** and ordered his soldiers to stab at the ocean to really teach him a lesson.[2] Afterwards they collected sea-shells for a rather disappointing war booty.

---

[1] It's pretty good.
[2] "It has been declared, 'an eye for an eye', so let us take our vengeance on this murderous ocean." -Nauclerus Evidens

Raetia

Size: 41,819 square Roman miles
Capital: Augusta Vindelicorum
Government: Imperial Province
Religion: Roman and Celtic Polytheism
Language: Latin, Gaulish
Established: DCCXXXIX A.U.C. (15 B.C.E.)
De-established: MCCXXIX A.U.C. (476 C.E.)

Raetia is the province directly north of Italia across the *Alpes.* There are a
few routes in and out of the province. Two from the south, crossing the
mountains, and two ways on the west and east borders each. Most of the
cities are along the roads, but a few are more isolated in the mountains.
The entire province is a bit sparse culturally, it's a frontier province
mostly filled with waystations on major trade routes, and Augustus
didn't settle large groups of his veterans here as he did in numerous other
provinces.

   Clavenna is the first city you'll come to as you enter the province from
Italia on the western route. It's a city well used to travelers, and you'll
find respite there. To the west in the mountains are **Oscela** and **Bilitio.**
Neither of which is really worth going out of the way to visit, **Bilitio** is a
military fort and **Oscela** a Gallic town.

   Further north are the small towns of **Curia** and **Clunia.** Next to *lacus
Raetiae Brigantinus* is **Brigantium,**[1] a fortified military post, and seat of

the navy in the great lake. **Arbor Felix** is another fortified lake town on the southern shore. To the east is **Cambodunum** which has a forum surrounded by temples and large baths.

North of **Brigantium** is a river crossing and the town of **Guntia.** **Aquileia** is the meeting place of several roads, one leads directly west out of the province, another north (which also goes out of the province) and one to the east. Thankfully, the city has thermal baths, as it does get very cold up in this region.

Alae is the town directly north of **Aquileia,** it has a cavalry fort nearby. The road passes northwest through **Gamundia Romana** and heads into Germania Superior.

Tridentum[1] is the first city you'll reach if you're coming up on the eastern route from Italia. It is renowned as a stopping place on the way to **Veldidena,** you'll be welcomed there. The city has fine vineyards thanks to the numerous surrounding hills. In the valley east of the city are **Belunum,** a small mining town bringing copper and iron from the mountains, and **Feltria,** this road continues and descends back into Italia.

North after **Tridentum,** you'll pass through several cities, each is a small mountain community without much to do, though **Vipitenum** does have an altar to Mithras. A garrison and small town are found at **Veldidena,** which also provides a crossing for the *Oenus.*

You'll enter a marshland and come to the town of **Parthanum,** then **Foetes,**[2] further along. The provincial capital, **Augusta Vindelicorum,** has numerous temples and warehouses, as it's a major crossway of rivers and roads. Heading north from **Vindelicorum** you'll come to a T intersection, west leads to Germania via **Aquileia,** east through a couple forts (**Regina** and **Batava**) before entering Noricum.

---

[1] And you thought Alexandrias were everywhere.
[1] Land of fresh breath.
[2] An okay place to rest your Foetes.

Noricum

Size: 24,056 square Roman miles
Capital: Virunum
Government: Imperial Province
Religion: Roman and Celtic Polytheism
Language: Latin and Gaulish
Established: DCCXCVI A.U.C. (41 C.E.)

Noricum is another frontier province occupying the eastern end of the
Alpes south of the *Danuvius*. It is well known for its steel production,
which makes the finest tools, weapons, and armor anywhere in the
Empire. There are a few roads crossing the province, one major across
the northern part of the province, following the river, one through the
center of the province, circumventing the *Alpes,* and a few smaller routes
crossing the southern areas.

Entering the province from Italia in the south brings you to **Virunum,**
the capital of the province. It has a forum, several temples, including a
Capitolium, two Mithraea, and a temple to Nemesis[1] as well as an
amphitheater which doubles as a circus, and the only theater in the entire
province.

If you enter the province on the southeastern corner, you'll pass
through **Celeia** on your way towards Pannonia. It has temples to Mars,
Hercules and Isis.

West of **Virunum** in the *Alpes* is **Teurnia,** a city with baths, a
Capitolium, forum and temple to Grannus.[2] On the eastern side of the
province, on the western bank of the *flumen Mura* is **Flavia Solva**. It has
a temple to the local cult of Isis and an amphitheater. It is connected to
Virunum by a minor trade route.

On the western side of the province is **Iuvavum,**[3] a town near the
border of Raetia, the road entering the province from the west splits here,
either heading southeast towards **Virunum** or northeast towards
Ovilava.

The city of **Ovilava** has an amphitheater and thermal baths. But its real
worth comes from the fact that it sits at a few major crossroads. Trade
goods pass through here from all directions, meaning you can buy some
trinket-souvenir from Italia or Gallia for a decent price here.[4]

---

[1] Nemesis is who comes for you if you commit crimes of hubris against the gods, not the guy
who microwaves fish in your small office breakroom.
[2] God of spas and those dumb foam things that keep toes separated after a pedicure.
[3] Mozart will be born here, but you'll have to wait 1700 years to meet him.
[4] If you are passing through on your way from either of these places, it's kind of like getting a

Northwest of **Ovilava** is **Boiodurum** on the border to Raetia. Going Northeast from the former you'll pass through **Lauriacum** and **Cetium** along the *Danuvius* before reaching Pannonia.[1]

---

souveneir from your home airport because you forgot to buy one when you were actually there.

[1] Hardly worth mentioning, but ink is cheap.

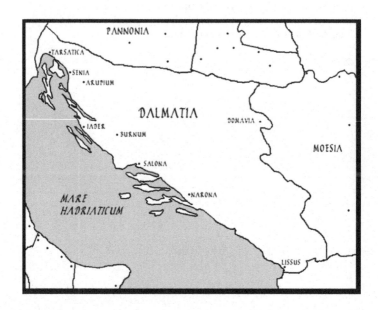

Dalmatia

Size: 38,527 square Roman miles
Capital: Salona
Government: Imperial Province
Religion: Roman, Illyrian, and Grecian Polytheism
Language: Latin, Illyrian and Greek
Established: DCCXXII A.U.C. (32 B.C.E.)
De-established: MCCXXXIII A.U.C. (480 C.E.)

Dalmatia[1] has one major route, the *Via Flavia* which followings the length of the *Mare Hadriaticum*. The *Via Argentaria* runs from **Salona** into Pannonia, a few other roads cross in and out of the province through the mountains.

Coming into the province along the *Via Flavia* brings you first to the old Illyrian fortress of **Tarsatica.** Further down the coast you'll reach **Senia** which has temples to Magna Mater[2] and Liber, as well as a nice

---

[1] You'd think if I made jokes about spotted dogs, they wouldn't actually line up. Well, they come from here, an historical district of modern Croatia. Shows what you know.

[2] Don't make the mistake of calling her "Big Momma", or at least explaining what that means

set of baths.

You'll pass through **Arupium** and before you hit the next town you can detour down to **Iader**, which has baths, a Capitolium, baths, a proper forum,[1] and amphitheater. Back on the *Flavia* is **Burnum** which has an amphitheater, baths, and several temples. The next city is **Salona**, the provincial capital, the *Via Argentaria* begins here and heads towards Sirmium in Pannonia. **Salona** has an amphitheater, theater, public baths, and a few temples. The city was favored over other cities in the province because it sides with Caesar against Pompey.

Further south is **Narona**, which has a temple to the Imperial Cult. Another road heads northeast from here, passing through the mining town of **Domavia** before leaving the province for Moesia. **Lissus** is the city furthest south in the province before you enter Macedonia.

---

to the locals.

[1] Way better than the lousy stores all throughout that advertise "Everything's I As"

Macedonia

Size: 35,407 square Roman miles
Capital: Thessalonica
Government: Senatorial Province
Religion: Grecian Polytheism
Language: Greek
Established: DCVIII A.U.C. (146 B.C.E.)

Macedonia has a few routes leading into it. There is the *Via Flavia* which runs parallel to the *Mare Hadriaticum* through Dalmatia. This links to the *Via Egnatia,* this crosses the province running west to east, the *Via Graeca* starts up in Dacia and runs north to south all the way through the province to the Peloponnese.

On the coast of the province is **Dyrrachium**[1], a major port and the start of the *Via Egnatia,* which is considered a continuation of the *Via Appia* in Italia. In addition to its busy port, the city has baths, an amphitheater and plenty of places to stay and rest after the voyage across the *Hadriaticum.*

To the southeast is the city of **Clodiana**, the road here turns northeast. You can stop and rest in **Mansio Scampa** which begins as a waystation for travelers before growing into a proper Roman city.

Heading east on the *Via Egnatia* you'll end up in **Heraclea Lyncestis** on the *lacus Lychnidus.* It's small town, but it's got a bath and a theater with regular gladiatorial fights, not too bad a place to rest up for a bit.

From **Heraclea** you'll pass through the small town of **Resen** and near **Florina** which will likely have been abandoned due to a fire by the time you're heading past. **Edessa** has a few temples and a theater, it is historically significant to the region, if you're interested talk to locals.

Further east is **Pella**, the birthplace of Alexander, apart from the obvious related sites to Alexander and his impressive lineage, there is a huge agora surrounded by stoae, temples to Aphrodite, Demeter and Cybele. The grand houses surrounding the agora have some of the most beautiful mosaics you'll never see, so we've heard.

Thessalonica is the capital of the province and a city of great historical heritage. Serving as a major trade hub and the intersection for both the *Via Graeca* and connecting Dyrrachium on the Adriatic coast to Byzantium as the gateway to Asia. The ancient temple to Aphrodite is the center of the religious district, built originally for Therma.[2] The gymnasium just north of the forum is a great place for you to relax and listen to a philosopher spout wisdom, or maybe get into a wrestling match and make a friend who can show you around the town.[3]

Conveniently located next to the gymnasium is a nice sized stadium where you can watch athletics or pretend you're an Olympian and run across the finish line. This is a good place to know how to get to if you're here in the Republican era, Thracians have a habit of raiding and you don't want to get caught in the open during the pillaging.

The Roman forum is flanked by two storied Stoae, given Thessalonica's fine position in the middle of everything you can restock on just about anything you need here. The theater here has drama,

---

[1] Don't drink the water. Just kidding. It's probably fine.

[2] One of the earliest examples of re-gifting we have.

[3] There just probably won't be much eye-contact after.

dancing competitions[1] and the occasional gladiatorial bout. It sits on the east side of the Forum. There are two large bath complexes located in the forum, they are beautifully decorated, and you can get in usually for an *obol* or less.

If you head northwest from **Thessalonica** towards Moesia, you'll reach the town of **Stobi.** The town has a large bath, temples to Nemesis and Isis, a synagogue, and a theater. Overall, a worthwhile place to stop and rest.

Southwest of **Thessalonica** is **Veria**, a must visit if you're a fan of athletic competition, they hold the Pan-Grecian *Alexandrian* games.

Entering the province on the *Via Graeca* from the north brings you to **Stobi,** a decently sized polis with a few things to check out. There are two baths, a Roman theater, and a decent shopping center. Temples and shrines dedicated to Nemesis, Hygeia and Telesphorus, Artemis, Apollo, Jupiter, Dionysus and Hera.

Amphipolis[2] is a little ways from the coast in the northeast of the province, just before Thracia. The city is on the *flumen Strymon* and has a couple things to do if you're there for the day. There is a nice gymnasium south of the acropolis. And south of the city, across the river is a monumental statue of a lion placed by one of Alexander's generals.

In the shadow of *Mons Olympus* is **Dion**, the city is centered upon a large altar dedicated to Zeus and the Muses. Alexander celebrated numerous victories here, made many sacrifices, and built a few monuments. It was sacked in DXXXV A.U.C. (219 B.C.E.) by the Aetolians but you could never tell by the state of it. The city serves as the religious center for all Macedonia, temples and sanctuaries of several deities can be found here, including Dionysus, Athena, Cybele, Demeter, Aesculapius, Artemis, Isis and Hermes. There are two theaters here, one built by the Macedonians and a later Roman one. Other amenities include the beautifully decorated baths and an agora.

♦ There is a sanctuary to Zeus atop the third highest peak of Olympus if you fancy a good hike to honor the king of the gods.

Larissa is a good place to stop if you're on the *Via Graeca* heading to or from Greece. There are a couple theaters and a temple to Athena here, stop in at the agora in the city center and pick up a gift if you plan on looking for a host to put you up for the evening. The polis is also renowned for being both the birthplace of Achilles, and the deathplace of Hippocrates of Kos, talk to the locals and one will surely give you a tour of the sites.[3]

---

[1] *Saltans Cum Astris*
[2] While it sounds like it should mean "Frogtown", it actually means "Around the City", referring to the *flumen Strymon* flowing around the city.

---

[3] Lots of other people died here too, it isn't like if you aren't named Kos you are immortal there.

Epirus

Size: 10,059 square Roman miles
Capital: Nicopolis
Government: Imperial Province
Religion: Grecian Polytheism
Language: Greek
Established: DCCCLXIII A.U.C. (110 C.E.)

There is one major road following the coast through Epirus as many of the cities are more easily accessed via ship.

Apollonia is the first town you'll reach, entering the province from Macedonia, originally and unfortunately named **Gylakeia**, after Gylax the founder. They thankfully changed it to something you can say without sounding like your mouth is full of rocks, even if it's way too common of a name. Due to the city's port, there is a spur of the *Via Egnatia* linking it all the way to Byzantium. There are several temples here, as well as a theater, odeon, and renowned school of philosophy.

Further south is **Aulon** which you'll pass through on the way to the city of **Phoenice.** The city has several temples and a Greek theater. On the nearby island is the city of **Corcyra** which has a fine temple to Artemis, theater and sea baths. **Nicopolis**, the provincial capital sits in the far south, it has a busy port. **Neapolis** has not only a theater, but also an odeon. The theater is found north of town near the stadium, the odeon west of the city walls. There is a stadium and nearby gymnasium just north of town. The largest bath complex is found adjacent to the theater. The city has a sanctuary sacred to Apollo. There is also a nymphaeum and monument to Augustus.

Achaia

Size: 19,381 square Roman miles
Capital: Corinthus
Government: Senatorial Province
Religion: Grecian Polytheism
Language: Greek
Established: DCCXXVII A.U.C. (27 B.C.E.)
De-established: MCDXLIII A.U.C. (690 C.E.)

The major land route entering Achaia is the *Via Graeca,* which runs all
the way down to the Peloponnese. The province is filled with historic
sights, cultured cities, excellent food, and good people. They turn their
nose up a bit at anyone they consider to be one of the βάρβαροι, but if
you'll speak a little Greek it'll go a long way.

The first stop is a layover in **Lamia**, while it's a tad unassuming as a
city, it has a storied past. Shortly after the death of Alexander the Great,
the Athenians rebel and push the Macedonians back to **Lamia**, where
they are eventually defeated by a massive army. Inside its walls it has an
agora, theater and an impressively fortified acropolis. Not too far south
of **Lamia**, is the pass of *Thermopylae* where the 300 Spartans and
several thousand Greek allies held back the Persian forces for a short
while.[1] The pass's name derives from the nearby hot springs, heated by
the blood of the Hydra washed off there by Hercules.[2] Here there is an
inscribed monument:

Ω ξεῖν, ἀγγέλλειν Λακεδαιμονίοις ὅτι τῇδε κείμεθα, τοῖς κείνων ῥήμασι
πειθόμενοι.

*Oh stranger, tell the Lacedemonians, that here, obedient to their laws,
we lie.*

After *Thermopylae,* you'll cut south into the mountains, passing
through several small towns which are frequented by travelers of all sorts
before you reach **Amphissa** which is just below **Delphi**. **Amphissa** has a
temple to Athena which is said to have been brought from Ilium after its
fall. **Delphi** is considered to be the center of the world by the Greeks, the
area below the temple has numerous shrines as well as amenities.

The temple itself is magnificent, and the oracle has been consulted on

---

[1] 300+ a couple thousand isn't a story that sells as many movie tickets, though.
[2] Considering it was this same Hydra venom, which when simply on a robe worn by Hercules
manages to kill him, I don't think I want to swim in Hydra water. How does it not
contaminate the water, hmm?

matters since time immemorial. In DCLXXI A.U.C. (83 B.C.E.) it is partially destroyed, and the site is in dire straits until restored by Hadrian. The temple is in the middle of town, you can't miss it.

There are several treasuries just below it, filled with tithes from the Greeks who support the oracle. (This may be why the area was sacked by the Phocians, the Thracians, the Romans, then the Romans again). There is a theater just above the temple on the side of the mountain, an Ionic stoa off to the north east, a gymnasium with baths, a stadium and a hippodrome. Due to the Pythian Games occurring every four years here (two years before or after each Olympic Games), there are numerous athletic statues upon which you may feast the eyes.[1]

After coming down the mountain you'll come to **Thebae**, renowned for incest, patricide and probably most importantly its gates. After it's razed by Alexander, the city pales in comparison to its Hellenistic ancestry, but still has a few things to check out. The Cadmea is on a hill on the south side of town, said to be built by Cadmus and where he grew his Spartoi. (Apparently the soil isn't as great now as it was back then).[2] East of the Cadmea is a small agora and the fountain of Oedipus, a temple to Artemis, and a shrine to Alcmene. There is a temple to Apollo south-east of the Electra gate. South of the Cadmea is a temple to Hercules and attached gymnasium where the Heraclea are often held. To the southwest is a temple to Athena. On the north side of the city is a theater and temple dedicated to Dionysus.

Next down the road is **Athenae**, there is plenty to see and do here. The Acropolis of **Athenae** is one of the more popular tourist destinations. Ruins of the Mycenaean era can be found atop the *Cecropia*, alongside numerous fortifications and structures. You can find the Parthenon dedicated to the virgin goddess Athena, the Erechtheum dedicated to Nike, the Eleusinion dedicated to Artemis, as well as numerous smaller shrines and sanctuaries. Here the Athenians end their procession of their grand *Panathenaea*. If you're in the region in time for a games, you absolutely must stop in, the wine drinking alone is worth it.

The area around the Acropolis is full of things to do. On the southern slope of the hill is a large theater dedicated to Dionysus as well as the odeon of Pericles. Between the two is the temple to Aesculapius where the ill often make offerings. To the northwest is an agora, which has stoae wrapping around three sides and the odeon of Agrippa in the center. The library of Pantainos lies east of the agora, the temples of Hephaestus and Apollo to the west, and a temple to Ares to the north. Just east of the acropolis is the temple of Zeus. The stadium for the

---

[1] And the games are played starkers, you know, so behold those statues, you pervert.

[2] You also have to plant dragon teeth to sprout legendary men, and use plenty of Miracle-Gro.

Panathenaea is a little ways east of the temple of Zeus. The Lyceum is located just outside the walls east of the stadium, and nearby is a gymnasium.

Corinthus is the provincial capital, while it is a fine city, it pales in comparison to Athenae, especially after the city is razed when the Romans conquer. The acropolis, known as the *Acrocorinthis* has impressive fortifications, as well as a temple of Aphrodite and sanctuaries to Demeter and Kore. The city center is dominated by an agora, temples to Apollo and Hercules, the fountain of Glauca, and the baths. Caesar ordered built an amphitheater here shortly after he recolonized the city. One of the most impressive feats of engineering in antiquity, the Diolkos runs across the Isthmus.

After **Corinthus** is the Peloponnese, which, for all its history, influence, and beauty, does not have much in it. The Spartans themselves admit that no one would ever know they were there a hundred years after they were gone, and they are quite correct.[1] **Megalopolis** in the center of the Peloponnese has a 20,000 seat theater and was the supposed site of the Titanomachy.[2] **Sparta** is a shadow of the military powerhouse it once was, now a tourist attraction if you want to observe Spartan customs. The coastal city of **Gythium** serves as a major port, but unless you plan on hitching your next ride out of there, it isn't worth the walk. One thing worth seeing in the Peloponnese is the statue of Zeus at **Olympia** on the western shore, it is one of the Seven Wonders of the Ancient World.[3]

---

[1] Which is why nobody ever talks about them, or writes books, comics, or movies about them.
[2] Where the Olympians overthrew the Titans after a 10 year battle. You'd think the land would be more scorched from something like that.
[3] Some of the only surviving period depictions of the epic statue of Zeus are commemerative coins, like pressed pennies from Disneyland.

Pannonia Superior

Size: 26,426 square Roman miles
Capital: Savaria/Carnuntum
Government: Imperial Province
Religion: Roman, Illyrian, and Grecian Polytheism
Language: Latin Illyrian, and Greek
Established: DCCCLVI A.U.C. (103 C.E.)
De-established: MLXI A.U.C. (308 C.E.)

Pannonia Superior is the western of the two Pannonian provinces. They are originally one province but are split in DCCCLVI A.U.C. by Trajan. There are three major east-west running roads, and one running north-south on the western side.

Entering the province in the southwest either from Italia or Dalmatia leads to **Siscia,** a city used as a major base of military operations during the Illyian wars. It has a major river port thanks to its location on the *flumina Strymon, Colapis* and *Savus.* It also has baths and a forum.

The road continues east and comes to **Servitium**, where you can find a port for the Roman river fleet. Here the road either turns south into

Dalmatia or further east into Pannonia Inferior.

Poetovium sits on the middle road in the province near the western border and is the starting point for the road running north to the upper road. It has numerous temples to Mithras, Jupiter, Vulcan, and Venus, the worshippers of Mithras are nothing short of fanatical here, so that may be a selling point to stop in or perhaps avoid the town.[1]

To the east of **Poetovium** is the small town of **Iovio Botivo,** the road then continues east into Pannonia Inferior. Before reaching **Iovio Botivo,** you'll come to **Aqua Viva**, a road starts here heading south through the town of **Pyrri** then **Andautonia** before joining up with the lower road at **Siscia**. After **Iovio Botivo** is **Aqua Balissae,** a city renowned for the healing properties of its hot spring baths. The city also has an amphitheater, large forum and temple frequented by A-list celebrities such as Emperors. Roads go out in seemingly all directions from the town.[2]

North of **Poetovium** is **Savaria**, the earlier provincial capital of Pannonia Superior. **Savaria** has an excellent forum due to its frequent visits of emperors and major trade route location. In the forum there is a Capitolium which has splendid statues of the capital triad, as well as a Mithraeum, decorated with expensive pigments. There is a temple to Isis of the basalt road, and a temple to Jupiter Dolichenus just east of that.

Off the Cardo Maximus[3] is a large bath complex. Attached to the Baths is a wrestling school if the mood strikes you to get all oiled up and grapple. The city's theater is found a short ways to the west of town.

The road here splits to the northwest and northeast. Heading northwest you'll pass through **Scarbantia** before meeting up with the upper road at **Vindobona.**

Vindobona is found on the western border with Noricum, just south of the *Danuvius*. Here in CMXXXIII A.U.C. (180 C.E.) Maximus Decimus Meridius under Marcus Aurelius, fights Germanic tribes and leads his legion to victory.

East of **Vindobona** is **Carnuntum**, the later capital of the province. The city boasts two amphitheaters, one (being considerably smaller) is found in the *castra*, the other with a seating capacity of 13,000 is located in town, you can't miss it, as it's one of the largest amphitheater in the entire Empire. There is a Capitolium and Mithraeum in the forum.

The city boasts a large palace used by the governing legate, visiting emperors and the like. The baths are located on the edge of the forum. Just outside the city walls is a magnificent gladiatorial school, rivaling

---

[1] Depending on your own level of fanaticism.
[2] As they say: All roads lead from Balissae.
[3] The Cardo Maximus is the primary north-south road in a Roman town. You could read this as "Main Street".

the *Ludus Magnus* in Roma.

The road follows the *Danuvius* through **Arrabona** and finally the fort-city of **Brigetio** before crossing over into Pannonia Inferior.

Pannonia Inferior

Size: 12,161 square Roman feet
Capital: Aquincum
Government: Imperial Province
Religion: Roman, Illyrian, and Grecian Polytheism
Language: Latin, Illyrian and Greek
Established: DCCCLVI A.U.C. (103 C.E.)
De-established: MLXI A.U.C. (308 C.E.)

The territory incorporated into Pannonia Inferior is a long tract of land west of the *Danuvius* as it turns south and then east again. It is bordered by Pannonia Superior on the west, Dalmatia and Moesia Superior to the south and Dacia to the east. A couple roads run east-west in the southern portion, and one major route runs north-south tracing the route of the river.

The lower road comes into the province from Pannonia Superior, on the western side is a way which links the two through the marshland. There is a waystation at **Marsonia** if you can convince them you're on official business, otherwise try you luck with the townspeople or you'll be sleeping in the swamps.

Continuing eastbound and down on the lower road brings you to **Sirmium.** The city has temples, baths, an amphitheater, theater and later a hippodrome. A city oft inhabited by Emperors and other persons of note. The road continues east and enters Moesia Superior.

The upper road also comes from Pannonia Superior, it goes through **Certissia** then comes to **Cibalae.** Here the road joins with the north-south road and continues east. **Ciccium** is the next town you'll come to, then following the road to the end it joins with the lower road and exits the province.

North of **Cibalae** is **Mursa,** a major trade route intersection with roads going out in all directions. It has an extensive number of *tabernae* which is good for you as a traveler. There are temples or local cults to Hercules,[1] Mercury, Cybele, Jupiter, Silvanus, Isis and Osiris, there is also a synagogue here. There is a stadium outside the city walls.

♦ Not a place to be in MXIII A.U.C. (260 C.E.) due to a bloody battle fought by two of the 'thirty tyrants' attempting to usurp the Imperial throne, Ingenuus and Aureolus. It's best to avoid these 1/15ths of the tyrants if you can.

In the northeastern part of the province is **Aquincum,** the provincial capital. A large city with 35,000 residents. The city boasts baths, a

---

[1] Nowadays they call this cult "Planet Fitness."

forum, temples, and two amphitheaters. The road here turns west into Pannonia Superior.

Moesia Superior

Size: 31,544 square Roman miles
Capital: Viminacium
Government: Imperial Province
Religion: Roman and Grecian Polytheism
Language: Latin and Greek
Established: DCCLIX A.U.C. (6 C.E.)
Divided: DCCCXXXVIII A.U.C. (85 C.E.)
Reformed: MXXIV A.U.C. (271 C.E.)

There are several roads across Moesia Superior. Two run approximately north-south and intersect at the **Naissus** before eventually reaching the *Danuvius.* The other major road follows the river.

Sculpi is the first city across the border from Macedonia. It's a fairly Hellenized city with baths and a theater. The theater here, unlike nearby Stobi in Macedonia, is only ever used for theatrical performance, and does not display violent spectacles.

If entering the province from the south of Dalmatia, the first major town you'll come to is **Ulpiana**. It is a city of mosaics and robust theatric culture.[1] The city of **Naissus** sits at an important crossroads in the

---

[1] People live there, too.

province, with roads intersecting and heading north and south, as well as the *Via Militaris* which cuts east through **Remesiana** and into Thracia. The city itself is a strong military outpost with a steady flow of traders in and out of the region, the forum always has goods at reasonable prices.

Northeast of **Naissus** is the fortified town of **Bononia** on the *Danuvius*. There are shrines to Jupiter and Neptune here. To the east is a castra, **Ratiaria**, and to the west the town of **Taliata**, here there is a river crossing.

Northwest of **Naissus** is the farming settlement and fort of **Horreum Margi**. Further up the road is **Viminacium**, the provincial capital. The amphitheater is found on the north-east side of town, next to the *castra*, and hosts fantastic beast fights including bears and camels.[1] There are baths just southwest of the amphitheater on the next *insula* over. The hippodrome is found just outside the wall on the south side of town. There are several temples surrounding the forum, and the theater is found on the western side of town, inside the city walls.

To the west is **Singidunum**, on the border of Pannonia Inferior. The city has baths directly off the forum, several temples, and a port on the *Danuvius*.

---

[1] See our companion guide, Fantastic Beast Fights and Where to Find Them.

Moesia Inferior

Size: 25,891 square Roman miles
Capital: Tomis
Government: Imperial Province
Religion: Roman and Grecian Polytheism
Language: Latin and Greek
Established: DCCLIX A.U.C. (6 C.E.)
Divided: DCCCXXXVIII A.U.C. (85 C.E.)
Reformed: MXXIV A.U.C. (271 C.E.)

Moesia Inferior has two main roads, one follows the path of the
Danuvius, and the other the western shore of the *Pontus,* known as the
Via Pontica. Like many other northern provinces, this area is fairly wild
and untamed.

Oescus is the first city you'll come to following the river route from
the west. It's impressively secure militarily. The city has well maintained
baths, a capitolium and temple to Fortuna.

Further east is the legionary fort **Novae,**[1] which helps keep the region
secured. **Durostorum** is another military fortress prepared to thwart the
barbarian horde.[2] **Troesmis** is the northernmost fort, there is a road to the
east leading to **Salsovia,** the last of the Danuvian castra**.**

Histria is a large city on the coast of the sea. Originally a Greek
colony, it has a theater, gymnasium, temples to Zeus, Aphrodite, the
great gods of Samothrace, and baths. Just down the *Pontica* is the
cultural metropolis of **Tomis,** the provincial capital. There are sizable
baths in town, where you can meet many metropolitan citizens and try to
find a place to stay for the night.

The city has a Greek style theater which has decent plays running
regularly. There is an impressive collection of mosaics in the local
warehouses, beautifully decorated storehouses. It may be best to try and
make a little cash and get a good look at these while you're in town. If
you're here between DCCLXI A.U.C. (8 C.E.) and DCCXXI A.U.C. (18 C.E.)
you may be able to catch Ovid here during his exile. Please bear in mind
he's fairly miserable about it all, so you'll not likely find him in a good
mood.[3]

---

[1] Literally just called "New Fort".
[2] This means YOU.
[3] If you can find out why he was banished, let us know. He was rather mum about it in official
records.

The city of **Odessus** is not too far from the border to Thracia. It's a robust trading post with excellent public baths. Further inland is **Marcianopolis** which has an amphitheater. To the west is **Nicopolis,**[1] a nice city with baths, a temple to Cybele, and even a *thermoperiatos,* which was a heated indoor shopping complex.

---

[1] Nice City.

Dacia

Size: 77,213 square Roman miles
Capital: Ulpia Traiana Sarmizegetusa
Government: Imperial Province
Religion: Grecian and Roman Polytheism
Language: Greek and Latin
Established: DCCCLX A.U.C. (107 C.E.)
Abandoned: MXXVIII A.U.C. (275 C.E.)

There is one road in Dacia which runs from Moesia Superior to the opposite border of the province, another road runs from Moesia Inferior and meets with the first at **Apulum**.

Taking the road from Inferior will bring you to **Romula**, where two legions are stationed at one point. The road continues up to meet with the other after a considerable distance.

Entering from Moesia Superior, you'll come first to **Drobeta**, here there is a massive bridge across the *Danuvius*. **Drobeta** contains temples to Jupiter, Cybele, Mithra and Venus, and maintains a Roman presence even after the rest of the province is abandoned.

West of the city is **Dierna**, a castra off the river bank of the *Danuvius*. Up the road is **Tibiscum**, here the road curves to the northeast towards the capital.

Ulpia Traiana Sarmizegetusa is the provincial capital, it is the largest city in all of Dacia and is a proper Roman city.[1] The city is built up around the original fort, the amphitheater is found a short ways north of the old *castra*. A small circus is located south of the amphitheater. The gladiatorial school is just southwest of the amphitheater. There are numerous temples around the city, temples to Aesculapius and Hygeia, Liber Pater, Nemesis, and Silvanus are all found south of town, just west of the amphitheater. The city's main baths are right off the forum.

Apulum is not far north of **Sarmizegetusa**, there is a significant Roman fortress here, along with a decent sized town surrounding it.

Further north is the fort at **Potaissa**, there area is known for its salt mines. There are baths in town if you have need. Continuing along the road you'll pass through **Napoca** before finally reaching **Porolissum**, the northernmost settlement in Dacia. Despite being so far away from the rest of civilization, it has temples to Jupiter, Liber Pater, Nemesis, as well as an amphitheater and baths.

---

[1] With proper naked wrestling and the letter Z in its name.

Thracia

Size: 39,175 square Roman miles
Capital: Heraclea Perinthus, Philippopolis
Government: Imperial Province
Religion: Grecian Polytheism
Language: Greek
Established: DCCCXCIX A.U.C. (46 C.E.)
De-established: MXLVI A.U.C. (293 C.E.)

Thracia is found in the far east of Europa and acts as the gateway to Asia.
Three major routes pass through the province, two run east-west, one
being the *Via Militaris,* and the *Via Pontica* follows the shore of the
Pontus.

Entering the province from Macedonia, along the coastal *Via Egnatia*
brings you to **Philippi**. Here the literal backstabber Marcus Iunius Brutus
met his end against the forces of Augustus and Marcus Antonius.[1] The
city has a theater, agora, forum, and a temple dedicated to their local
hero.[2] The theater is expanded under Roman rule to allow for games to
take place in addition to theatrical performances. Further down the road,
on the coast is **Neapolis.** This small town is important due to its harbor
and location of the *Egnatia.* Just east of here is the city of **Abdera,** which
is renowned for the stupidity of its residents. The Abderans make up

---

[1] Et tu, Antone?
[2] Not Brutus.

approximately a third of the butt of all Roman jokes.[1]

A considerable distance down the road is **Traianoupolis**, which is known throughout the region for the quality of its baths. Next are the towns of **Kypsala** and **Aproi,** the latter being a veteran colony.

Heraclea Perinthus is the original capital of the province. While that sort of title implies some grand city, it is actually a relatively plain town, perhaps why the capital was in fact moved to somewhere more interesting. Next is the village of **Selymbria** before you reach the edge of the continent.

Entering the province from Moesia on the *Via Militaris* in the northwestern corner of the province you'll soon arrive at **Serdica**. The city has high walls, baths, and an amphitheater. Further down the road is the second provincial capital, **Philippopolis.** The city has a Grecian theater to the northeast of town. The odeon is Roman-built and found near the forum next to the library. The stadium is west of the theater, and north of the forum. There are two main baths, one north of the forum, and the other east of there a short ways. The city has a synagogue and a temple to Aesculapius next to the eastern bath complex. Apollo is honored near the stadium with Pythian games.

The road continues, passing through **Hadrianopolis** and then finally meeting with the *Via Egnatia* at Byzantium.

Mesembria is the first town you'll come to on the *Via Pontica* from Moesia. It has an agora, baths, and temple to Apollo. Along the shores is **Apollonia Pontica,** named for its famed temple to Apollo, the colossal statue is pilfered away to Roma when the city is sacked by the Romans.[2] The city has an important port,[3] which will grant you access to areas around the *Pontus.* **Deultum** has a temple to the imperial cult and baths. The *Pontica* continues south to Byzantium.

---

[1] An Abderite sees a eunuch talking with a woman and asks him if she's his wife. The guy responds that a eunuch is unable to have a wife. "Ah, so she's your daughter?"

[2] Who lost it in the back of a closet behind some shoes or something.

[3] It is imPORTant.

VIII Africa

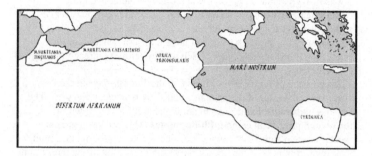

Africa is hot, really hot, you might think standing near a fire is hot, or a dip in the caldarium is hot, but that's just peanuts to Africa. The region is vast stretches of parched wasteland with the occasional oasis or river valley bringing life with it.

Still some of wealthiest provinces in the Empire are found here; Roma's greatest enemy once lived on the coast. It is a wonderful place to visit with plenty of things to see and do, as long as you can take the heat.

Mauretania Tingitana

Size: 28,020 square Roman miles
Capital: Tingis
Government: Senatorial Province
Religion: Roman, Berber, Punic, Grecian Polytheism
Language: Latin, Berber, Punic, Greek
Established: DCCXII A.U.C. (42 B.C.E.)
Reduced: MXXXVIII A.U.C. (285 C.E.)

Tingis, the provincial capital, is the most likely place you'll enter the province if you're not coming from the road east. The city has a couple baths, as well as other amenities, but the major focus it the port itself, which can get you anywhere you want to go in the western Mediterranean. From here you can head east towards Caesariensis or south.

Traveling south along the coast, you'll come to **Lixus,** an ancient city and one of the few in western Africa to have an amphitheater. It has one of the oldest sanctuaries to Hercules you can find anywhere. And rumor has it that the Garden of the Hesperides is located somewhere nearby.[1]

Further south is the Augustan colony of **Iulia Valentia Banasa** which is a beautifully decorated city. It has a forum, capitolium, and baths. The mosaics are some of the nicest you'll see and you'd never expect them so far from civilization.

The *end of the road* so to speak is the colony of **Sala,** originally a Phoenician city, it was taken by the Romans as a port. The city has a forum, baths, and even a triumphal arch. To the south of the city are the southern limits of the Roman Empire. Beyond that there is the Berber city of **Anfa,** which the Romans partially control and use for commercial

---

[1] It's a secret garden.

trading. Unless you've got bulk wares to sell, this is as far as you'll probably ever need to go from Roma.

If you head inland from **Sala** you'll come to the city of **Volubilis,** a city renowned for its quality olives. It also has an arch dedicated to Caracalla, two baths, a temple to Saturn, a capitolium, and a forum. The city is captured in MXXXVIII A.U.C. (285 C.E.) so perhaps consider skipping a visit around that time unless your Berber is excellent.

Heading southeast from **Tingis** will bring you to **Iulia Constantia Zilil,** another colony of Augustus. It has an amphitheater, baths, and plenty of drinking water, which is very important during these long stretches of road.

The road east towards Caesariensis is long and hot, gather water whereever you can, and be wary of the local wildlife. The next major city you'll come to is **Rusadir.** If you can afford it, book a vessel east towards any of the major ports further along the coast.

Mauretania Caesariensis

Size: 52,921 square Roman miles
Capital: Caesarea Mauretaniae
Government: Senatorial Province
Religion: Roman, Berber, Punic, Grecian Polytheism
Language: Latin, Berber, Punic, Greek
Established: DCCXII A.U.C. (42 B.C.E.)

There is a long road, the *Via Claudia* which traverses the province entirely, with a second route splitting off at **Siga** and rejoining at **Saldae** (if traveling from west to east, otherwise… just reverse that). There are several ports along the coast giving you access to the province.

The first city you'll reach entering the province from the west is **Siga.** The city has baths, here the road splits to either cut across the province or follow the outline of the coast. Further along the shore is **Aresenaria**, also known as **Portus Magnus,** where you can hitch a ride on any number of grain and salt barges bound for elsewhere in the empire.

You next stop down the coast is **Quiza Xenitana**, you need to make sure you have plenty of water from here, as it's a long stretch to the next town. **Cartennas** is a port city right next to a river. It's a colony established by veterans of Augustus and has most amenities you'll require during your visit.

The city, **Caesarea Mauretaniae** (formerly **Iol**) is a proper Roman one. As the capital of the province, there is plenty to do. There is a library not far from the forum. The amphitheater is found on the east side of town, it has two tunnels for beasts, and with Africa's wealth of fauna, there is never a dull fight here. The theater is just a short walk east from the amphitheater.

The hippodrome is northeast of the amphitheater, not too far from the shore. There are numerous temples including a Capitolium, a temple to Diana, and numerous earlier Punic and Numidian sanctuaries. The city has its own academy and school of philosophy near the forum. The city's baths are near the shore and are rather majestic, the sea air does wonders to the vapors of the steam room. The city has a small lighthouse on an island just offshore.

Tipasa is just east of **Caesarea**, its forum is located up on a rocky promontory with a Capitolium, further south is the amphitheater and the baths. The port is found underneath the cliffs.

Next is **Icosium**, which has baths that are quite nice. **Rusguniae** on the other side of the bay also has fine baths with delightful mosaics. **Rusucurru** is another stopping point on the road before reaching **Saldae**. **Saldae,** like **Caesarea** has plenty to do. The city has multiple baths, an amphitheater, theater, circus, temples to Saturn and Oceanus as well as others. The city is decorated with beautiful mosaics. The last city you'll pass through before Africa Proconsularis is **Igilgili.** It's a site of major crossroads and a full Roman colony.

If you were to take the southern route from **Siga,** you'd come first to **Gunugus,**[1] which is a small town. Further east is **Zuccabar**. The colony has a small amphitheater where new gladiators are often showcased. One such gladiator, known as Maximus or *Hispanus* once shouted "*Nonne spectamini?*" "Are you not entertained?"

To the south of **Zuccabar** is **Oppidum Novum**, and **Aquae Calidae**[2] is just a ways northeast. **Aquae** is a small but rich cities, its local hot springs provide waters for its famous baths, the city also has a library, forum, and theater.

Auzia is a ways east of **Aquae,** it's a smaller farming community with a forum and temple in the town proper, as well as a nearby *castra.* **Setifis** has baths and a circus. The road here cuts back northeast, passing **Tubusuctu** which has baths and a contingent of soldiers. The road rejoins the main one at **Saldae.**[3]

---

[1] Not *those* Gungans.

[2] Nothing like a Hot Tub after a nice day in the blazing equitorial sun.

[3] Saldae is one of the many places taken over by the Germanic Vandal tribe, whose legendary sacking and looting gives us the term vandalism. They tend to get all the blame when it may have also been at the hands of other barbarians and Byzantines or even just bored local teenagers.

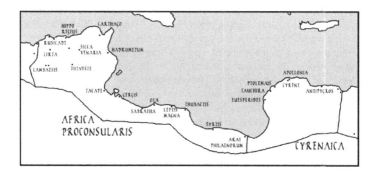

Africa Proconsularis

Size: 117,360 square Roman miles
Capital: Carthago
Government: Senatorial Province
Religion: Roman, Greek and Punic Polytheism
Language: Latin, Greek, and Phoenician
Established: DCVIII A.U.C. (146 B.C.E.)
Conquered: MCLXVIII A.U.C. (415 C.E.)

There are two main routes across Africa. The first is the *Via Claudia* following along the coast, and the other cuts across the interior of the province in the south running west to east from Mauretania and meeting the *Claudia* at **Tacape.**

Upon entering the province from Mauretania, you'll pass by **Chullu** and come to **Rusicade**, which apart from robust wheat farms surrounding it, has an amphitheater, theater, and mithraeum. South of **Rusicade**, about halfway between the two main roads is **Cirta**, the capital of Numidia (after CMXLVI A.U.C.), there is a mix of cultures here, including Roman, Greek, and Punic.

Further south is **Lambaesis,** which has an amphitheater, baths, a couple triumphal arches, a Capitolium and temple to Aesculapius. Just west of here is **Thamugadi**, a large veteran colony on a major road intersection. It has most amenities you'll need, including several baths, a theater, numerous markets surrounding the forum, library, a Capitolium as well as temples to Saturn, Mercury, and Ceres.

On the *Via Claudia*, east of **Rusicade** is the port of **Hippo Regius.**[1] You can reach far across the sea from here. There is a theater, baths,

---

[1] Regal Hippo, the horse meaning, not the Hippopotamus one. Still a good name for a rock band.

forum, markets, and several temples. South of **Hippo** is **Thagaste**, which is in a wooded area and is the hometown of novelist Apuleius. Further from the coast, on the southern road is **Theveste**, which has an amphitheater, theater, baths, and temple to Minerva. The city of **Sicca Veneria**[1] is found northeast of **Theveste** on the road to **Carthago**.

Carthago is the capital of Africa Proconsularis and the former chief city of the Carthaginians *(if you hadn't already guessed)*. The city was founded by Queen Dido, who, was rather clever when she settled the area. She was given an oxhide and told she could build her city on whatever land she could cover with the hide, so she cut it into strips and surrounded a nearby hill, tricking the Berbers out of additional land while still being technically correct.[2]

The amphitheater can be found on the western side of town. The hippodrome is found south of the amphitheater, on the western edge of town. The city's theater and odeon are located on opposite sides of the hill from each other in the middle of the city.

Carthago has several baths, the greatest however are those of Antonius, which sit near the shore on the eastern side of the city. They are some of the most splendid baths in the entire Empire, and certainly in all Africa. There are several temples throughout the city, one of Eshmun is found on the Byrsa hill in the citadel. There is one to Tanit just east of Eshmun's.

♦ *Carthago delenda est!* If you happen to find yourself in Africa around DCVIII A.U.C. (146 B.C.E.) Do your duty to Roma and help sack the child-sacrificing barbarian descendants of Dido and grab yourself a handful of salt to finish the job right.

Further along the coast to the southeast is **Hadrumentum**, which, having abandoned the rest of the Carthaginians during the Punic wars, escaped being razed.

Moving east, you'll pass through **Tacape** and **Gergis** before you come to the city of **Sabratha**, which has a theater, amphitheater, baths, forum, harbor, and temples to Liber Pater,[3] Serapis, Hercules and Isis.

Phoenician remains the dominant language in **Oea**, east of **Sabratha**, so you may consider skipping the city if you're a little rusty. Further east is **Leptis Magna**, which has a theater, amphitheater, baths, two large fora, nymphaeum, and temples to Augustus, Jupiter, Liber Pater and Hercules.

You'll pass through the towns of **Thubactis** and **Syrtis** as you head eastwards. **Syrtis** is renowned for the waters in the surrounding gulf.

---

[1] You'd be Sicca Vaneria too if you didn't have access to penicillin.

[2] The best kind of correct.

[3] Free Daddy.

They are notoriously dangerous for ships due to numerous sandbars. You'd be better off heading to literally any other port, seriously, go somewhere else.

The last landmark you'll reach in the province is **Arae Philaenorum.** This monument stands as the border between **Carthago,** and therefore the province and Cyrenaica. The legend says that the brothers Philaeni chose to be buried alive in this spot to secure a border for their home town.[1]

---

[1] Carthage and neighboring Cyrene wanted to solve a border dispute by having a pair of runners leave their towns, and where they met, the border would be. The Carthaginian brothers were accused of cheating because they made better time, so to make up for it they were buried alive there instead. Or so the Cyrenians said...

Cyrenaica

Size: 67,040 square Roman miles
Capital: Gortyn (in Creta)
Government: Senatorial Province
Religion: Roman, Berber, Punic, Grecian Polytheism
Language: Latin, Berber, Punic, Greek
Established: DCLXXVI A.U.C. (78 B.C.E.)
Restructured: MXLIX A.U.C. (296 C.E.)

There is the *Via Claudia* acting as the primary road which runs west-east across Cyrenaica. The province begins at the Arae Philaenorum in Africa Proconsularis, and at **Catabathmus Magnus** to the east, which marks the boundary between the continent of Africa and Asia.[1] The province technically falls under the administration of Creta.

Euesperides is the first Pentapolis you'll come to in the province, it may be known as **Bernice**, depending on when you arrive. Afterwards you'll continue through **Tauchira**, before reaching **Ptolemais.** The city has a few things to see and do, including an amphitheater, theater, odeon and also a decently sized port.

Cyrene has several temples to Zeus, Apollo, and Demeter and Persephone. Apollo's temple has a theater adjoining. If you're in the area, pick up some *silphium*[2] here where you can get it cheaply. It fetches a hefty price throughout the Empire outside of Africa. **Apollonia** is the port city of **Cyrene**, while it does have a theater of its own, it's mostly just worth visiting to try and find some temporary work in the warehouses or hitch a ride to elsewhere.

The city of **Antipyrgos** sits roughly across from Pygros on Creta. Further east is **Petras Maior**, which we can tell you is much better than Petras Minor, so much so the lesser Petras isn't even worth mention, so we're sorry that we did…

The end of the line so to speak is the pass known as **Catabathmus Magnus**. West of the pass is Cyrenaica, and therefore Africa, to the east is Aegyptus, and consequently Asia.

---

[1] In Hellenistic Geography, Egypt is in "Asia". To anyone who has looked at a globe, it is clearly almost entirely in Africa, with that tiny bit on the Arabian peninsula on the other side of the Red Sea and modern day Suez canal.

[2] Silphium was a popular contraceptive and spice, so popular in fact, that the Romans harvested it into extinction, after losing their plan B, they had to move on to plan Γ.

IX Asia

Asia is expansive and diverse, many of the most alien creatures and cultures known to the Empire come from its dark corners.[1] But it is filled with strong and proud peoples who contribute many things to the Empire. The exotic architectures, languages, cuisines[2] and religious perspectives mean that every province you visit will bring you to something new.

---

[1] It's a regular Mos Eisley Cantina out there, except all the aliens are people.

[2] Chinese food is the best when Americans invent it in about 1950.

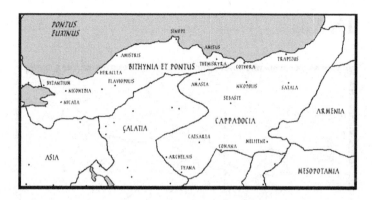

Bithynia et Pontus

Size: 39,386 square Roman miles
Capital: Nicomedia
Government: Senatorial Province
Religion: Grecian Polytheism
Language: Greek
Established: DCXC A.U.C. (64 B.C.E.)
De-established: MCCCXCV A.U.C. (642 C.E.)

There are several options for entering the province of Pontus et Bithynia, the first and most obvious is the *Via Egnatia* from Europa. Others come up from Galatia and Cappadocia in the south.[1]

Approaching from Europa on the *Egnatia* brings you to the city of **Byzantium**. One day this will be the capital of the entire Eastern Roman Empire, but for the last days of the Republic and early days of the Empire is an important trade post controlling access to the *Pontus* from the *Aegaeum*. Severus expands the city, adding a theater, hippodrome, and larger baths.

East of **Byzantium** is the provincial capital, **Nicomedia.** The capital has a theater, baths, and temples to Augustus, Commodus, Roma, and Demeter. The road here continues east, or heads south.

♦ You may want to avoid the city in MVI A.U.C. (253 C.E.) as it is sacked by the Goths then.[2]

The city of **Nicaea** is a favorite of Pliny the Younger, it sits south of

---

[1] Digging up from underneath is ill-advised.
[2] They are very moody and mostly just going through a phase.

Nicomedia. The road here heads east into Galatia. The city has a gymnasium, baths, theater, and temples to Aesculapius, Dionysus, and Tyche.

To the northeast of **Nicomedia** is the town of **Heraclea Pontica**, south of that is **Claudiopolis.** Previously **Bithynium,** known for its pastures and cheeses. **Flaviopolis,** also known as **Cratia,** is east of **Bithynium.** The road proceeds south into Galatia.[1]

Amistris is east, up the coast from **Heraclea.** The townspeople are industrious, taking advantage of quality soil, timber, and fishing to act as a trading powerhouse in the area. There isn't much culture here however. Much further east is **Sinope**, the source of the *sinopia* red pigment found throughout the Empire.

At the head of the trans-Anatolia road is **Amisus** on the coast of the *Pontus.* The city is the unofficial commercial capital of the province, owing to its land and sea routes. The road south leads into Cappadocia.

East of **Amisus** is the legendary city of **Themiscyra**, home of the Amazons.[2] You may think a visit to a city occupied solely by women would be a fine way to spend your temporal vacation, but you'd be wrong, friend. The Amazons do not take kindly to strangers, especially male strangers, visit at your own peril.

---

[1] Not to be confused with Galaxia, land of dairy. This would be an awesome name for Wisconsin.

[2] Word is they have magic bracelets and whips. And they provide free 2-day shipping to any member of their tribe.

Cappadocia

Size: 70,310 square Roman miles
Capital: Caesarea
Government: Imperial Province
Religion: Grecian and Roman Polytheism
Language: Greek, Anatolian and Latin
Established: DCCLXXI A.U.C. (18 C.E.)
Reorganized: MCCCXCV A.U.C. (642 C.E.)

Roads crisscross all throughout the province of Cappadocia. Most entrances to the province are in Galatia and Cilicia, as well as a few ports along the shores of the *Pontus*.

Entering the province from Galatia, you'll come to **Sebaste**, the road here splits in all directions.[1] **Amaseia** is northwest of the city on the way to Pontus and Bithynia. It is a city of philosophers, writers, and artists.[2] Northeast of **Sebaste** is **Nicopolis**, which has temples to Zeus and most importantly Nike. Further up the road on the coast is **Cotyora**, a costal town with sanctuaries to Cybele, Pan and Dionysus.

Far to the east of **Sebaste**, past **Nicopolis** is **Satala**, which has a large statue of Aphrodite. North of here is **Trapezus**[3] with an expanded port and Mithraeum. The *Classis Pontica* is also stationed here for a time. **Melitene** is far southeast of **Sebaste**, near the border Syria. Procopius of Caesarea writes in that it has nice temples, theaters, and agorae.

The provincial capital is **Caesarea**, like **Sebaste**, the road splits here in multiple directions. [4] **Comana** is east of the capital, with a temple to Enyo which is widely celebrated and beloved. The Romans later reassign it to Bellona. The city also has a small theater near its river.

You're bound to find hospitality in **Tyana** to the far south of **Caesarea**. Initially it was reported that the citizens were stingy and unwelcoming, until Zeus and Hermes stopped in for a visit, and upon being refused by everyone but a pair of peasants, smote the whole town via flood. We think they've probably learned their lesson by now.

---

[1] Including up and down.
[2] They all work retail, like every other philosophy and English major you know.
[3] It's a swinging good time.
[4] Including sideways and slantways and longways and backways.

Asia

Size: 51,882 square Roman miles
Capital: Ephesus
Government: Senatorial Province
Religion: Roman and Grecian Polytheism
Language: Latin and Greek
Established: DCXXI A.U.C. (133 B.C.E.)
Divided: MXLVI A.U.C. (293 C.E.)

There are numerous choices one has for entering the province of Asia. First and foremost is the *Via Asiana* which enters the province in the north and travels along the coast hitting most of the major cities before going into Lycia et Pamphylia. The *Via Augusta Nova* and *Via Galatia* both cut through the mountains and enter Galatia in the north and south respectively. Additionally, one can enter the province through the ports in any of the major coastal cities.

Coming along the *Asiana* from Pontus and Bithynia, you'll reach **Cyzicus** on a narrow isthmus on northern shore of the province known as Arctonnesus.

According to legend, Alexander had his soldiers heap dirt into the sea until the then island of Arctonnesus was connected to the land. The city boasts one of the largest amphitheaters in the entire Empire, as well as a theater, nice baths, and temples to the Imperial cult.

There are a number of cities which are off the main road through Asia which are still attractive locations to visit for their cultural and historical relevance. **Lampsacus** for example is the supposed birthplace of Priapus, so his temple and idols are found aplenty here if you're into that.[1] A number of philosophers, mathematicians, and talented satirists are also born here throughout the years.

Troia or **Ilium** is found further south, near the coast. The city was originally named **Wilion** by the Greeks, but they had *twuhble* with the *Wuh* sound, thus dropping the digamma to call is Ilion. The city has numerous amenities, including music, theater, racing, splendidly decorated temples with the largest dedicated to Athena and of course the culture of the Trojans who share a common ancestry with the Romans.[2] **Alexandria Troas** is the largest port city in the province, and in fact, in most of the region. The city will be considered as a candidate for the new capital by Constantine, but we already know where he chooses to have his city. The city has a fine stadium, baths, and gymnasium should you choose to visit.

The city of **Pergamum** has numerous attractions and is found along the *Via Asiana*. There are several temples, including one to Aesculapius, which is expanded into a spa. There is also a large forum, amphitheater, theater, and stadium. The physician Galen is eventually born here, if you find yourself coming down sick with something, just remember that you'll never have him as your doctor.

Cyme or **Cumae** was supposedly founded by an Amazonian woman of the same name. The *Via Augusta Nova* begins at **Smyrna** heading inland. **Smyrna** has several beautiful statues to Zeus, Hestia, Hermes, Dionysus, Eros and Hercules in the agora. **Sardis** is found along the *Augusta* in the interior of the province. It has a great bath-gymnasium complex with attached synagogue, and a temple to Artemis. In DCCLXX A.U.C. (17 C.E.) the city is devastated by an earthquake, so avoid around that time. The *Via* continues to **Dorylaeum**, which during the early Empire is a trading post, the road continues from here into Galatia.

Ephesus is the capital of the province and has numerous things to see and do. There are two agorae in the city, the State Agora in the southeast, and the Lower Agora southwest of the theater. Each agora is surrounded by plenty do to, as well as good shopping. There are several temples spread around the city, with concentrations near the agorae. The temple to Artemis is found north of town and is listed as one of the Seven

---

[1] Be careful doing an image search for this guy. NSFW.

[2] Not to mention their wealth of contraceptives.

Wonders of the Ancient World.

♦ Artemis' temple was destroyed before in the past by some arsonist trying to achieve immortal fame.[1]

The Temples of Domitian, Divus Iulius, Dea Roma, and Hestia are found around the State Agora. On the road down towards the theater is the nymphaeum, and temple of Hadrian. There is also a temple of Serapis on the west side of the Lower Agora. The city has an impressive Greek style theater on the eastern side of town near the lower agora at the end of the harbor road.

The city's library is on the south side of the Lower Agora. The western gymnasium, near the harbor, is the nicer of the two found in Ephesus. It has a grand bathhouse attached to the complex. The other gymnasium is found northwest of the theater. A small stadium is on the north side of town. The odeon is just north of the State Agora. While it pales in comparison to the city's theater, it still has worthwhile performances regularly.

Magnesia[2] is an Ionian city, found along the *Maeander*. The city has temples to Artemis, Zeus and Dindymene and a nice theater. Here the *Via Galatia* heads inland, and the *Via Asiana* continues southward.

South of **Magnesia** is the city **Miletus**, which has a theater, stadium, renowned school of literature, temples to Athena and Apollo, agorae and gymnasium. On the way to the next town, it's worth the trip to check out **Halicarnassus**, where the Tomb of Mausolus is found, one of the Seven Wonders of the Ancient World. The road continues along the coast before eventually coming to **Caunus.** Near the border to Lycia and Pamphylia, this city has an amphitheater, bath-palaestra, and several Grecian temples.

Tralles is a short ways east of **Magnesia**, much further to the northeast is the commercial center known as **Laodicea ad Lycum.** The city, in addition to having large markets and a surplus of trading goods for you to sift through, has many temples, baths, a stadium, theaters, and a gymnasium. **Apamea ad Maeandrum** sits right near the border of Lycia and Pamphylia. A road running north-south exits the province to the south and ends at **Dorylaeum** in the north.

---

[1] We can't seem to recall his name at the moment.

[2] Don't drink milk from here.

Lycia et Pamphylia[1]

Size: 14,303 square Roman miles
Capital: Attaleia
Government: Imperial Province
Religion: Grecian and Roman Polytheism
Language: Greek and Latin
Established: DCCXXVII a.u.c. (74 c.e.)
De-established: MLXXVIII a.u.c. (25 c.e.)

One major road, the *Via Asiana* runs along the southern coast of the province. Several smaller roads head up into the mountains and there are numerous ports along the shores.

Patara is a coastal city on the western side of the province. It is noted for its oracle at its temple to Apollo. The city also has baths and a theater. Further east is **Myra**, which has temples, a theater and baths, the city also has an abundance of Murex shells and the dye can be bought *slightly* cheaper here than in most of the Empire if you want to have a regal look to you. The city of **Gagae** is renowned for its magical healing stones. They drive away serpents, diagnose epilepsy, relieve feminine hysteria, evacuate worms, treat heart problems and remove sexually transmitted infections.[2] Just north-east of **Gagae** is Mount Chimaera where flames from its battle with Bellerophon can still be seen to this day.[3]

Attaleia is the provincial capital. It has an impressive harbor, augmented by the surrounding terrain. East of here is **Side**, which has a temple to Apollo, theater, baths, and nymphaeum.

In the western part of the province, off the coast is the city of **Tlos**. With an impressive theater, some rather nice baths, a palaestra, stadium, agora and a few temples, it's definitely worth a visit. Nearby **Nisa** also has a stadium and theater, and well used agora.

North of **Tlos** is **Oenoanda**, which has a few amenities including a theater. Further north near the border of Asia is **Cibyra.** A large multi-cultured city, it has numerous public buildings including a theater, odeon, stadium, baths, and temples.

---

[1] Meaning "Brochure Lovers", but not in a weird way, like those Pampheros creeps.
[2] Works just about as well as anyone selling a salt lamp promising the same effects.
[3] Mount Chimaera is half mountain, half hill, and half caverns. Three halves, that's right.

There are a cluster of cities in the eastern interior of the province. **Perga** has fine baths with an attached palaestra, theater, stadium, agora and temple to Artemis. West of **Perga** is **Termessos**, here you can find an odeon and theater, as well as six temples, including one to Zeus and another to Artemis. Other cities, such as **Ariassus**, **Pednelissus** and **Sagalassos** further inland are interesting enough, but probably not worth a visit unless you're passing through to Galatia.

Galatia

Size: 47,335 square Roman miles
Capital: Ancyra
Government: Imperial Province
Religion: Roman, Grecian, Celtic and Phrygian polytheism
Language: Latin, Greek, Gaulish
Established: DCCXXIX A.U.C. (25 B.C.E.)

There are two main routes through Galatia, one northern, the *Via Augusta Nova* and one southern, the *Via Galatia.* The two routes are connected by smaller approximately north-south running roads in the neighboring provinces. Starting from either Bithynia et Pontus or Cappadocia and taking the northern route will bring you to **Ancyra,** the provincial capital, founded by the legendary King Midas.

 The Galatians here built a castle upon a rocky promontory, which the Romans further fortified, it is an excellent place to see what Celtic architecture looks like so far east. The city has a temple to Augustus and Roma built on an earlier site dedicated to Man, found northwest of the citadel. The city has a palaestra and gymnasium for local athletes. Late imperial baths are found just northwest of the temple to Augustus. The theater is built into the side of the west side of the citadel; it is well decorated with beautiful statues.

Heading southeast along the road will bring you into Cappadocia. Galatia, and much of this region in general could be considered a *sail-past province* as in "there's nothing here, might as well just *sail-past.*"[1]

After passing through **Archelais,** and come to **Tyana,** just west of the city you'll re-enter Galatia. A ways down the road is **Heraclea Cybistra.** An important choke-point on the route through the Cilician Gates, the city serves as a regular check-point for the Roman military.[2] While it has strategic importance, there isn't much for you to do here, apart from rest before heading on.

Iconium is a city of Greeks, Romans and a small population of Hebrews. It's a good place to stop for water and food in what is a largely hot and fairly inhospitable stretch of terrain.

A shining bastion of Roman culture in a strongly barbarian area is the city of **Antiochia Caesareia,** Latin is the official language of the city and spoken regularly, alongside Greek, Gaulish and Hebrew. The city has a theater, a nympheum, forum partially surrounded by a stoa, baths, a stadium, synagogue, and temples to Augustus and Mens Askaenos.[3]

From Antiochia you can cross into the province of Asia, then turn north, then east again to come back into the province. **Pessinus** is south of the colony of **Germa.** It is the seat of the cult of Cybele. The city has a robust temple district with several sanctuaries, including a theater temple. It also has a gymnasium and palaestra, as well as a forum and baths.

Heading towards Ancyra you'll pass the ruins of **Gordium**, a city made famous by its Gordian knot, according to prophecy, whoever managed to untie it would become the ruler of all Asia. Alexander the Great managed to loosen the knot by either cutting it or pulling a pin from the cart it was tied to. He then proceeded to technically conquer all of Asia, but that didn't really last too long, kind of a waste of a prophecy…

---

[1] You could also call them flyovers if'n you have a magic wine cup.

[2] You definitely want to go through the checkpoint over the choke-point.

[3] God of the moon, Now you can worship at any Mens Warehouse.

Cilicia

Size: 22,688 square Roman miles
Capital: Tarsus
Government: Imperial Province
Religion: Grecian and Roman Polytheism
Language: Anatolian, Greek, Latin
Established: DCXCI A.U.C. (63 B.C.E.)
De-established: ML A.U.C. (297 C.E.)

The main route running through Cilicia is the *Via Asiana* which follows the coast of the Mediterranean through the entire province. A few other routes cut through the mountains heading north into Galatia and Cappadocia.

Entering the province from the west, you'll follow the *Asiana* for some time before reaching **Anemurium** at the province's most southern point. It has a port, theater, odeon, and nice baths. To the northeast is **Seleucia ad Calycadnum**, found a few miles up from the mouth of the *Calycadnus*. It has an exquisite temple district, with a resplendent temple to Jupiter. The road here goes inland towards Galatia. **Corycus** is a few miles southeast of **Seleucia** and is its port town. Not far from town is a cave which was once the lair of Typhon[1] and is where the best saffron in the world grows.

The provincial capital **Tarsus** is the civil and religious metropolis for the region. It has numerous temples, a gymnasium, stadium, baths, academy, as well as an important port and shipyard. There is a road from here heading up towards Cappadocia. The small port town of **Myriandros** sits near the provincial border headed into Syria.

---

[1] Typhon is a half man, half snake, but not in the mermaid sense. Many illustrations show him with his two legs replaced by two separate snake bodies without any feet at the end; he must have walked like some kind of awkward octopus. His wife is also snake from the waist down, and together they are often cited as the parents of most if not all other mythological monsters.

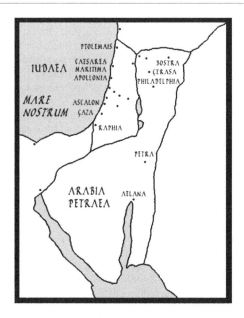

Iudaea

Size: 8,483 square Roman miles
Capital: Caesarea Maritima
Government: Imperial Province
Religion: Roman, Grecian and Punic Polytheism, Judaism, Christianity
Language: Latin, Greek, Phoenician, Hebrew and Aramaic
Established: DCCLIX A.U.C. (6 C.E.)
Reorganized: DCCCLXXXVIII A.U.C. (135 C.E.)
As Syria Palestina: MCXLIII A.U.C. (390 C.E.)

Iudaea is primarily accessible through its numerous ports along the
Mediterranean coast, there is a main road that follows along the coast,
and a secondary road which cuts off the main one heading inland towards
Hierosolyma. The province is bordered on the eastern side by the *flumen
Iordanes* which separates it from Arabia Petraea.

Entering the province from Aegyptus in the south, you'll come to the
town of **Raphia** which is built up by Gabinius in the 1st century B.C.E. Just
north of there is **Gaza**, which is an impressive city favored by the
Emperors.

It has an immense stadium where wrestling, boxing and oratorical competitions are held.[1] The city also has numerous temples to Zeus, Apollo, Helios, Aphrodite and Athena with the city's chief temple dedicated to Marnas. There are also synagogues and early churches here, the Christians purge most of the other temples in the early 5th century so you don't have to worry about missing anything as long as you're here on the earlier side of the 4th century.[2]

The road splits at **Ascalon**, a city built up by Herod with magnificent public buildings. The road here continues northwards or east into the middle of the province. **Lydda** is to the northeast of **Ascalon**, you may want to pass on through; however, it is razed in the later 1st and again in the early 2nd centuries for rebellion. At the dawn of the 3rd century it is finally elevated to the level of city by Septimus Severus.

Ioppe is a known pirate port and maybe not the safest place to sail from or to. **Apollonia**, however, to the north of **Ioppe** is a safe port and expansive commercial center for the region. The provincial capital of **Caesarea Maritima** is found on the coast. **Caesarea** has a hippodrome which is later converted into a theater, and occasionally used for water games. Just before reaching the city the road splits with the eastern fork heading to Arabia. The city of **Ake-Ptolemais** is the last major port you'll come to before entering Syria. It has baths and a gymnasium built by Herod. The road continues onwards to Tyrus.

Heading east from **Ascalon** you'll reach the major road hub of **Eleutheropolis**. It is an important city in the region, from here you can head in numerous directions. To the northeast is **Aelia Capitolina**, also known as **Hierosolyma**. The city was built up by Herod in the 1st century C.E. and then razed in DCCCXXIII A.U.C. (70 C.E.) so completely that no sign of previous habitation remains. Visit earlier if you'd like to see the second temple before its destruction. Also, Jewish travelers may consider skipping this city after the province is reformed as Syria Palestina, as all Hebrews are banned from the city save one day a year during Tisha B'Av, but Christians are welcome in the 4th century.

♦ If visiting during DCCLXXXIII A.U.C. – DCCLXXXIX A.U.C. (30 C.E. – 36 C.E.) be wary of the *Populi Frons Iudeae,* who are a radical cell of Hebrews who are said to hate the Romans, *a lot!* They even go as far as painting *Romanes eunt domus* once, and *Romani ite domum* one hundred times onto the walls of the governor's palace. Don't worry as much about running into the *Iudeae Populi Frons,* they're reportedly wankers.

Scythopolis is in the northeastern corner of the province, the city

---

[1] It's kind of like how comedians perform in multipurpose sports complex arenas.

[2] Gaza will later get taken over by Byzantine Christians, razed, by Persian Muslims, razed again, the Western Christians came back, razed some more, then back and forth between the Christians, Jews, and Muslims until the sun burns out.

flourishes under Roman rule and has a Hippodrome, nymphaeum, baths and a Roman style theater. The road here heads westwards towards the coast, or a couple routes head east across the *Iordanes* into Arabia.

Arabia Petraea

Size: 38,233 square Roman miles
Capital: Petra, Bostra
Government: Imperial Province
Religion: Nabataean, Roman and Grecian Polytheism, Judaism,
Christianity
Language: Arabic, Aramaic, Latin, Greek, Hebrew
Established: DCCCLIX A.U.C. (106 C.E.)
De-established: MCCCLXXXVI A.U.C. (633 C.E.)

Arabia Petraea is a massive province bordered by Aegyptus on the west,
the *Mare Arabicum* to the south and Iudaea and Syria to the northwest
and north respectively. Most of the cities are focused in the northern part
of the province with a couple in the south. The main road stretches from
Aela in the south headed through **Petra** and then splitting in the north
heading into the other provinces.

   The coastal city of **Aela** or **Aelana** sits on the northernmost tip of the
Mare Arabicum. It is a major port and you can easily barter passage to
southern Aegyptus from here.

   The first provincial capital, **Petra**, is north of the sea. Here there is an
ingenious set of dams and canals which direct the flow of flash flood
water for storage. The city early on is a major hub for caravan trade but
declines as sea trade increases.[1] The road splits here, heading west to
Gaza or continuing north.

   Philadelphia is in the northern part of the province. It is a robust city
with a theater, odeon, nymphaeum and temple to Hercules on its citadel.[2]
A road here heads northwest into Iudaea, another to **Gerasa** and a third
to **Bostra.** The city of **Gerasa** has large temples to Zeus and Artemis, a
triumphal arch, nymphaeum, two theaters, baths, a hippodrome and
bizarrely ovular forum which is nearly unique in the entire Empire.

---

[1] This leads to gangs of unemployed camels, sitting around trying to look cool in leather
jackets and smoking cigarettes.
[2] In Old Philadelphia, born and raised, in the forum is where I spent mosta my days...

North of **Gerasa** is **Capitolias**, which has a Roman theater, west of here is **Gadara** birthplace of the Grecian poet Meleager. The city is razed as a result of the Jewish revolt in the 1st century, so steer clear during that time. **Bostra** is the second provincial capital and is found in the far northeast of the province. **Bostra** is a busy town with a few sights, the theater is as the south end of the Cardo Maximus, the stadium is west of that. The hippodrome is south of the stadium and can accommodate 30,000 spectators, and the Trajan baths are found on the eastern end of the Decumanus.

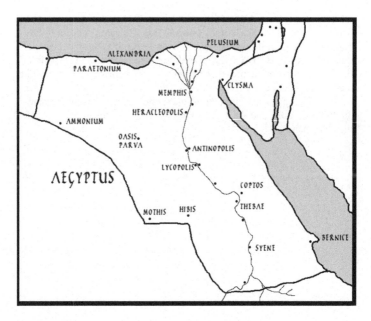

Aegyptus

Size: 249,236 square Roman miles
Capital: Alexandria
Government: Imperial Province
Religion: Grecian and Egyptian Polytheism, Judaism
Language: Latin, Greek, Egyptian, Hebrew
Established: DCCXXIV A.U.C. (30 B.C.E.)
Conquered: MCCCXCIV A.U.C. (641 C.E.)

Aegyptus is a large province and serves as the western boundary of Asia.
There are two main roads, one generally following along the coast and
the other down the shores of the *flumen Nilus.* It is a beautiful and
wealthy province with history millennia older than Roma herself.

If you enter the province from Africa to the west, you'll come to
Paraetonium after a short while. It has a major military port built for the
Egyptian navy. The road continues to the east, but another heads south
into the desert. **Ammonium** is an oasis in the far south, it has an oracular
temple to Amun which is worth a visit. To the east is another oasis,
Oasis Parva and the road continues east towards the *Nilus.*

The provincial capital of **Alexandria** is found to the east of

Paraetonium. The city has several temples of note, the primary being dedicated to Poseidon, with temples to Saturn, Serapis and Osiris on the west side of town, and a temple of Hephaestus near the lighthouse. The main baths[1] are adjacent to the temple of Osiris. The city's main theater is near the temple of Poseidon in the center of town, off the forum, built into the side of a hill. The Musaeum is the most popular tourist attraction, particularly because of its library. It is partially destroyed multiple times during its existence, first when Caesar sacks the city, then later by the Emperor Aurelian when suppressing a revolt, thankfully if you get books just before that, there won't be any late fees. There is also a small theater attached to the complex. The gymnasium and attached palaestra are found on the eastern side of town. The ships found at the docks, guided by their magnificent lighthouse, can take you just about anywhere in the world. Along the coast you'll spot the Great Lighthouse of Alexandria, one of the Seven Wonders of the Ancient World.

Naucratis is found to the southeast of the capital. It was an important port city before the founding of **Alexandria**, and a prominent Greek city and trading post. Herodotus writes in to tell us that the prostitutes here are described as peculiarly alluring.[2]

Heading southward and following the river delta brings you to **Heliopolis**, a beautiful city filled with massive temples and impressive obelisks. The city is the center of the cult of Ra-Atum and holds numerous records on Egyptian history. **Memphis** is further up river, while it is largely abandoned in favor of **Alexandria**, its magnificent temples are worth seeing. There is a gargantuan temple complex to Ptah[3] with several smaller temples adjoining. There are also temples and sanctuaries dedicated to Hathor, Mithras, Astarte, Sekhmet, Apis, Amun and Aten. Just north of Memphis are the Great Pyramids and the Great Sphynx, the largest of these three pyramids is one of the seven wonders of the ancient world.[4]

On your way further south you'll pass through **Aphroditopolis** and **Heracleopolis**, the latter of which has a temple to Heryshef. Much further up river are the cities of **Antinopolis** and **Hermopolis Magna** on opposite sides of the *Nilus*. The former is built by Hadrian to commemorate the loss of a lover, Antinous who drowned near the city. It has numerous temples, a circus and theater, with annual races to celebrate their eponym. The latter has temples to the gods Thoth and

---

[1] You're going to need it with all the sand blowing around.

[2] He wrote the oddest postcards. "Wish you were here".

[3] Egyptian deity of craftsmanship and architects. It is said he created the world just by thinking about it.

[4] And the last one standing. It goes to show, it's a lot easier to pillage a giant bronze statue after an earthquake brings it down than it is to disassemble 6 million tonnes of sandstone, despite the limestone facing being pillaged to build mosques in Cairo.

Typhon and is primarily a resort town. Just south of **Antinopolis** is the oracle of **Besa**.

Lycopolis and **Hieracon** are likewise located on opposite sides of the river from one another. The latter of which has a Roman cohort detachment stationed there. **Ptolemais Hermiou** is a Greek city further up-river with temples to both Greek and Egyptian gods, most prominently, Zeus, Dionysus and Isis. There is a strong theatrical presence here with quality plays regularly shown at the theater.

The city of **Coptos** has several large temples dedicated to Min and Isis, Geb, and Horus.[1] The *Via Hadriana* leads south-east from **Coptos** to the city of **Berenice** on the coast which connects Aegyptus to India and Arabia. **Thebae** was the religious center of all of Egypt before Greek and later Roman occupation. Its chief deity Amun-Ra and his wife Mut and son Khonsu are principally worshipped. There are also temples to Ptah, Hathor and Isis. The nearby valleys of the Kings and Queens are beautifully decorated, and the Colossi of Memnon are impressively tall.

Further south are the cities of **Hierakonpolis**, **Syene** and **Hierasykaminos**, while they have some things to see and do, they're not really worth visiting unless you're committed to taking that much longer to get back to civilization.

Northeast of **Heliopolis** is the city of **Boubastis**, a city which has a dedication to Bastet and therefore an unhealthy dedication to cats as well.[2] On the eastern side of the delta is **Pelusium** which sits on two military roads and has a decent port. South of here is **Clysma** which provides a sea trade route which stretches down the coast. The road continues east from **Pelusium** into Iudaea.

---

[1] We're not going to tell you what all these represent here. See Chapter XVIII for a list of the various deities, their roles, and their cross-pantheon equivalents.

[2] It is the world's second largest repository for mummified cats, after one crazy lady in Fort Wayne, Indiana.

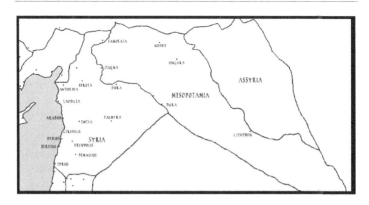

Syria

Size: 67,610 square Roman miles
Capital: Antiochia
Government: Imperial Province
Religion: Grecian, Roman, and Punic Polytheism, Judaism
Language: Greek, Phoenician, Aramaic
Established: DCXC A.U.C. (64 B.C.E.)
De-established: MCXLIII A.U.C. (390 C.E.)

Syria occupies a region on the eastern shores of the Mediterranean. There is the main road, which runs north-south along the coast passing through many major cities. Other roads run parallel further inland, and a few connect the major routes in between.

The provincial capital, **Antiochia**[1] is found just south of the provincial border with Cilicia. The city has a forum in the center of town and an agora to the south with a temple of Jupiter adjacent. The theater is between the forum and the agora, and the amphitheater is south of the latter. Most of the city's baths are found in the northern portion of town, where the river splits. The stadium and attached gymnasium are south of the Palatium. The circus is found in the north of the city, just east of the Palatium. There is also a temple of Apollo, and a synagogue. The nymphaeum found right off the forum.[2]

To the south is **Laodicea**, which is a city noted for its wine production,

---

[1] Similarly important to Christian, Jewish, and Islamic combatants as was the Holy Land in Gaza. Everyone on a religious crusade passed through and subsequently left their mark on the city.
[2] It also becomes well known later for its manufacture of Hand Grenades with very specific timing.

the nearby hills almost entirely covered in lush vineyards. The Punic island of **Aradus** is just off shore between **Laodicea** and **Tripolis**. It has a proud and illustrious history steeped in naval tradition.

Tripolis has a temple to the Imperial cult and a stadium if you're in town. The city is mostly a financial center but has a bustling port, so you can at least catch a ride here.

Byblos is a thriving port city and the main exporter of Egyptian papyrus. If you're not looking to get involved in the paper trade there is a theater here, as well as a site sacred to Isis and Osiris, and temples to Resheph and Adonis. If you're looking to hear some Latin spoken in the region, stop by **Berytus**. Founded by Augustus, it is a proper Roman colony. Here you can find baths, a theater and amphitheater, several temples and a prestigious school of law. [1]

The city of **Tyrus** is renowned throughout the ancient world for its shellfishy purple dye and for being the city from which Phoenician naval dominance spread across the early Mediterranean, founding Punic cities in Africa, Sicilia and Hispania. The city was once an island, until Alexander decided to change that fact when he sacked the city.[2] The city has temples to Melqart and Hephaestus, a hippodrome, and theater. The road continues south into Iudaea.

In the interior of the province, along the eastern road heading north from Iudaea is **Damascus**. It sits on a convergence point of a few trade routes from Egypt, Iudaea and even the silk route from India. It has a theater and temple to Jupiter. Just north of **Damascus** is **Heliopolis**, a town sacred to Ba'al Haddu equated to Helios.[3] There are three main temples, one to Jupiter Heliopolitanus (Ba'al), Venus Heliopolitana (Ashtart) and Bacchus (just Bacchus). There is also an oracle here which is even consulted by Emperors.

The city of **Emesa** sits on a crossroads, the citizens here are most proud of their temple to the sun god El-Gabal. There is a road here heading east to **Palmyra**, north towards **Beroea** or west towards **Aradus**. **Palmyra** to the east has a lot to see in do, there are nice baths, a proper Greek agora, Roman theater and a bunch of temples dedicated to Bel, Baalshamin, Nabu, Al-lat, Baal-hamon. The road from **Palmyra** heads north towards the *Euphrates*.

---

[1] It's that friendly kind of feeling, like finding a McDonald's in Malaysia.
[2] He had much of the city demolished and used the stone to connect to the mainland.
[3] This was the Roman way. What gods do you have? We have that too! But ours is better! Call theirs ours! Speak proper Rom'n, yeh barbarian hicks.

Mesopotamia

Size: 101,986 square Roman miles
Capital: Amiba, Dara, Nisibis
Government: Imperial Province
Religion: Grecian and Mesopotamian Polytheism
Language: Greek, Aramaic
Established: DCCCLXIX A.U.C. (116 C.E.) CMLI A.U.C. (198 C.E.)
De-established: DCCCLXX A.U.C. (117 C.E.) Conquered: MCCCXC A.U.C.
(637 C.E.)

The province of Mesopotamia only lasts for a year the first time around, the second time the province is created, it is constantly a hotbed for military activity, it's probably not worth the visit. If you are incredibly determined to stop in, the cities of **Amiba, Dara** and **Nisibis** are nice when not under siege. **Circesium** sits on the border of Syria and is probably safe to visit. In **Babylon** you will however, find the Hanging Gardens, one of the Seven Wonders of the Ancient World.[1]

---

[1] Maybe. Conflicting surviving accounts carry little evidence of their location or even their very existence forward in time. If you do visit them, geotag for us, will you?

Armenia

Size: 77,499 square Roman miles
Capital: Artashat
Government: Imperial Province
Religion: Grecian and Mesopotamian Polytheism
Language: Greek, Aramaic
Established: DCCCLXVII A.U.C. (114 C.E.)
De-established: DCCCLXXI A.U.C. (118 C.E.)

Don't Bother.

Assyria

Size: 63,165 square Roman miles
Capital: Ctesiphon
Government: Imperial Province
Religion: Grecian and Mesopotamian Polytheism
Language: Greek, Aramaic
Established: DCCCLXIX A.U.C. (116 C.E.)
De-established: DCCCLXXI A.U.C. (118 C.E.)

No, *Really...* Don't Bother.

X Mare Nostrum

The Mediterranean, *Mare Nostrum* or *Mare Internum* in Latin, or ἡ μεγάλη θάλασσα in Greek is the sea spanning from the Pillars of Hercules in the west to Aegyptus in the east. It contains several other smaller seas including the Aegean, *Mare Aegaeum* or Αρχιπέλαγος, the Adriatic, *Mare Hadriaticum* or Αδριατική θάλασσα, the Ionian, *Mare Ionium* or Ιόνιον Πέλαγος, the Libyan, *Libycum Mare* or Λιβυκόν Πέλαγος, and the Tyrrhenian, *Tyrrhenum Mare* or Τυρρηνικόν Πέλαγος.[1]

---

[1] Looks like the Greeks spell it "Tupp'nvikov". Silly Greeks and their dumb original alphabet.

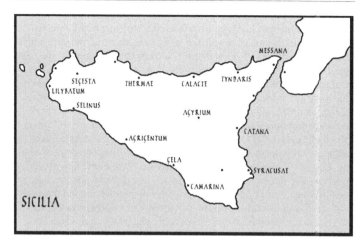

Sicilia

Size: 10,724 Roman square miles
Capital: Syracusae
Government: Senatorial Province
Religion: Roman, Greek, and Punic Polytheism
Language: Latin, Greek, Punic
Established: DCIII A.U.C. (241 B.C.E.)
De-established: MCCXXIX A.U.C. (476 C.E.)

As an island province in the southern Tyrrhenian, there is only one way to Sicilia and that is by boat. Well, we suppose you could in fact swim, but you'd probably get tired by the time you arrived unless you are a demi-god. The cheapest place to cross is from Rhegium in Italy. However, do not take the ferry if you can help it. There are far too many locals who make the trip daily or weekly to bother paying for a ride. Do a favor for one of them and get a ride across, and maybe one back if they remember you. The *Via Valeria* follows the coast around the island, bringing you to around to the larger cities on the perimeter.

   Messana is easily spotted on your approach from Italia due to its lighthouse. It is a typical Greek colony city, with an agora, theater, and gymnasium. The important part of Messana is the port however, which serves to bring goods to Italia from all over Sicilia.
♦ In DCCXVIII A.U.C. (36 B.C.E.), Augustus squares off against Sextus Pompey, after the latter took the town as a base for his revolt against the former.[1]

Heading counter-clockwise from Messana brings you to **Tyndaris.** Here Mercury is much beloved, but sadly their statue of him was stolen not just once, but twice. First by the Carthaginians as a spoil of war, then by some jerk named Verres, who broke it as soon as he fled the island. [1] **Calacte,** down the coast, has a strong fishing economy if you're looking for some day work. **Thermae** is a city rich in the arts as well as bath temperature. They too have statues returned to them after they were retrieved from the Carthaginians. **Panormus** is a city of mixed Roman and Punic cultures. The city was held by Carthage and resisted Greek attempts at dominance multiple times before finally being abandoned to the Romans. You can take in the architecture of the Punic fortress and walls, or the numerous Roman additions. The city has a sizable dock, and you may be able to find work, or a ship headed further around the coast.

A short ways inland is **Segesta**, supposedly originally named Egesta, the Romans changed that due to that name just being crap. There is a nice theater here, and an unfinished Doric temple which lacks ornamentation entirely. **Eryx** stands on a mountain in the northwest corner of the island. There is a magnificent temple here built by Aeneas himself, the city is named after his brother, who was killed in a wrestling match with Hercules.[2] **Dreponum** is its port city on the coast. To the south is the city of **Lilybaeum,** described as a most splendid city. The forum is located at the city center. The further west you go of the *Cardo Maximus,* the pricier and newer things get. You'll want to stick to the older, Punic side if you want to get things for a more reasonable price.

The acropolis of **Selinus** has wonderous temples, most of which are destroyed as the Carthaginians toppled the city as they were withdrawing from Sicilia. It is still a fun place to visit if you want to explore the ruins and poke around for salvage and relics. The *Via Selinutina* begins here and heads east. Further along the southern coast you'll come to **Agrigentum**, probably the place where you can find the cheapest clothes and fabrics in the Empire. The city also has the Valley of the Temples, with shrines and sanctuaries to Concordia, Hera, Heracles, Zeus, Castor and Pollux, Hephaestus, Aesculapius and shrines to the underworld deities. The city is still administered in Greek fashion despite its Roman status.

Gela sits near where the road cuts east across the interior of the island towards **Syracusae.** To the south is **Camarina**, the ancient citizens

---

[1] "You've committed one of the classic blunders! The most famous is never get involved in a land war in Asia. But only slightly less well known is this: Never go against a Sicilian when death is on the line!" The Sicillian here gets it too. Well, he wasn't from Sicily, but still.
[1] A tradition carried on by drunk idiots from rival colleges to this very day.
[2] Probably died naked after grappling with another dude in the hot sun all afternoon. Not the most dignified way to go.

accidently caused their own destruction by draining marshes to their north to avert a plague. With the marsh drained the Carthaginians were able to march across dry land and sack the city. Currently it is a small town with an agora and temple to Athena. **Acrae** sits east of **Gela** on the *Selinutina,* built up on a hill it is highly defensible and serves as the main watch post for the region. It has a temple to Aphrodite and small theater.

Syracusae is the capital of the province. It has a few sights to see and a healthy port for hitching a ride. It has a rich history which is well worth learning about, from its initial colonization from Corinthus to the expulsion of their upper class, the subsequent reclaiming, and then later battles with the Carthaginians. Be careful who you offend here though, you don't want to end up pressed into labor in the quarries near the theater.

Right off the coast of **Syracusae** is the island of Ortygia, where there is a major temple of Apollo, Athena's sanctuary is just south of there.[1] The fountain of Arethusa on Ortygia is where the nymph, transformed into a stream by Artemis, came to form the pool as we know it today.

The theater here is one of the largest ever built by Greeks. The Romans modified it to also act as a circus, the theater seats forming one of the turns. Here Aeschylus produced his plays, *Persai* and *Aetnae.*[2] Near the theater is a sanctuary of Demeter. The city's amphitheater is an impressive bit of architecture, the Romans cut much of the arena out of the living rock, and then built the structure up around it.[3]

In the city there is the Altar of Hieron, built at the same time as the theater by Hiero II. The surrounding area had been used for sacrifices and votives for a long time before the altar was built. Commemorating Zeus in CCLXXXVIII A.U.C. (466 B.C.E.) 450 bulls were sacrificed in a single offering. A triumphal arch is found near the city, built during the early empire commemorating Augustus' victory over the Sicilian revolt. Lastly, there is a temple to Zeus on a hill south of town.

North of **Syracusae** is the town of **Catana**, which sits in the shadow of *Aetna Mons.* The volcano is believed to be where Hephaestus forges thunderbolts for Zeus, and where Typhon is sealed. In the 2nd century B.C.E., Hephaestus' carelessness causes hefty damage to **Catana**, with ash raining so heavily it collapsed roofs. **Tauromenium,** halfway between **Catana** and **Messana** has a fine Greek style theater and a few temples.

---

[1] Consult with a preist of Aesculapius to determine if Ortygia is right for you.
[2] He is known as the father of Tragedy, so expect these to be real upbeat. Great date night shows, these.
[3] You should know it's much more difficult than digging it out of plain old dead rock.

Sardinia et Corsica

Size: 13,962 square Roman feet
Capital: Caralis
Government: Senatorial Province
Religion: Roman, Etruscan, Greek, and Punic Polytheism
Language: Latin, Etruscan, Greek, Punic
Established: DXVI/DXVII A.U.C. (238/237 B.C.E.)
Split: DCCLIX A.U.C. (6 C.E.)
Conquered: MCCVIII A.U.C. (455 C.E.)

Sardinia and Corsica, being islands in the middle of the Tyrrhenian are
also only reachable by boat. Lilybaeum, Ostia, Tarraco, Massalia,
Carthago and Narbo all have ships that pass through either of the islands,
and it's not hard to find a ship crossing the *Fretum Gallicum* strait
between the two. Corsica is the less populous of the two; it is mostly
Greek and Etruscan in culture. Sardinia was held by the Greeks and
Carthaginians prior to Roman occupation.

Corsica has few major cities of note, mostly ports for importing and exporting local goods. **Mariana** and **Aleria** are found on the east coast. Aleria is an excellent place to get some fresh oysters, as they are harvested from the lake just north of town.[1] The city has a temple to Augustus and Roma on the eastern side of the forum, there are baths to the north. There are traces of Punic, Grecian, and Etruscan architecture here alongside the more modern Roman structures, but it's better to just visit Italia if that's what you're about. **Adiacium** is a harbor on the south-western side of the island.

Olbia is a port city on the northeastern shore of Sardinia, it has a temple to Ceres, as well as a Punic temple. There are baths not too far from the forum. Ships frequent Ostia from here.

Turris Libyssonis is a larger city founded by Caesar on the northern side of the island. The *Via Sarda* connects it with **Caralis** in the south. The city has a port, forum, baths, and a temple of Fortuna. Headed south from Turris you'll pass through **Bosa**,[2] further down you'll pass through **Corus** and **Othoca,** Othoca is a producer of wine and vinegar,[3] which ships through nearby **Tharros.**

Caralis is the largest city on the island and the provincial capital. It serves as an important port, with trade routes stretching in a wide arc from the city reaching Africa, Gallia, Italia, Sicilia and Hispania. The amphitheater of Caralis is fairly sized, holding 10,000 spectators. Its appearance is striking against the landscape, carved into the side of a hill and built up with local white limestone, it shines beautifully against the surrounding greenery. Caralis hosts one of the oldest temple theaters in the Empire which was built by the Phoenician colonists. The city has a nice forum, with great *Piscatores,* much of the local cuisine is seafood based, and you can get great deals on fresh fish.

---

[1] Being that you are in a time before refrigeration, you really do not want non-fresh oysters.

[2] It experiences some eventual decline, but it is reestablished in 1112 as Bosa Nova.

[3] They won't tell you which is which.

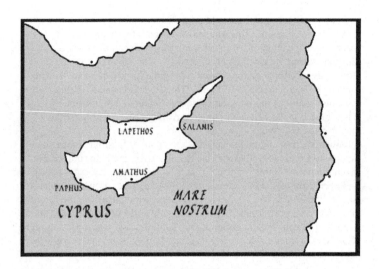

Cyprus

Size: 3,884 square Roman miles
Capital: Paphus
Government: Senatorial Province
Religion: Grecian and Roman polytheism
Language: Greek, Latin
Established: DCXCVI A.U.C. (58 B.C.E.)
Went with the East in the divorce: MCXLVIII A.U.C. (395 C.E.)

Cyprus is most easily reached from Syria to the east or Cilicia to the north. The island itself is comparable in size to Creta. The main road runs along the southern coast.

Lapethos is on the northern coast, is a major producer of copper and earthenware products, so if you've lost or broken anything, it's a nice place to pick something up on the cheap.

On the eastern side of the island is **Salamis**.[1] A vast cultural center, and prior seat of governance in the province. The city amphitheater is incorporated into larger stadium on the northern side of town. The theater is found just to the south. North of the stadium-amphitheater complex is the gymnasium and palaestra with attached baths. There are two more bath houses to the north-east (Greek style) and south-west (Roman style)

---

[1] Besides cured meats, there is also a town called that.

of the amphitheater. The city's fine fish markets are near the Roman baths, well, the market is fine, the fish less so later in the day, but you'll be able to tell by the smell. The main agora is on the southern side of town, with a temple to Zeus at its southern end.

Further west there is a temple to Aphrodite and nice agora in **Amathus. Paphus** is the provincial capital during the Roman period, it has a theater, odeon, agora, a robust harbor and a temple to Apollo. There are exquisite mosaics in the houses here if you can find your way inside. Also, Aphrodite emerged from the sea here, after being birthed from genital froth.[1]

---

[1] A really bad name for a rock band. Or anything. We apologise for this phrase.

Creta

Size: 3,499 square Roman Miles
Capital: Gortyn
Government: Senatorial Province
Religion: Grecian and Minoan Polytheism
Language: Greek
Established: DCLXXXVII A.U.C. (67 B.C.E.)
De-established: ML A.U.C. (297 C.E.)

Creta is an island just south of Achaia in the southern *mare Aegaeum*, it
can be reached by dozens of ports on the surrounding shores.[1] There is a
network of roads connecting the cities, some are of Greek or Roman

---

[1] All of them run by Cretans.

construction, others much older than Roma itself.

Cydonia sits on the northwestern shore of the island. Renowned for its archers, stop by if that's something that interests you. Much further eastward, along the northern coast is **Cnossos, Knossos** or **Colonia Iulia Nobilis**. The city has a wonderous Minoan palace, thousands of years old, various temples, an amphitheater, theater, and baths.

The capital for both the island, the province of Creta and Cyrenaica is **Gortyn**, found in the interior of the island. There are two theaters: the larger of the two is on the other side of the river, the other is near the agora. The odeon is near the eastern bank of the river, up near the larger theater. The amphitheater is found a ways southeast of the agora. There is a concentration of temples in the center of town near the agora, there is a nymphaeum, and sanctuaries dedicated to Apollo and Isis. The stadium doubles as a circus and is found south of the amphitheater. The city's baths are near the great gate on the south side of town. There is a public display of laws known as the Gortyn Code[1] for the city near the odeon.

The city of **Lyctus** is northeast of Gortyn, a short way inward from the shore. **Hierapytna** is on the eastern side of the island and is the only city on the southern shore. It has a couple theaters, an amphitheater, baths, and a harbor.

---

[1] Rule 1: You do not talk about the Gortyn Code. Rule 2: You do not talk about the Gortyn Code!

Mediterranean Islands

Thasos is found in the northern *mare Aegaeum*, south of Thracia. It is known mostly for its timber and mining industries. **Lemnos** is the place upon which Hephaestus was thrown by Zeus. It's also in the northern Aegean. Its chief city is **Hephaistia**, the island has a thriving tradition in theater. The island of **Lesbos**[1] is famous for its poet Sappho, from the town of **Eresos**. It is found in the northern Aegean and the capital of the island is **Mytilene.** The island of **Skyros** is found in the middle Aegean, east of Achaia. It is the place from which Achilles set off for Ilium, and where Theseus met his end.

Lovers of Greek wine will want to visit the northern Aegean island of **Chios**. The wine made here is of exceptional quality. **Icaros** is found in the middle Aegean, it is named after Icarus, the son of Daedalus who fell here after flying too close to the sun. The island has a beautiful temple to Artemis at **Oenoe**, and a smaller one on the northwestern coast used primarily by sailors, so if you're travelling through, it wouldn't hurt to make a small sacrifice.

Patmos is a small island in the eastern *Aegaeum*, raised from the bottom of the sea by Artemis and Apollo.[2] Fans of the artichoke should stop by the island of **Kinaros**, which is named after the vegetable and grows it plentifully. **Cos** or **Kos** is an island very amicable to the Roman people. It is found in the south-eastern portion of the *mare* near **Rhodus.** It has a few things to do and see including an odeon, and temple to Aesculapius.

The island of **Rhodus** is famous for its Colossus of Helios, one of the Seven Wonders of the Ancient World, which as of DXXVIII A.U.C. (226 B.C.E.) has fallen and cannot get up. Keep in mind that you should beware the various tourist traps and scam artists around the statue, but definitely check it out if you're in the area.[3] The island hosts plenty to see, there is a temple to Apollo, theater, and stadium up on the acropolis. **Carpathus** is found in the southeastern *Aegaeum,* and along with **Rhodus**, forms the edge of the sea.

The Cyclades are a group of islands surrounding **Delos** in the *Aegaeum.* **Amorgos** is the easternmost of the Cyclades in the Aegean, there is a temple to Aphrodite here. **Anaphe** is one of the southernmost

---

[1] Do not make any jokes about homosexual women here, the natives do not think that it's clever.

[2] They didn't have a magic fishhook and were not voiced by Dwane "The Rock" Johnson, though.

[3] They didn't fix it because they believed the gods were unhappy with them, so it lay for almost 800 years until some Muslims melted it down and carried it out on 900 camels.

islands, it has a temple to Apollo, and was used as a safe harbor by the Argonauts during their voyage.[1] The volcanic island of **Thera** is just east of **Anaphe**, supposedly it was created by the Argonaut Euphemus, who threw a clump of dirt into the sea after having had sex with another clump of dirt which he had apparently nursed with milk from his breast, the concept of *Euphemism* was probably invented so no one would ever actually have to tell that story again. **Naxos** is on the eastern edge of the middle Cyclades, it has few temples including one to Apollo and another to Demeter.

The island of **Delos** is famous as being the birthplace of the god Apollo and in some stories, his sister Artemis. The island is a major trade port after the Romans raze Corinthus in the days of the Roman republic, but wains in the time of the Empire. The island has several agorae, a theater dedicated to Dionysus along with large stone phalluses, the main temple to Apollo, temples to Isis and Hera, and a synagogue.

Kimolos and **Milos** are two of the more western Cyclades. It's very important to recognize that the Athenians of **Kimolos** hate the Spartans of **Milos** and the two islands are frequently at odds. The island of **Siphnos** was originally fueled by its mining industry but has suffered considerably since the mines which had not previously dried up are a tad too wet now due to flooding.[2]

The island of **Syros** hosts the city of **Hermoupolis**, which rivals Piraeus and serves as the chief city in the Cyclades region. **Mykonos** and **Tenos** surround **Delos** to the east and north respectively. Supposedly **Mykonos** is covered with the petrified testicles of giants left there after Hercules killed them.[3] **Andros** is the northernmost of the Cyclades and has a temple dedicated to Dionysus.[4] **Ceos** near mainland Achaia has a strong poetic tradition.

---

[1] Using this naming convention, when you go on a cruise you become a Carnival Spiritnaut or a Disney Wondernaut.
[2] Too bad they couldn't Siph'n the water out.
[3] Really rocky mountain oysters.
[4] He also really hates that Star Fox McCloud.

XI Working in Roma

During your travels you're bound to find yourself strapped for cash at some point or another but worry not! For there are numerous opportunities to make some money whilst you're out and about. This section details some of the various odd jobs you can do. Some require some basic skills obviously, while others are menial and just require you to show up.

COQUUS. If you have some experience in the kitchen, you may consider hiring yourself out at the *forum coquinum* as a cook for the day. While many wealthy families use slaves for their cooking they often hire on extra help when providing banquets to their clients and friends. We recommend you find a copy of *De re coquinaria* if you're wanting to cook the fancier fare. Roman cuisine is largely game based, with vegetables and pulses. But a dramatic flair is always appreciated.

PISCATOR. If you have a love for the sea, then perhaps you'll consider taking up nets with a *piscator*. You can stop in at the local docks or even the *forum piscatorium* to see if you can find a fisherman who needs help for the next few days. It's physically demanding work, and the pay isn't great but it's the perfect way to get a good reputation down at the docks, and if you do good work your employer might have a friend with a ship who's headed in the same direction you are.

SCRIBA. If you've got excellent handwriting, and a stupid amount of patience, you might want to work as a *scriba*. This job can be monumentally boring, often transcribing documents, books, edicts again and again onto papyrus. There are numerous military, civil and private opportunities available depending on where you're at, just make sure your Roman cursive is good and you can read *scriptio continua* which is where the words lack any sort of spacing in-between creating a single continuous line.

GLADIATOR. Contrary to popular belief, being a *gladiator* is not a certain death sentence, nor is it an exclusively slave profession. You can take up the *gladius* and compete in the games, for money and fame, but in doing so you are labeled *infamis* which means you're forever labeled with a negative reputation in public life. While people will praise and celebrate you, they will not likely want to be seen in public with you for fear of damaging their own reputations. Gladiatorial combat does not often end in death, but rather when one of the combatants is wounded, obviously beaten, or too tired to continue, it's only much later that Emperors begin demanding the deaths of the losers.

TEXTOR/TEXTRIX. Men or women with a lot of patience can take up weaving, simple cloths are easy to make if you know how to work a loom. It's a stable way to make consistent income, and there are weavers everywhere in the Empire. Even when you're finished working for the day, you may be able to convince your employer to allow you to make cloth for yourself to use for clothing.

AGRICOLA. Men with a strong back can consider taking up the plough to help out in the local fields, farmers always need help ploughing, clearing areas out for new fields, tending to wines, or any other number or chores. Check with them when you're still outside of town or in the market with their wares, depending on the season.

PROSTITUTUS/PROSTITUTA. No matter how desperate you get, don't turn down this road. For one, you have to be licensed with the local government, and your name gets recorded publicly forever. Imagine returning to your home time period after your done and everyone already knows what you were up to on your vacation. You will suffer the same status of *infamis* as *gladiatores*, but without the fame and celebration.

FABER. With a little know-how and experience with ancient tools, you may want to try your hand as a *faber*. Between expansive public works projects, and private construction of *insulae* and homes you can find work wherever you go. It's a respectable profession and it pays well but pay is directly linked to your skill and reputation.

POETA. If your Latin or Greek is excellent and you have a mastery of meter, you could try to write some poetry. Keep in mind your audience when writing however, some of the best poetry is filthy smut and insults, some of the worst is vain and heroic tales of how the author saved the republic single-handedly.

ORATOR. If large crowds don't make you nervous, you may find work as an *orator* satisfying. There are various types of oration you can do, such as acting as a *praeco,* a town-crier, or as an advocate for another in court (make sure you know the laws well if you don't want your client exiled, executed or fined).

PARASITUS/PARASITA. If you're content living off someone else's good fortune, consider taking up the mantle of parasite. It's easy enough to do, just make sure you're never late to dinner.

TESTARIUS. If you're able to do repetitive work in hot conditions you could be a *testarius* and bake bricks next to a hot kiln, bricks are used in many construction projects and you can find work doing it pretty much anywhere. Just make sure you don't anger the *Daemones Ceramici,* who haunt pottery and will destroy your work.

MERCENNARIUS. If you are essentially unskilled, you can always pick up something heavy and carry it somewhere else, dig ditches, push things, pull things, or whatever else the *mercedarii* in the forum need done for the day. There is always someone willing to pay you to do something, it may not be glamorous or prestigious, but it's a living.

MILES OR NAUTA. If you're looking for a life of adventure and have time to devote to the cause, consider enlisting in the Roman army or navy. While your vacation isn't probably long enough to endure a full career, it is a good way to see the Empire, if you don't mind the battles, fast paced marches, uncomfortable sleeping arrangements and heavy equipment. Naval service trades marches for the unpleasant amount of time you'll spend at sea, but you've got to make sacrifices if you'll survive in the military service.

XII Doing as Romans do

How to put on a toga

The toga is the epitome of Roman men's fashion, while it is expensive to acquire, it is thankfully easy to put on. To put it on start by draping a third over your left shoulder and down towards your feet, with the fabric spread down towards your elbow. Taking the rest of the toga in your right hand you'll wrap it around your body and toss it over your left shoulder. You will need to practice a few times before you are public ready.

How to put on a peplos

As an unmarried woman, one of the more popular options for dress is a peplos, a sleeveless tunic. It consists of two pieces of fabric sown together with two flaps at the top left unsewn. Dropping the garment over your head, you'll allow the flaps to fold over. You pin the creases of the folds together over your shoulders and belt the garment under the breasts either over or under the folds.

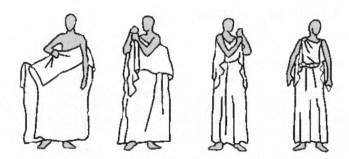

How to put on a chiton

Similar to a peplos in principle, the chiton is a sleeved dress, it goes on over the head as well, but uses several pins to affix the front and back of the dress, it is also typically belted under the breasts, but variations exist.

How to apply ancient cosmetics

Men typically do not wear cosmetics, with few exceptions, but it's better to just go without. Acceptable makeup for men was the painting of the face red to symbolize a victorious Jupiter Optimus Maximus during a triumphal procession.

Women often undergo various processes to fit in to beauty standards. Amongst the upper class, fair skin is supreme. Lanolin can be applied before bedtime, but it reeks. You can also use juices of various kinds, powdered seeds, horns, excrement, honey, plants, placenta, marrow, vinegar, bile, urine, sulfur, vinegar, eggs, incense, frankincense and myrrh, ground oyster shells, onions, and white lead.

After baths you can apply chalk, crocodile dung, or white lead to your face for the sake of beauty.[1] Aside from the head, all hair should be removed by shaving, plucking or waxing. Rouge is used to add natural color to the face and give a healthy and vibrant look.

The good stuff is ground red ochre from Gallia Belgicum, the cheap alternative is wine dregs and mulberry juice. Some women use cinnabar or red lead to color their faces. Dark eyebrows are also preferable, and an almost unibrow is viewed as attractive.

Perfumes are common and come in many varieties. Some perfumes have specific purposes such as curing ailments. Keep in mind to not overdo it on the makeup, too much and you'll be labeled a prostitute.
♦ We would like to remind you at this time that lead and cinnabar are toxic, and we do *not* advocate rubbing them on your face.

How to row on a trireme

So, you've found yourself rowing on an ancient vessel, luckily the rowing isn't too complicated once you get into rhythm. The rule of thumb is this: *Up – Backwards, Down – Forward.* That is to say when the end of the oar you're holding is angled up so that the paddle is in the water, you pull backwards. When the end of the oar your holding is down, so that the paddle is out of the water, you push forward, preparing for the next oar strike. Just listen to the commands and follow along with everybody else.

Also, you needn't worry about being pressed into service on a galley as a slave or prisoner of war, as some Charioteering Hebrews would have you believe, galley crews consist of freedmen and mercenaries, when slaves do enter service they are freed beforehand.

How to get rid of a curse

If you find you've been cursed, then it's a good thing you've been able to find this section, because we may be able to help you out, and if we can't try referring to the next passage to help take your mind off things.

If you can find the person who cursed you, you can try pleading your case with them to remove the curse.

If you can find the tablet accompanying your curse, you'll at least know

---

[1] Nothing better than a crocodile poop bronzer.

which god the curse is addressed to and make counteractive offerings to said deity.

If neither are available, you can make offerings to the *Di Inferi,* those infernal gods are typically associated with curses, Pluto, Charon, Hecate, Persephone, etc. See **Chapter XVIII** for a more complete list.

If a god has cursed you, for say… taking the daughter of one of his priests as war booty, just give her back and say you're sorry. Also, don't take it personally and take someone else's girl, this typically ends poorly.

If the consequences of the curse aren't too bad, have you considered just living with them?

If you are not cursed, but merely transformed into an animal, such as a donkey, try eating roses, but be sure to not eat rose-laurels which are poisonous. If you cannot find roses, then turn to Isis, as she's been known to rescue the metamorphosed in peril.

Also, be careful what you wish for, as some gifts from the gods wind up being curses in their own right. You may wish for the power to turn anything you touch into gold and find yourself unable to eat or drink. You may wish to live forever only to have your wife required to die in your place. It's perhaps best to just avoid dabbling in the affairs of deities and magicians.

How to tell a joke in Latin

Romans are a major fan of humor, so if you're stuck somewhere and a little bored as tends to happen on long journeys, you can always try breaking the ice with a short joke. Try this one, for example:

Ineptus in tempestate navigat. Servi eius clamare incipiunt, eis imperat, "Nolite trepidare; in testamento meo, manumittam vos."

A fool is sailing in a storm. His slaves begin to wail, he says to them, "Don't panic; in my will, I will set you free."[1]

---

[1] Wakka wakka.

How to throw a *pilum*

The *pilum* is the primary ranged weapon of the Roman infantryman, why you'd need to throw it is anyone's guess but we're here, so this is how to do it. Typically, when throwing a *pilum*, you remain stationary, charging two steps forward to throw it will only break ranks and defeat the purpose, leaving you to get cut down for your foolishness.

Grip the javelin underhanded (with your thumb facing backwards) in your right hand, a little ways forward of the mid-point, bend at the knees and rotate your hips so that your left shoulder is forward. Rotating from the hips, bring your arm forward quickly and release the *pilum* sending it sailing into the shield of your enemy, and hopefully impaling them. If you have time, practice beforehand, if not and the enemy is currently charging your position, then we wish you the best of luck.

How to use a *xylospongium*

The *xylospongium,* also known as a *tersorium* is a simple tool used for cleaning yourself after defecation. It is simple enough to use, using one hand to cover the front end you can use the other hand to make use of the tool to clean yourself. Roman latrines have an opening on the front side, so you have room to do this allowing you to preserve some modicum of modesty, so if you clean yourself standing, it's officially weird. After use the brush is washed in a bucket of vinegar and brine, we advise bringing your own with you and cleaning it thoroughly instead of sharing fecal germs with everyone who passes through.

How to take a bath

Bathhouses are found throughout the Empire as you have no doubt seen. While they are used for personal cleanliness, they are often the perfect place to socialize and get to know the people of the town.

Men and women sometimes have separate entrances, but regardless of gender, you'll enter an *apodyterium* first, where you'll store your possessions while bathing. Be wary of thieves, who may make off with your things, perhaps don't bring anything you cannot afford to lose. And don't walk off with someone else's things either, there are mounds of curse tables dedicated to such vagrants.

The first bath room is the *frigidarium,* which has cold water to refresh yourself in. Sometimes the *frigidarium* contains individual tubs or small multi-person tubs, other times it holds large pools capable of supporting many bathers at once.

Next is the *tepidarium,* which is a warm air room and typically finely decorated. After warming up from your cold bath, you'll proceed to the *caldarium,* where you would take a hot bath. You can return to the *tepidarium* to be massaged and anointed with oil, or once perspiration begins, enter the *laconium* to sweat more.

Bathhouses are often attached to Palaestra, which can be used for exercise, sometimes they are attached to a stadium where you can compete.

You, knowing better, should avoid the baths if you are sick. Do not go to the baths if you have an open wound, as you will be at great risk for gangrene, and there won't be any antibiotics for a very, very long time.[1]

How to feast

Feasting is commonplace amongst the upper classes, if you find yourself lucky enough to receive and invitation to a *cena,* it's best you behave appropriately. You should show up for dinner wearing a toga, if you do not have one, alert your host when you receive your invitation, he may have one you can borrow, or know someone who can lend you one.

There is a reclining order and you'll be told where to lay or sit depending on your relationship with the host. You typically start the meal by reclining, propped up on your left elbow, but if that's uncomfortable it's not uncommon to move about and adjust as needed. (Perhaps wait for someone else to do so first).

You should be served finger food typically, when that is the case, eat with your first two fingers and your thumb. The first course is usually an egg dish of some sort, followed by various courses of vegetables and meats, and often ends with a fruit desert.

Since you are eating with your hands, you need to bring your own napkin, it is a status symbol of sorts, so the nicer napkin you have, the fancier you are. It is considered poor decorum to walk off with another's napkin, and don't try to play it off as a jest, we all know what you're up to. Servants will also come by periodically with water, so you may rinse your hands.

Don't worry too much about dropping food on the floor, as it is an offering of sorts to the gods, a sort of accidental libation. The servants will tend to it later.

You should also note that weapons of any sort are banned from the

---

[1] You should probably clean wounds with vinegar or learn how to distill stronger alcohols for sanitation purposes.

dinner table. If you have rings you should symbolically transfer them to the other hand or leave them out altogether.

How to escape an inescapable labyrinth

For some reason or another, ancient kings occasionally build inescapable labyrinths. If you followed our suggested packing lists and brought thread, then you'll have no trouble. Just tie it to the door and feel free to explore carefree.[1]

How to defend yourself in court

Our advice is… don't. If you find yourself in legal trouble, and you didn't accidently sign up for a Roman law class while you were drunk in your junior year, you don't know the ins and outs of the Roman legal system. It's better to rely on someone who does. If you have a *patronus,* they're obligated to defend you, if you were taken in as a guest, your host is similarly beholden (and in some ways, on the hook for your behavior). Lacking either of these, take to asking around for orators who may be willing to help. Cicero is renowned to be the best, but he is an insufferable, pompous jackass, so if he's not available, perhaps seek out another insufferable, pompous jackass and hope for the best.

How to fight a…

While we can't prove mythological creatures existed, you can't prove they didn't either.

BASILISK. The basilisk can be thwarted with a simple treatment of weasel urine, so maybe keep some in a sealed bottle when traveling through their territory.[2]

CENTAUR. Centaurs are particularly vulnerable to hydra venom, even immortal ones, so get a little of that in their system and they're done for, just be absolutely sure to not wear any clothes they offer as they lay dying under any circumstances.

CHIMERA. The Chimera is very easily defeated, all you need is a flying

---

[1] You can also try the computer-maze solving technique of following the right-hand wall. As long as the walls are all interconnected, you should find the exit eventually.

[2] Where you get the weasel urine from…?

horse and to add a block of lead to the tip of your spear.

CYCLOPS. A Cyclops can be defeated with a swift poke to the eye.

HYDRA. The Hydra is a water serpent who sprouts heads for each one cut off, simply cut off the head, then cauterize the stump with a fire-brand. The last head is immortal so just put a big rock on it.

ONOCENTAUR. This creature is a mix of a man and a donkey, you won't need to fight one, we just wanted you to know this pathetic thing exists. The Ichthyocentaur is similarly bizarre, which is half man, half horse, half fish. Figure that one out.

SIREN. Just plug up your ears when passing by.

SPHINX. The sphinx is a lion-bodied, human-headed beast who will consume you if you cannot solve its riddle. Try practicing a couple before taking on head on.

τί ἐστιν ὃ μίαν ἔχον φωνὴν τετράπουν καὶ δίπουν καὶ τρίπουν γίνεται;

The answer here is obviously ὁ ἀνήρ[1]

Ego sum principium mundi et finis saeclorum attamen non sum deus.

A similarly easy one, M[2]

---

[1] What has one voice, but goes on four feet, than two, than three? A man (as a *infans* crawling, an *adulescens* walking, and a *senex* with a cane.

[2] I am the beginning of the world (mundi) and the end of the ages (saeclorum) yet I am not a god.

How to play *Rota*

If you're bored during your travels, you'll probably wind up playing *Rota* (wheel) at some point or another. The game is simple, first you draw out the playing surface in the following fashion.

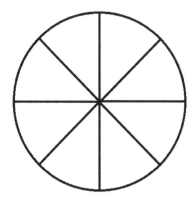

- Each player receives three stones distinguished from the other player's by color.

- Each player takes turns placing a stone on any point where two lines intersect, including the center intersection.

- Once all three pieces are placed, players take turns moving their piece to an adjacent spot, they cannot jump other pieces, even their own.

- The game is won when a player has three stones in a row. It cannot end in a tie.

How to read your future

There are five types of Augury you can conduct (unofficially of course, unless you're a priest).

Ex caelo: If lighting strikes it, it's a bad sign, avoid whatever was struck.

Ex avibus: There are two classes of birds to observe: *Oscines,* who cry, and *Alites,* who fly. The *Oscines* are ravens, crows, owls, and hens, who give either favorable or unfavorable omens depending on their song. The *Alites* are eagles, vultures, and falcons, who give either favorable or unfavorable omens depending on where they fly into a designated area from. Some birds play for both teams.

Interpretation is fluid at best, one guy might say, "I saw birds first!" The other might say, "I saw twice as many!" Then naturally, the victor is the one who kills the other first.

Ex tripudiis: This augury involves the observation of sacred chickens' eating patterns. First, get some sacred chickens, open their enclosure and toss bread, or cakes or similar in front of them. If they refuse to exit their domicile, flap their wings, cry out or fly away, then it's bad. If they are messy eaters, then it's great.

Ex quadrupedibus: This is simply the observation of four legged animals of any kind crossing one's path or being found in an unusual location. Interpret as you will.

Ex diris: Loosely translated as: from any other crap. This is the interpretation of sneezing, stumbling, or anything out of the ordinary you can use to excuse your circumstances.

Bibliomancy: Bibliomancy is a lesser form of fortune telling, to perform, find a book which you believe holds truth. Place the book on its spine and allow it to fall open, then pick a passage at random with your eyes closed. (Probably not the best to try with this guide)

XIII Tips and comments from travelers

From time to time, travelers in the Ancient World will send in their advice to be ignored or heeded at your own discretion. Some advice seems more specific than others, but it's always good to learn from someone else's personal experiences.

A bit of earwax is the best way to counter Sirens, won't be any bother to you if you can't hear them.
    Perimedes

If you're visiting a strange foreign land, be wary of what food items they might serve you. You don't want to be dragged off by an angry travelling companion after dining on too many lotus flowers.
    Polites

Be extra careful when sailing around Lamos, giants tend to throw rocks down upon you. Also, watch your step when drinking, that's a right way to end up paying passage to Charon.
    Elpenor

Learned this the hard way, if you're told some cattle are sacred to the sun god, then they are sacred to the sun god. Better to be hungry than drowned at the bottom of the sea.
    Eurylochus

If someone bothers to give you mixed bags of wind to assist you in your travels, make sure you explain to *everyone* around you what they are, and why it would be *tremendously* bad if they were to, say, unleash them all at once.
    Aeolus

If you're at a crossroads and a charioteer attempts to run you down, just let it go and save yourself considerable trouble and eye-pain later.
    Oedipus

When your friend is murdered by witches in the night, make sure you have good rope.
    Aristomenes

When travelling with a group be sure you don't get separated, if it happens to you, try and find another group to tag along with.
  Achaemenides

A little travelling music can always lift the spirts.
  Orpheus

Watch out for snakes while travelling in Lybia.
  Mopsus

Be cautious of those boars near the Acheron.
  Idmon

Elephants do not do well crossing the Alpes…
  Hannibal

If you decide to visit the Oracle of Delphi, just remember that some prophecies are more figurative than others.
  Brutus

There is a shortcut which really cuts down on travel-time if there is a block at the pass of Thermopylae.
  Ephialtes

If you want favorable winds, you have to be prepared to commit to getting them.
  Agamemnon

Travel is guaranteed to give you fresh perspective, whether you want to gather a little material to write about or transform your city-state into a military powerhouse which is elevated to near mythical status in the future.
  Lycurgus

Be wary of whom you accept as a house guest, and if you're a house guest, stealing wives is really uncool.
  Menelaus

Always inspect any vehicle you're travelling in for potential safety hazards.
  Oenomaus

Be very careful when you're travelling through woods sacred to Artemis, or at the very least, leave your hounds at home that day.
Actaeon

If you have something you don't want a guest consuming, make sure you hide it out of sight.
Pholus

If you're starving and down to your last two obols… save them.
Charon[123]

---

[1] It is long debated what the obol (small coin) for the ferryman of the dead is for. Does Charon need bribed to do his only job? Will he leave you on the bank of the river Styx if you don't pay him, in a sort of purgatory, unable to join the afterlife yet unable to retun to the world of the living? Will he take you to a better dead neighborhood if you pay him? Will you be tossed into the river of souls and lose any concept of an afterlife at all?

[2] What does he spend it all on? Boat repairs? Spooky lantern oil?

[3] How about people who die in battle or get eaten by a lion or immolated or something? Only those whose families force-feed them a nickel when they are on a slab get to go on?

XIV Festivals

The Roman people frequently celebrate festivals throughout the year. Some of these are culturally tied, like Greek speaking cities celebrating festivals of Dionysus or Zeus, others are based on local traditions, and some can be found throughout all Roman territory.

The Roman calendar was originally lunar, but no longer complies with lunar orbit after Caesar reforms it. The **Kalends** is the first day of the month. The **Nones** is the 5th or 7th day of the month depending on if the month has 31 days or less. The **Ides** is on the 13th or 15th. It's terribly confusing, so we'll just lay it out for you here.

Month	Kalends	Nones	Ides
Ianuarius	1st	5th	13th
Februarius	1st	5th	13th
Martius	1st	7th	15th
Aprilis	1st	5th	13th
Maius	1st	7th	15th
Iunius	1st	5th	13th
Iulius/Quintilis	1st	7th	15th
Augustus/Sextilis	1st	5th	13th
September	1st	5th	13th
October	1st	7th	15th
November	1st	5th	13th
December	1st	5th	13th

After the Julian reforms, the calendar becomes much simpler, with the Nones always on the 5th, and the Ides always on the 13th with the exception of Martius, Maius, Iulius/Quintilis and October.

Kal. Kalends
Non. Nones
Eid. Ides
DN. Dies natalis: A deity's birthday or anniversary of temple dedication
DF. Dies ferialis: A festival day
DR. Dies religiosus: A day sacred to the individual honored
NL. Nova Luna: New Moon

Roman Festival Calendar

IANUARIUS

Kal.	Consular Inauguration,	*Consules*
	DF.	Aesculapius
		Vediovis
3-5	*Compitalia¹*	Lares Compitales
Non.	*DN.*	Vica Pota
9	*Agonalia*	Ianus
11	*Carmentalia*	Carmenta
	Iuturnalia	Iuturna
15	*Carmentalia*	Carmenta
24-26	*Sementivae*	Tellus
27	*DN.*	Castor et Pollux

FEBRUARIUS

Kal.	*DN.*	Iuno Sospita
2	*Sementivae*	Ceres
Non.	*DN.*	Concordia
Eid.	*Faunalia*	Faunus
13-22	*Parentalia*	Ancestors
15	*Lupercalia*	Lupercus
17	*Fornacalia²*	Fornax
	Quirinalia	Quirinus
21	*Feralia*	*Di inferi*
22	*Caristia*	*Familia*
23	*Terminalia*	Terminus
24	*Fugalia*	*regifugium*
27	*Equirria*	Mars

MARTIUS

Kal.	*DN.*	Mars
	Matronalia³	Iuno Lucina
Non.	*DF.*	Vediovis
9	*DR.*	Mars
14	*Equirria*	Mars
Eid.	*DF*	Iuppiter
		Anna Perenna
16-17	*Argei*	Saturnus aut Tiber
17	*Liberalia⁴*	Liber

---

¹ Festival of crossroads, not the Britney Spears movie, though.

² Festival of ovens, not fornication.

³ Pretty much Roman Mother's day.

	Agonalia	Mars
19	*Quinquatria*	Minerva
		Mars
23	*Tubilustrium*	*Tubae*
31	*DN.*	Luna

APRILIS

Kal.	*Veneralia*	Venus
4-10	*Megalesia*	Cybele
Non.	*DN.*	Fortuna Publica
12-19	*Cerialia*[1]	Ceres
Eid.	*DN.*	Iuppiter Victor
15	*Fordicidia*	Tellus
21	*Parilia*	Pales
	DN.	Roma
23	*Vinalia*	Iuppiter, Venus
25	*Robigalia*	Robigus
27/28	*Floralia*	Flora

MAIUS

Kal.	*Floralia*	Flora
	DN.	Bona Dea
	DF.	Lares Praestites
9, 11, 13	*Lemuria*	Mania, *Mortui*
Eid.	*Argei*	Mars Invictus
21	*Mercuralia*	Mercurius
23	*Tubilustrium*	*Tubae*
	DF.	Volcanus
25	*DN.*	Fortuna Primigena

IUNIUS

Kal.	*DN.*	Mars
		Iuno Moneta
		Tempestates
		Cardea
3	*DN.*	Bellona
4	*DN.*	Hercules Custos
Non.	*DN.*	Dius Fidius
7	*Ludi Piscatorii*[2]	*Piscatores*

---

[4] This day is sort of a Roman male coming of age day. Think of it as a Roman Bar Mitzvah, but with less money from your Bubbe that you will use to buy an Xbox.

[1] This festival is where people tie torches to foxes' tails, because a boy tried to burn a thieving fox once and it fled, flaming into some sacred fields and burned them, so all foxes must be ceremonially punished.

7-15	*Vestalia*	Vesta
8	*DN.*	Mens
11	*Matralia*	Mater Matuta
	DN.	Fortuna (*in foro boario*)
Eid.	*DF.*	Iuppiter
13-15	*Quinquatria*	*Tibicines*
19	*DN.*	Minerva
20	*DN.*	Summanus
24	*DF.*	Fors Fortuna
27	*DN.*	Iuppiter Stator
29	*DN.*	Hercules Musarum

QUINTILIS / IULIUS

Kal.	*DN.*	Iuno Felicitas
5	*Poplifugia*	*populifugia*
6-13	*Ludi Apollinares*	Apollo
6	*DN.*	Fortuna Muliebris
Non.	*Caprotinia*	Iuno
	DF.	Consus
8	*Vitulatio*	Vitula
Eid.	*Transvectio equitum[1]*	*Equites*
17	*DN.*	Honor *et* Virtus
	DF.	Victoria
18	*Dies ater*	**NO BUSINESS!**
19, 21	*Lucaria*	*luci*
20-30	*Ludi victoriae Caesaris*	Caesares
22	*DN.*	Concordia
23	*Neptunalia*	Neptunus
25	*Furrinalia*	Furina
30	*DN.*	Fortuna Huiusque diei

SEXTILIS / AUGUSTUS

Kal.	*DN.*	Spes
3	*Supplicia canum*	Iuventas *et* Summanus
Non.	*DF.*	Salus
9	*DF.*	Sol Indiges
12	*DF.*	Hercules Invictus
Eid.	*DF.*	Diana, Vortumnus Fortuna
		Equestris Hercules Victor
		Castor *et* Pollux Flora
		Camenae
17	*Portunalia[2]*	Portunus
19	*Vinalia rustica*	Iuppiter
		Venus

---

[2] Fish Games. A celebration of fishermen.

[1] This is a big horse parade day. You may want to see it, but you don't want to smell it.

[2] This festival people honor the god of doors and locks by throwing keys in a fire.

21	*Consualia*	Consus
23	*Volcanalia*	Volcanus
	DF.	Maia
		nymphae
		Ops Opifera Hora
24	*DF.*	Luna
25	*Opiconsivia*	Ops Consivae
27	*Volturnalia*	Volturnus
28	*Ludi in circo maximo*	Sol *et* Luna

SEPTEMBER

Kal.	*DF.*	Iuppiter Tonans, Iuno Regina
Non.	*DN.*	Iuppiter Stator
5-19	*Ludi Romani*	*Populi Romani*
Eid.	*DN.*	Iuppiter Optimus Maximus
	Epulum Iovis	
14	*Equorum probatio*	*Equites*
23	*DN.*	Apollo
	DF.	Latona
26	*DN.*	Venus Genetrix

OCTOBER

Kal.	*DF.*	Fides
		Tigillum Sororium
3-12	*Ludi Augustales*	Augustus
4	*Leiunium Cereris*	Ceres
6	*Dies ater*	**NO BUSINESS!**
Non.	*DF.*	Iuppiter Fulgur
		Iuno Curitis
9	*DF.*	Genius Publicus
		Fausta Felicitas
		Venus Victrix
10	*DN.*	Iuno Moneta
11	*Meditrinalia*	*Di et Deae*
12	*Augustalia*	Augustus
13	*Fontinalia*	Fons
14	*DN.*	Penates Dei
Eid.	*Feriae*	Iuppiter
	Equus October	Mars
16	*Lupinalia*	*Lupi*
19	*Armilustrium*	Mars
26-Kal.	*Ludi victoriae Sullanae*	Sulla

NOVEMBER

| Kal. | *Ludi circenses* | Sulla |
| 4-17 | *Ludi Plebii[1]* | *Plebes* |

Eid.	*Epulum Iovis*	Iuppiter
	DF.	Feronia
		Fortuna Primigena
14	*Equorum probatio*	*Equites*

DECEMBER

Kal.	*DF.*	Neptunus, Pietas
3	*DF.*	Bona Dea
Non.	*Faunalia*	Faunus
8	*DF.*	Tiberinus Pater
		Gaia
11	*Agonalia*	Indiges
12	*DF.*	Consus
Eid.	*DN.*	Tellus
15	*Consualia*	Consus
17-23	*Saturnalia[1]*	Saturnus
18	*Eponalia*	Epona
19	*Opalia*	Ops
21	*Divalia*	Angerona
	DF.	Hercules
		Ceres
22	*DN.*	Lares Permarini
23	*Larentalia*	Lares
	Sigillaria	Saturnus
	DF.	Diana
		Iuno Regina
		Tempestates
25	*DN.*	Sol Invictus
	Brumalia	Saturnus *et* Ceres

---

[1] So, pretty much with Roman holidays, if it says Ludi expect there to be games, races, theatrical performances, gladiatorial exhibitions, etc. Festivals often also include sacrifices of animals for one reason or another, and are often associated with various harvest seasons, or sending the military to or from war.

[1] Where some modern Christmas traditions, mainly feasting and gift-giving come from.

Greek Festival Calendar

ἙΚΑΤΟΜΒΑΙΩΝ / HEKATOMBAION
4	*Aphrodisia*	Aphrodite
12	*Kronia*	Cronus
15-16	*Synoikia*	*Synoecism*
28	*Panathenaea*	Athena

ΜΕΤΑΓΕΙΤΝΙΩΝ / METAGEITNION
2	*Heracleia*	Hercules
15-18	*Eleusinia*	Eleusis
16	*DF.*	Artemis
		Hekate
20	*DF.*	Hera Thelchinia
25	*DF.*	Zeus Epoptes

ΒΟΗΔΡΟΜΙΩΝ / BOEDROMION
2	*Niketeria[1]*	Nike
3	*Plataia*	Plataia
5	*Genesia[2]*	The honored Dead
6	*Charisteria*	Artemis Agrotera
7	*Boedromia*	Apollo
15-21	*Eleusinian Mysteries[3]*	Demeter
		Persephone
18	*Epidauria*	Asclepius
27	*DF.*	*Nymphae*
		Achelous
		Alochus
		Hermes
		Gaia

ΠΥΑΝΕΨΙΩΝ / PYANEPSION
5	*Proerosia*	Demeter
7	*Pyanepsia*	Phoebus Apollo
7	*Oschophoria*	Wine harvest
8	*Theseia*	Theseus
9	*Sternia*	Demeter
		Persephone
11-13	*Thesmophoria*	Demeter
		Persephone
30	*Chalkeia*	Hephaistos

---

[1] Festivals, just do them.

[2] Greek Halloween, but before the invention of candy.

[3] Kind of like frat pledge week for the cult of Demeter and Persephone. Ancient Greek Life.

ΜΑΙΜΑΚΤΗΡΙΩΝ / MAIMAKTERION
16	*Pompaia*	Zeus
		Hermes

ΠΟΣΕΙΔΕΩΝ / POSEIDEON
8	*Poseidea*	Poseidon
16	*DF.*	Zeus Horios
19	*DF.*	Dionysus
26	*Haloa*	Demeter
		Dionysus

ΓΑΜΗΛΙΩΝ / GAMELION
2	*Theogamia*	Zeus
		Hera
8	*DF.*	Apollo Apotropaeus
		Apollo Nymphegetes
		Nymphae Erchiae
9	*DF.*	Athena
12-15	*Lenaia*	Dionysus
26	*Gamelia*	Zeus, Hera

ἈΝΘΕΣΤΗΡΙΩΝ / ANTHESTERION
2	*DF.*	Dionysus
9-13	*Anthesteria*	Dionysus
23/28	*Diasia*	Zeus Meilichios

ἘΛΑΦΗΒΟΛΙΩΝ / ELAPHEBOLION
6	*Elaphebolia*[1]	Artemis
8/9	*Asklepieia*	Asclepius
9-13	*Dionysia*[2]	Dionysus
14/17	*Pandia*	Zeus
15	*DF.*	Cronos

ΜΟΥΝΙΧΙΩΝ / MOUNICHION
4	*Feast of Eros*	Eros
6	*Delphinia*	Apollo Delphinus
6/16	*Mounichia*	Artemis
19	*Olympieia*	Zeus Olympius

ΘΑΡΓΗΛΙΩΝ / THARGELION
4	*DF.*	Leto

---

[1] The festival of the deer slayer. Our dad had a Ford Escort wagon that he hit two deer in that we also called the *Deer Slayer*.

[2] Festival of wine and theatrical performances. Greek festivals are generally heavier on the theater and sport and lighter on the combat and animal torture.

		Zeus
		Apollo
		Dioscuri
		Hermes
6	*DF.*	Demeter
6-7	*Thargelia*	Apollo *et* Artemis
16	*DF.*	Zeus Epacrios
25	*Plunteria*	Athena

ΣΚΙΡΟΦΟΡΙΩΝ / SKIROPHORION

3	*Arrhephoria*	Athena
3	*DF.*	Athena
		Zeus
		Poseidon
12	*Skiraphoria*	Demeter
		Persephone
14	*Dipolieia*	Zeus
29/30	*DF.*	Zeus
		Athena

Celtic Festival Calendar

SAMONIOS
    Litha   Summer Solstice

DUMANNIOS
    Lughnasadh   Between Summer Solstice and
                                      Autumnal Equinox

RIUROS
    None

ANAGANTIO
    Mabon   Autumnal Equinox

OGRONNIOS
    None

CUTIOS
    Samhain   Between Autumnal Equinox
                                      and Winter Solstice

GIAMONIOS
    Yule[1]   Winter Solstice

SEMIUISONNA
    Imbolc   Between Winter Solstice and
                                      Vernal Equinox

EQUOS
    Ostara   Vernal Equinox

ELEMBIUOS
    None

AEDRINIOS
    Beltaine   Between Vernal Equinox and
                                      Summer Solstice

CANTLOS
    None

---

[1] The only one that has survived Christianization into modern western traditions. Most of the rest of the Celtic days are only recognized as being the literal first days of each season, based on the solstices and equinoxes, unless you are a Neo-Pagan, Wiccan, Neo-Wiccan, or Neo-Neo-Wiccan-Pagan

Egyptian Festival Calendar

AKHET THOTH
1	*Wepet-Renpet*	Osiris
15	*DF.*	Hapi
		Amun
18	*Wag*	Osiris
20	*DF.*	Thoth

AKHET PHAOPHI
15	*Opet*[1]	Amun
		Mut
		Khonsu

AKHET ATHYR
9	*DF.*	Amun
30	*DF.*	Anuket

AKHET CHOIAK
1	*DF.*	Hathor
26	*DF.*	Seker

PERET TYBI
1	*DF.*	Nehebkau
20	*DF.*	Wadjet
29	*DF.*	Bast
30	*DF.*	Sakhmet

PERET MECHIR
1	*DF*	Anubis

PERET PHAMENOTH
1	*DF.*	Ptah
21	*DF.*	Amenhotep

PERET PHARMUTHI
4-5	*DF.*	Bast
25	*DF.*	Renenutet

SHEMU PACHONS
1	*DN.*	Neper
10		Anubis

---

[1] This festival includes carrying statues of the three honored gods more than a mile between temples in Karnak and Luxor.

| 11 | *DF.* | Khnum |

SHEMU PAYNI
| *NL.* | *Heb nefer en inet[1]* | The honored dead |

SHEMU EPIPHI
| 15 | *DF.* | Hapi |
| | | Amun |

SHEMU MESORE
| 30 | *New Year's Eve* | |

EPAGOMENAE
1	*DN.*	Osiris
2	*DN.*	Horus
3	*DN.*	Seth
4	*DN.*	Isis
5	*DN.*	Nephthys

---

[1] Beautiful Festival of the Valley. But the dishonored dead don't get a festival.

XV Weights and Measures

These tables convert Roman and Attic measures to Imperial units for your convenience. These systems of measurement are widespread, but you need to take note of local variations in your travels.

Roman measures of Length

Roman unit	English name	Equal to	Imperial
digitus	Finger *dealer's choice as to which	$\frac{1}{16}$ pes	0.73 in
uncia pollex	inch (thumb)	$\frac{1}{12}$ pes	0.97 in
palmus	palm	$\frac{1}{4}$ pes	0.24 ft
palmus major	palm length	$\frac{3}{4}$ pes	0.73 ft
pes	foot	1 pes	0.97 ft
palmipes	foot and a palm	1 $\frac{1}{4}$ pedes	1.21 ft
cubitum	cubit	1 $\frac{1}{2}$ pedes	1.46 ft
gradus, pes sestertius	step	2 $\frac{1}{2}$ pedes	2.43 ft
passus	pace	5 pedes	4.85 ft
decempeda, pertica	perch	10 pedes	9.71 ft
actus (length)		120 pedes	116.5 ft
stadium	stade	625 pedes	607.14 ft
mille passus, mille passuum	mile	5000 pedes	4854 ft 0.92 mi
leuga	(Gallic) league	7500 pedes	7281 ft 1.38 mi

Greek measures of Length

Greek name	English name	Equal to	Imperial
δάκτυλος	daktylos (finger)		0.76 in
κόνδυλος	kondylos	2 daktyloi	1.52 in
παλαιστή, δῶρον	palaiste (palm)	4 daktyloi	3.04 in
διχάς, ἡμιπόδιον	hemipodion half foot	8 daktyloi	6.07 in
λιχάς	lichas	10 daktyloi	7.58 in
ὀρθόδωρον	orthodoron	11 daktyloi	8.34 in
σπιθαμή	spithame (span of fingers)	12 daktyloi	9.10 in
πούς	pous (foot)	16 daktyloi	12.13 in
πυγμή	pygme (forearm)	18 daktyloi	13.65 in
πυγών	pygon	20 daktyloi	15.17 in
πῆχυς	pechys (cubit)	24 daktyloi	18.20 in
ἁπλοῦν βῆμα	haploun bema (step)	2 ½ podes	2.5 ft
βῆμα, διπλοῦν βῆμα	bema (pace)	5 podes	5.1 ft
ὄργυια	orgyia (fathom)	6 podes	6.1 ft
κάλαμος, ἄκαινα, δεκάπους	kalamos	10 podes	10.1 ft
ἄμμα	hamma	60 podes	20.2 yd
πλέθρον	plethron	100 podes	33.7 yd
στάδιον	stadion (⅛ Roman mile)	600 podes	202.2 yd
δίαυλος	diaulos	2 stadia	404.5 yd
ἱππικόν	hippicon	4 stadia	808.9 yd
μίλιον	milion (Roman mile)	8 stadia	1,617 yd
δόλιχος	dolichos	12 stadia	1.379 mi

| παρασάγγες | *parasanges*
(Persia league) | 30 stadia | 3.447 mi |
| σχοινός | *schoinos*
(Egyptian
league) | 40 stadia | 4.596 mi |

Roman Area measures

Roman unit	English name	Equal to	Imperial
pes quadratus	square foot	1 pes qu.	0.943 sq ft
scrupulum or decempeda quadrata	10 x 10	100 pedes qu.	94.3 sq ft
actus simplex	4 x 120 ft	480 pedes qu.	453 sq ft
uncia		2400 pedes qu.	2260 sq ft
clima	60 x 60 ft	3600 pedes qu.	3390 sq ft
actus quadratus or acnua		14400 pedes qu.	13600 sq ft
iugerum		28800 pedes qu.	27200 sq ft 0.623 acres
heredium		2 iugera	54300 sq ft 1.248 acres
centuria		200 iugera	125 acres
saltus		800 iugera	499 acres

Divisions of *Iugera*

Roman unit	Roman square feet	Fraction of iugerum	Imperial
dimidium scrupulum	50	$\frac{1}{576}$	47.1 sq ft
scrupulum	100	$\frac{1}{288}$	94.3 sq ft
duo scrupula	200	$\frac{1}{144}$	188 sq ft
sextula	400	$\frac{1}{72}$	377 sq ft
sicilicus	600	$\frac{1}{48}$	566 sq ft

semiuncia	1200	$\frac{1}{24}$	1130 sq ft
uncia	2400	$\frac{1}{12}$	2260 sq ft
sextans	4800	$\frac{1}{6}$	4530 sq ft
quadrans	7200	$\frac{1}{4}$	6790 sq ft
triens	9600	$\frac{1}{3}$	9050 sq ft
quincunx	12000	$\frac{5}{12}$	11310 sq ft
semis	14400	$\frac{1}{2}$	15380 sq ft
septunx	16800	$\frac{7}{12}$	15840 sq ft
bes	19200	$\frac{2}{3}$	18100 sq ft
dodrans	21600	$\frac{3}{4}$	20380 sq ft
dextans	24000	$\frac{5}{6}$	22640 sq ft
deunx	26400	$\frac{11}{12}$	24900 sq ft
iugerum	28800	1	27160 sq ft

Greek Area measures

Greek name	English name	Equal to	Imperial
πούς	*pous* (square foot)		1.02 sq ft
ἑξαπόδης	*hexapodes* (6 x 6 ft)	36 podes	36.8 sq ft
ἄκαινα	*akaina* (10 x 10 ft)	100 podes	102.3 sq ft
ἡμίεκτος	*hemiektos*	833 $\frac{1}{3}$ podes	853 sq ft
ἕκτος	*ektos*	1666 $\frac{2}{3}$ podes	1,704 sq ft
ἄρουρα	*aroura*	2500 podes	2,556 sq ft
πλέθρον	*plethron*	10000 podes	10,200 sq ft

Roman wet measures

Roman unit	Equal to	Imperial	US
ligula	$\frac{1}{288}$ *congius*	0.4 fl oz	0.39 fl oz
cyathus	$\frac{1}{72}$ *congius*	1.58 fl oz	1.52 fl oz
acetabulum	$\frac{1}{48}$ *congius*	2.39 fl oz	2.30 fl oz
quartarius	$\frac{1}{24}$ *congius*	4.79 fl oz	4.61 fl oz

hemina or cotyla	$\frac{1}{12}$ *congius*	9.61 fl oz	9.23 fl oz
sextarius	$\frac{1}{6}$ *congius*	19.22 fl oz	18.47 fl oz
		0.96 pt	1.15 pt
congius	1 *congius*	5.75 pt	3.46 qt
		0.72 gal	0.86 gal
urna	4 *congii*	2.88 gal	3.46 gal
amphora quadrantal	8 *congii*	5.76 gal	6.92 gal
culeus	160 *congii*	115.3 gal	138.4 gal

Roman dry measures

Roman unit	Equal to	Imperial	US
ligula	$\frac{1}{288}$ *congius*	0.401 fl oz	0.02 pt
cyathus	$\frac{1}{72}$ *congius*	1.58 fl oz	0.08 pt
acetabulum	$\frac{1}{48}$ *congius*	2.39 fl oz	0.12 pt
quartarius	$\frac{1}{24}$ *congius*	4.79 fl oz	0.25 pt
hemina or cotyla	$\frac{1}{12}$ *congius*	9.61 fl oz	0.5 pt
sextarius	$\frac{1}{6}$ *congius*	0.96 pt	0.99 pt
semimodius	1 $\frac{1}{3}$ *congii*	0.96 gal	0.99 gal
modius	2 $\frac{2}{3}$ *congii*	1.92 gal	1.98 gal
modius castrensis	4 congii	2.84 gal	2.94 gal

Greek wet measures

Greek name	Equal to	Imperial	US
κοχλιάριον	*kochliarion*	0.16 fl oz	0.15 fl oz
χήμη	2 *kochliaria*	0.32 fl oz	0.31 fl oz
μύστρον	2 ½ *kochliaria*	0.40 fl oz	0.39 fl oz
κόγχη	5 *kochliaria*	0.80 fl oz	0.77 fl oz
κύαθος	10 *kochliaria*	1.60 fl oz	1.54 fl oz
ὀξύβαθον	1 ½ *kyathoi*	2.40 fl oz	2.31 fl oz
τέταρτον, ἡμικοτύλη	3 kyathoi	4.80 fl oz	4.61 fl oz
κοτύλη, τρύβλιον, ἡμίνα	6 *kyathoi*	9.60 fl oz	9.22 fl oz
ξέστης	12 *kyathoi*	0.96 pt	1.153 pt

χοῦς	72 *kyathoi*	5.75 pt	6.9 pt
κεράμιον	8 *choes*	5.8 gal	6.9 gal
μετρητής	12 *choes*	8.6 gal	10.4 gal

Greek dry measures

Greek name	Equal to	Imperial	US
κοχλιάριον	*kochliarion*	0.16 fl oz	0.15 fl oz
κύαθος	10 *kochliaria*	1.60 fl oz	1.54 fl oz
ὀξύβαθον	1 ½ *kyathoi*	2.40 fl oz	2.31 fl oz
κοτύλη, ἡμίνα	6 *kyathoi*	9.60 fl oz	9.22 fl oz
ξέστης	12 *kyathoi*	0.96 pt	1.153 pt
χοῖνιξ	24 *kyathoi*	1.92 pt	2.3 pt
ἡμίεκτον	4 *choinikes*	0.96 gal	1.15 gal
ἑκτεύς	8 *choinikes*	1.92 gal	2.31 gal
μέδιμνος	48 *choinikes*	11.5 gal	13.8 gal

Roman measures of Weight

Roman unit	English name	Equal to	Imperial equivalent
uncia	Roman ounce	$\frac{1}{12}$ *libra*	0.97 oz
sescuncia or sescunx		$\frac{1}{8}$ *libra*	1.45 oz
sextans		$\frac{1}{6}$ *libra*	1.93 oz
quadrans, teruncius	quarter-pound	$\frac{1}{4}$ *libra*	2.90 oz
triens		$\frac{1}{3}$ *libra*	3.87 oz
quincunx		$\frac{5}{12}$ *libra*	4.83 oz
semis or semissis	half-pound	$\frac{1}{2}$ *libra*	5.80 oz
septunx		$\frac{7}{12}$ *libra*	6.77 oz
bes or bessis		$\frac{2}{3}$ *libra*	7.74 oz
dodrans	three quarter-pound	$\frac{3}{4}$ *libra*	8.70 oz

dextans		$\frac{5}{6}$ *libra*	9.67 oz
deunx		$\frac{11}{12}$ *libra*	10.64 oz
libra	Roman pound		0.73 lb

Subdivisions of the Uncia

Roman unit	English name	Equal to	Imperial equivalent
siliqua	carat	$\frac{1}{144}$ *uncia*	0.0067 oz
obolus	obolus	$\frac{1}{48}$ *uncia*	0.02 oz
scrupulum	scruple	$\frac{1}{24}$ *uncia*	0.04 oz
semisextula		$\frac{1}{12}$ *uncia*	0.08 oz
sextula	sextula	$\frac{1}{6}$ *uncia*	0.16 oz
sicilicus, siciliquus		$\frac{1}{4}$ *uncia*	0.24 oz
duella		$\frac{1}{3}$ *uncia*	0.32 oz
semuncia	half-ounce	$\frac{1}{2}$ *uncia*	0.48 oz
uncia	Roman ounce		0.97 oz

Greek measures of Weight (Attic)

Greek name	English Name	Equal to	Imperial equivalent
ὀβολός	*obol* or *obolus*		0.03 oz
δραχμή	*drachma*	6 obols	0.15 oz
μνᾶ	*mina*	100 drachmae	15.2 oz
τάλαντον	*talent*	60 minae	57.0 lb

XVI Who rules when

This chapter details when Emperors rule and what travel concerns you may need to look out for while they're in charge. During the third century there are numerous barbarian incursions and wars with the Persians in the east. During that time it's best to stay in Southern Europa, Africa, and some parts of Asia like Aegyptus.

Augustus	DCCXXVII A.U.C. DCCLXVII A.U.C.	27 B.C.E. 14 C.E.	One of the best times to travel in the early Empire is under Augustus, he brings Gallia, Hispania, Aegyptus, Syria, Cilicia and Cyprus under Roman control while founding colonies of Romans across the expanding territory.
Tiberius	DCCLXVII A.U.C. DCCXC A.U.C.	14 C.E. 37 C.E.	Apart from an early issue in Pannonia and Germania, travel is relatively safe under Tiberius, as long as you have nothing to do with Seianus.
Caligula	DCCXC A.U.C. DCCXCIV A.U.C.	37 C.E. 41 C.E.	The early part of Caligula's reign is blissful, but the latter half of his rule was filled with heavy taxation, executions, exiles, famine and soldiers stabbing the sea.
Claudius	DCCXCIV A.U.C. DCCCVII A.U.C.	41 C.E. 54 C.E.	Claudius brings peace to Achaea and Macedonia, and brings Thracia, Noricum, Pamphylia, Lycia, Mauretania, Iudaea, and Britannia under Roman rule. He is also fond of public games, so it is an entertaining time for sure.

Nero	DCCCVII A.U.C. DCCCXXI A.U.C.	54 C.E. 68 C.E.	Nero is the final emperor of the Judio-Claudian dynasty. At times during his rule, Roma burns, Britannia revolts and Iudaea rebels, so maybe avoid visiting those places during his rule.
Galba	DCCCXXI A.U.C. DCCCXXII A.U.C.	68 C.E. 69 C.E.	Widely unpopular, Galba heavily taxes the provinces and causes revolts in Germania.
Otho	DCCCXXII A.U.C. DCCCXXII A.U.C.	69 C.E. 69 C.E.	His rule is short and ends in suicide to prevent a civil war.
Vitellius	DCCCXXII A.U.C. DCCCXXII A.U.C.	69 C.E. 69 C.E.	While desiring to govern more wisely he is a ravenous glutton who sends the Roman navy to procure rare foods from far off lands, you may be lucky enough to catch a ride on one of these ships though.
Vespasian	DCCCXXII A.U.C. DCCCXXXII A.U.C.	69 C.E. 79 C.E.	First of the Flavian dynasty, he brings considerable stability after a brief civil war with Vitellius, barbarians in Dacia and Germania are fond of the Emperor. Sadly he is forever memorialized through association with latrines due to a tax on collected urine, much like poor John Harington and Thomas Crapper.
Titus	DCCCXXXII A.U.C. DCCCXXXIV A.U.C.	79 C.E. 81 C.E.	The rule of Titus is largely without military or political conflict, he finishes the *Ampitheatrum Flavium*. However, there is a war continuing in northern Britannia, a fire

			in Roma and the eruption of Vesuvius.
Domitian	DCCCXXXIV A.U.C. DCCCXLIX A.U.C.	81 C.E. 96 C.E.	Domitian, the last of the Flavian dynasty reduces the influence of the Senate and increases the efficiency of the bureaucracy. The war in Britannia continues during his rule, and he fights defensive campaigns in northern Gallia and Dacia.
Nerva	DCCCXLIX A.U.C. DCCCLI A.U.C.	96 C.E. 98 C.E.	Nerva's reign is short, but during his brief tenure he does preform repairs to the Roman road network, so travelling after his rule is a bit more comfortable.
Trajan	DCCCLI A.U.C. DCCCLXX A.U.C.	98 C.E. 117 C.E.	Trajan's rule sees expansion of the Empire in Dacia, Arabia Petraea and bringing the Greek city-states to heel. He also holds a three month long session of public games in the *Amphitheatrum Flavium*.
Hadrian	DCCCLXX A.U.C. DCCCXCI A.U.C.	117 C.E. 138 C.E.	Hadrian spends much of his rule travelling throughout the Empire. He constructs a massive wall across the northern border of Britannia, and quashes another rebellion in Iudaea, afterwards erases the province from existence and renaming it Syria Palestina. During his travels he restores and raises up many of the provinces he visits.
Antoninus Pius	DCCCXCI A.U.C. CMXIV A.U.C.	138 C.E. 161 C.E.	Antoninus Pius rules peacefully from Roma for the duration of his reign

			save for a military expedition north of Hadrian's wall.
Lucius Verus	CMXIV A.U.C. CMXXII A.U.C.	161 C.E. 169 C.E.	Co-Emperor with Marcus Aurelius, Lucius spends much of his career fighting wars in the far east in Armenia and Mesopotamia.
Marcus Aurelius	CMXIV A.U.C. CMXXXIII A.U.C.	161 C.E. 180 C.E.	Co-Emperor with Lucius Verus, Marcus sends Lucius to deal with wars in the far east in hopes of taming his debaucheries, in the second decade of his rule he pushes back Germanic invaders who sweep across Europa. Lucius brings a plague back with him and succumbs to it. His empire was also in contact with Han China in the far east.
Commodus	CMXXX A.U.C. CMXLV A.U.C.	177 C.E. 192 C.E.	Commodus serves as co-Emperor with his father for his first three years, and while his solo career is not plagued by constant warfare as his father's had been, it is full of political strife. He became increasingly obsessed with himself as time goes on, refounds Roma in his own name, renames the months, and competes regularly in gladiatorial games before he is finally assassinated bringing an end to the Nerva-Antonine dynasty.
Pertinax	CMXLVI A.U.C. CMXLVI A.U.C.	193 C.E. 193 C.E.	1/5 He really makes the Praetorians angry with him.
Didius	CMXLVI A.U.C.	193 C.E.	2/5 Buys the title of

Julianus	CMXLVI A.U.C.	193 C.E.	Emperor, goes out with a whimper, not a bang.
Pescennius Niger	CMXLVI A.U.C. CMXLVI A.U.C.	193 C.E. 193 C.E.	3/5 Holds support amongst the eastern provinces but was defeated by Severus.
Clodius Albinus Septimius Severus	CMXLVI A.U.C. CMXLVI A.U.C. CMXLVI A.U.C. CMLXIV A.U.C.	193 C.E. 193 C.E. 193 C.E. 211 C.E.	4/5 Holds support in Gaul, defeated by Severus 5/5 The victor of the year of 5 Emperors, he fights in wars all across the Empire, expands Africa and Syria and attempts to invade Caledonia before falling ill and dying in Britannia.
Caracalla	CMLI A.U.C. CMLXX A.U.C.	198 C.E. 217 C.E.	Fights a brief war in Germania and fortifies the northern border. He, in Alexandrian fashion decides to fight against Parthian and is stabbed to death by a disgruntled employee who he denied promotion.
Geta	CMLXII A.U.C. CMLXIV A.U.C.	209 C.E. 211 C.E.	Joint Emperor with Caracalla before succumbing to a bad case of fratricide.
Macrinus	CMLXX A.U.C. CMLXXI A.U.C.	217 C.E. 218 C.E.	Deeply unpopular with the Roman people due to financial hardship. Is executed and declared an enemy of the state.
Diadumen- ian	CMLXX A.U.C. CMLXXI A.U.C.	217 C.E. 218 C.E.	Declared co-Emperor, similarly executed as his father and also declared an enemy.
Elagabalus	CMLXXI A.U.C. CMLXXV A.U.C.	218 C.E. 222 C.E.	Disliked by the Senate and Roman people for his religious and personal eccentricities, he is eventually executed and declared an enemy of the

state.

Severus Alexander	CMLXXV A.U.C. CMLXXXVIII A.U.C.	222 C.E. 235 C.E.	The last of the Severan dynasty, he deals with wars in the far east and Germania, the military during this period suffers from lack of discipline and he is assassinated by the Legio XXII Primigenia.
Maximinus Thrax	CMLXXXVIII A.U.C. CMXCI A.U.C.	235 C.E. 238 C.E.	1/6 Consolidates power and secures the borders of the Empire, he is assassinated outside of Roma during the chaos caused by the Senate's support of the Gordians.
Gordian I	CMXCI A.U.C. CMXCI A.U.C.	238 C.E. 238 C.E.	2/6 Attempts to rebel in Africa with his son, hangs himself after his son dies in battle.
Gordian II	CMXCI A.U.C. CMXCI A.U.C.	238 C.E. 238 C.E.	3/6 Attempts to rebel in Africa with his father, dies in battle before his father hangs himself.
Pupienus	CMXCI A.U.C. CMXCI A.U.C.	238 C.E. 238 C.E.	4/6 Declared co-Emperor with Balbinus, murdered by Praetorians.
Balbinus	CMXCI A.U.C. CMXCI A.U.C.	238 C.E. 238 C.E.	5/6 Declared co-Emperor by Pupienus, also murdered by Praetorians.
Gordian III	CMXCI A.U.C. CMXCVII A.U.C.	238 C.E. 244 C.E.	6/6 After dealing with border incursions in Germania, he dies during a war against the Sassanid Empire in the east.
Phillip the Arab	CMXCVII A.U.C. MII A.U.C.	244 C.E. 249 C.E.	Spends much of his time dealing with the border incursions in Moesia, but does hold the monumental *Ludi Saeculares* in Roma. Celebrated the 1,000[th] birthday of the city. He is betrayed and killed in battle by Decius.
Phillip II	M A.U.C. MII A.U.C.	247 C.E. 249 C.E.	Son of Phillip the Arab, serves alongside him and dies alongside him.
Decius	MII A.U.C.	249 C.E.	Fights incursions from the

	MIV A.U.C.	251 C.E.	Goths in Moesia and Thracia and dies. During his rule he does persecute Christians, so beware that.
Herennius Etruscus	MIV A.U.C. MIV A.U.C.	251 C.E. 251 C.E.	Co-Emperor with Decius, he also dies in the battle of Abrittus.
Hostilian	MIV A.U.C. MIV A.U.C.	251 C.E. 251 C.E.	Shortly ruling alongside Trebonianus Gallus after his brother and father's deaths, he dies of plague not long after.
Trebonianus Gallus	MIV A.U.C. MVI A.U.C.	251 C.E. 253 C.E.	During his brief tenure, Syria, Cappadocia, Moesia and Armenia are in turmoil and unsafe for travel. He is murdered by his own troops.
Volusianus	MIV A.U.C. MVI A.U.C.	251 C.E. 253 C.E.	Serves and is murdered alongside Trebonianus.
Aemilian	MVI A.U.C. MVI A.U.C.	253 C.E. 253 C.E.	Defeats Trebonianus then his promptly murdered by his own troops in favor of Valerian.
Valerian	MVI A.U.C. MXIII A.U.C.	253 C.E. 260 C.E.	The first Emperor to be taken as a prisoner of war by the Persians, also persecutes Christians during his rule.
Gallienus	MVI A.U.C. MXXI A.U.C.	253 C.E. 268 C.E.	His long rule is filled with tumultuous revolts as he puts out one fire for another to break out. Revolts in the east and the succession of the Gallic Empire and Palmyrene Empire lead to a period of civil war and difficulty for anyone wanted to travel.
aloninus	MXIII A.U.C. MXIII A.U.C.	260 C.E. 260 C.E.	Served as co-Emperor with his father.

Claudius II	MXXI A.U.C. MXXIII A.U.C.	268 C.E. 270 C.E.	Routs the Goths in Pannonia and Illyricum before dying of plague.
Quintillus	MXXIII A.U.C. MXIII A.U.C.	270 C.E. 270 C.E.	Didn't last very long at all…
Aurelian	MXIII A.U.C. MXXVIII A.U.C.	270 C.E. 275 C.E.	The *Restitutor Orbis*, Aurelian conquers the Palmyrene Empire, reclaims the Gallic Empire and abandons Dacia to the Goths. He also expels barbarian intruders from northern Italia. He is murdered over a paperwork mistake.
Tacitus	MXXVIII A.U.C. MXXIX A.U.C.	275 C.E. 276 C.E.	Fights campaigns against the barbarians before succumbing to a fever.
Florianus	MXXIX A.U.C. MXXIX A.U.C.	276 C.E. 276 C.E.	Has to deal with a revolt in Asia Minor, his troops murder him because the climate is too hot.
Probus	MXXIX A.U.C. MXXXV A.U.C.	276 C.E. 282 C.E.	After defeating Florianus he pushes the Goths out of the Empire and gets a peace treaty then begins work on restoring the devastated regions of Gallia and securing the border along the *Rhenus*.
Carus	MXXXV A.U.C. MXXXVI A.U.C.	282 C.E. 283 C.E.	Further stabilizes Gallia and heads east against the Persians, he apparently offends Jupiter in some way or another, because divine justice strikes him down.
Numerian	MXXXVI A.U.C. MXXXVII A.U.C.	283 C.E. 284 C.E.	Co-Emperor with his father Carus and brother, dies while travelling back to Roma.

Carinus	MXXXVI A.U.C. MXXXVIII A.U.C.	283 C.E. 285 C.E.	Co-Emperor with his father Carus and brother, is killed by Diocletian.
Diocletian	MXXXVII A.U.C. MLVIII A.U.C.	284 C.E. 305 C.E.	Diocletian's rule marks the splitting of the Empire into the Western and Eastern Roman Empires, please see the *Hitch-hiker's* *Guide to Byzantine Rome:* *Roman through the streets* *of Byzantium* and the *Hitch-hiker's Guide to* *Medieval Europe:* *Plagues, Popes and* *Patriarchal Monarchy* for more information.

XVII Historic Routes

For those of you who would like to travel along the routes of your favorite heroes or maybe see some specific sites, here are a few suggested trips you can take to recreate the experience.

The route of Odysseus

I: Ilium, Asia
II: Ismara, Thracia
III: *Insula Lotophagorum*, Africa Proconsularis
IV: *Insula Cylopum,* Sicilia
V: Aeolia, southwest of Sicilia
VI: Telepylos, Africa Proconsularis
VII: *Insula Circae,* west of Italia
VIII: *Insula Sirenum,* off of the west coast of southern Italia
IX: *Fretum Siciliense,* between Sicilia and Italia
X: Thrinacia, south of Italia
XI: Ogygia, *Mare Ionium*
XII: Ithaca, Achaia

The route of Aeneas

I: The grave of Polydorus, Thracia
II: Delos, *Mare Aegaeum*
III: Knossos, Creta
IV: Strophades, Achaia
V: Actium, Achaia
VI: Buthrotum, Achaia
VII: Caraunia, Achaia
VIII: Tarentum, Italia
IX: *Insula Cyclopum,* Sicilia
X: Carthago, Africa Proconsularis
XI: Sicilia
XII: Cumae, Italia
XIII: Latium, Italia

The route of the Argonauts

I: Iolcus, Achaia
II: Magnesia, Achaia
III: Lemnos, *Mare Aegaeum*
IV: Samothrace, *Mare Aegaeum*
V: Cyzicus, Asia
VI: *Prusius ad Mare,* Bithynia et Pontus
VII: Gulf of Olbia, Bithynia et Pontus
VIII: Thynia, Bithynia et Pontus
IX: Thynias, Bithynia et Pontus
X: Heraclea Pontica, Bithynia et Pontus
XI: Tomb of Sthenelus, Bithynia et Pontus
XII: Sinope, Bithynia et Pontus
XIII: Themiskyra, Bithynia et Pontus
XIV: *Insula Aris,* Bithynia et Pontus
XV: Aea, Colchis
XVI: *flumen Halys*, Cappadocia
XVII: Narex, Moesia Inferior
XVIII: *Sinus Flanaticus,* Dalmatia
XIX: *Insula Electris,* Italia
XX: Hyllus, Dalmatia
XXI: *flumen Padus,* Italia
XXII: *Insulae Stoechades,* Gallia Narbonensis
XXIII: Elba, Italia
XXIV: *Insula Circae,* west of Italia
XXV: Eryx, Sicilia
XXVI: Corcyra, Macedonia
XXVII: Syrtis, Africa Proconsularis
XXVIII: Creta, *Mare Nostrum*
XXIX: Anaphe, *Mare Aegaeum*
XXX: Aegina, *Mare Aegaeum*

The route of Hercules

I: Nemea, Achaia
II: Lerna, Achaia
III: Ceryneia, Achaia
IV: Erymanthia, Achaia
V: *Stabula Aegeae,* Achaia
VI: Lake Stymphalia, Achaia
VII: Creta, *Mare Nostrum*
VIII: Bistonia, Thracia

IX: Themiskyra, Bithynia et Pontus
X: Gades, Hispania Baetica
XI: *Mons Atlans,* Mauretania Tingitana
XII: The Underworld, see **Chapter** – for directions.

The Seven Wonders of the Ancient World

I: The Great Pyramid, NW of Memphis, Aegyptus
II: The Hanging Gardens, Babylon, Mesopotamia
III: Temple of Artemis, Ephesus, Asia
IV: Statue of Zeus, Olympia, Achaia
V: Mausoleum at Halicarnassus, Halicarnassus, Asia
VI: Colossus of Rhodus, Rhodus, *Mare Nostrum*
VII: Lighthouse of Alexandria, Alexandria, Aegyptus

XVIII O Di Immortales

The ancient world is absolutely teeming with deities, you can seemingly find one of every river, tree and hill in the Empire, we've compiled a short list for you to reference if you find yourself joining a cult and are unsure of who you may be pledging your life to. Greek, and Egyptian deities are denoted. Due to the tribal nature of Gauls, you will not likely find yourself worshipping a Gallic deity, perhaps being sacrificed to one, but not likely worshiping. Additionally, deities of individual springs, rivers, cities and tribes are not listed as their name is typically associated with the subject of their influence.

Name	Role
Abnoba	The goddess of the Black Forest.
Abundantia	The goddess of abundance and prosperity.
Achlys	The Greek goddess of poison.
Adolenda	The goddess of the burning of trees struck by lightning.
Aequitas	The goddess of equality and fairness.
Aesculapius	The god of healing.
Aeternitas	The god of eternity.
Aether	The Greek god of light and the upper atmosphere.
Aion	The Greek god of the ages.
Aius	The god of warning the Romans of the approach of the Gauls in 389 B.C.E.
Aken	An Egyptian god of earth.
Alernus	The god of beans.
Altercatio	The goddess of disputes, debates, and arguments. (especially angry ones)
Ambisagrus	The Gallic god of thunder and lightning, the sky, wind, rain, and hail.
Amor	The god of love.
Amun	The Egyptian creator god.
Amunet	The Egyptian goddess of being married to Amun.

Ananke	The Greek goddess of compulsion and necessity.
Angerona	The goddess of relieving pain and sorrow.
Anhur	The Egyptian god of hunting and war.
Anna Peranna	The goddess of the returning year.
Annona	The goddess of marketable output.
Antevorta	The goddess of cephalic birth and the future.
Anubis	The Egyptian god of embalming and having a dog head.
Anuket	The Egyptian goddess of southern Aegyptus.
Aphrodite	The Greek Venus.
Apollo	The god of prophecy, music, poetry, archery, medicine.
Ares	The Greek Mars.
Artemis	The Greek Diana.
Ascensus	The god of surmounting things.
Astraea	The goddess of justice.
Aten	An Egyptian god of the sun.
Athena	The Greek Minerva.
Atum	An Egyptian creator god.
Aurae	The goddesses of the breezes.
Aurora	The goddess of the dawn.
Averruncus	The god of calamity aversion.
Bacchus	The Roman Dionysus.
Bastet	The Egyptian cat-goddess.
Bat	The Egyptian cow-goddess.
Bellona or Duellona	The goddess of war.
Bennu	The Egyptian creator bird-god.
Bibesia	The goddess of banquet and drink.
Biviae	The goddesses of cross-roads.
Bona Dea	The goddess of women.
Bonus Eventus	The god of good outcomes.

Boreas	The god of the north wind.
Britannia	The Gallic goddess of Britannia.
Bubona	The goddess of cattle.
Caca	The goddess of fire.
Cacus	The god of fire.
Caeculus	The god of blindness.
Caelus	The god of the sky.
Calliope	The goddess of epic poetry and chief Muse.
Cardea	The goddess of hinges.
Carmenta	The goddess of prophecy and childbirth.
Carna	The goddess of the heart and internal organs.
Ceres	The Roman Demeter.
Chaos	The Greek goddess of nothingness.
Chronos	The Greek god of time.
Clementia	The goddess of forgiveness.
Clivicola	The god of slopes.
Cloacina	The goddess of sewers.
Commolenda	The goddess presiding of the grinding or pounding down of ritually burned objects.
Concordia	The goddess of agreement, understanding, and marital harmony.
Consivius	The god of procreation.
Consus	The god of the storing of the harvest.
Copia	The goddess of abundance.
Cronos	The Greek father-Titan.
Cuba	The goddess who protects a child in bed.
Cunina	The goddess of the cradle.
Cupido	The god of carnal desire.
Cupra	The fertility goddess of Cupra.
Cura	The goddess of caring.
Cybele	The Great Mother goddess.

Cynthia	The goddess of Mount Cynthus, Diana.
Cypria	The goddess of Cyprus, Venus.
Dea Dia	The goddess of growth.
Dea Tacita	The goddess of the dead.
Decima	The goddess of the last month of a woman's pregnancy.
Demeter	The Greek Ceres.
Deverra	The goddess of brooms and midwives.
Di Conserentes	The gods of procreation.
Diana	The Roman Artemis.
Dies	The goddess of the day.
Dione	The goddess of being the mother of Venus.
Dionysus	The Greek Bacchus.
Disciplina	The goddess of discipline.
Discordia	The goddess of discord and strife.
Dius Fidius	The god of oaths.
Edusa	The goddess presiding over a child's eating.
Egeria	The goddess of water.
Enyo	The Greek goddess of war.
Epona	The Gallic goddess of horses, donkeys and mules.
Erebus	The god of darkness.
Erebus	The Greek god of darkness and shadow.
Eros	The Greek god of desire.
Fabulinus	The god of story-telling.
Fama	The goddess of fame.
Farinus	The god of speech.
Fascinus	The god of protecting from the evil eye with his phallus.
Fatum	The god of fate.
Fauna	The goddess of prophecy.
Faunus	The god of flocks.
Febris	The goddess of fever.

Fecunditas	The goddess of fertility.
Felicitas	The goddess of good luck.
Ferentina	The goddess of Ferentinum.
Feronia	The goddess of the wilderness and plebians.
Fides	The goddess of loyalty.
Flora	The goddess of flowers or the flowering season.
Fontana	The goddess of springs.
Fontus	The god of springs.
Fornax	The goddess of ovens.
Fortuna	The goddess of luck and fortune.
Fufluns	The god of wine and natural growth.
Fulgora	The goddess of lightning.
Furiae	The goddesses who take vengeance for guilt.
Gaia	The Greek personification of the Earth herself.
Geb	An Egyptian god of earth.
Genius	The god of you, personally.
Hades	The Greek Pluto.
Haket	The Egyptian frog-goddess of childbirth.
Hapi	The Egyptian god of the Nile flood.
Hathor	The Egyptian goddess of sexuality, motherhood, music and dance.
Hebe	The goddess of waitressing.
Hecate	The goddess of crossroads.
Heh	The Egyptian deity of infinity.
Hemera	The Greek goddess of the day.
Hephaestus	The Greek Vulcan.
Hera	The Greek Iuno.
Hercules	The god of strength.
Hermes	The Greek Mercurius.
Hesat	The Egyptian maternal cow-goddess.

Honor	The god of military power and virtue.
Honos	The god of honor.
Hora Quirini	The goddess of being married to Romulus.
Horus	The Egyptian god of the sky, sun, kingship, protection.
Hygia	The goddess of health.
Hymen	The god of marriage.
Hypnos	The Greek god of sleep.
Ianus	The two-faced god of doors and beginnings.
Iesus Christus	Hebrew demigod.
Ilithyia	The Greek goddess of childbirth.
Imentet	The Egyptian goddess of the afterlife.
Imporcitor	A god of agriculture.
Inachus	The god of the Inachus.
Intercidona	The goddess of protecting children directly after birth.
Inuus	The god of herdsmen.
Invidia	The goddess of envy and wrong-doing.
Iris	The goddess of the rainbow, the messenger of the gods.
Isis	The Egyptian goddess of funerals, motherhood, magic.
Iuno	The Roman Hera.
Iupiter	The Roman Zeus.
Iustitia	The goddess of justice.
Iuturna	The goddess of fountains, wells, springs.
Iuventas	The goddess of youth.
Kek	The Egyptian deity of chaos and darkness.
Khepri	The Egyptian solar creator god.
Khnum	The Egyptian ram-god.
Khonsu	The Egyptian moon god.
Lactans	The god of the growth of young crops.
Latona	The goddess of light.

Laverna	The goddess of thieves.
Levana	The goddess of father's accepting a newborn child.
Liber	The god of vegetation and agriculture.
Libera	The goddess of agriculture.
Libitina	The goddess of funerals.
Lua	The goddess of captured weapons.
Lucifer	The god of the morning star.
Lucina	The goddess of bringing children into the world, either Iuno or Diana.
Luna	The goddess of the moon.
Luperca	The goddess of being the wife of Lupercus.
Lupercus	The god of shepherds and wolves.
Maahes	The Egyptian lion-god.
Maat	The Egyptian goddess of truth, justice and order.
Mana Genita	The goddess of infant mortality.
Manturna	The goddess of the preservation of marriage.
Mars	The god of war.
Meditrina	The goddess of healing.
Mephitis	The goddess of exhalations and volcanic vapors.
Mellona	The goddess of bees.
Memoria	The goddess of memory.
Mena	The goddess of menstruation.
Menhit	An Egyptian lioness-goddess.
Mens Bona	The god of sanity.
Mercurius	The Roman Hermes.
Minerva	The Roman Athena.
Mithras	The Persian god of the sun.
Molae	The goddess of grain grinding.
Montu	The Egyptian god of war and the sun.
Mors	The deity of death.

Murcia	The goddess of sloth and laziness.
Mutinus	The Egyptian goddess of seeing Amun on the side.
Mutinus	The goddess of phallicy marriage.
Myiodes	The Greek god of fly repulsion.
Naenia	The goddess of funeral lamentations.
Natio	The goddess of childbirth.
Nebula	The goddess of fog and mist.
Nefertum	The Egyptian god of lotus blossoms.
Nehebkau	An Egyptian serpent-god.
Neith	The Egyptian goddess of hunters.
Nekhbet	The Egyptian vulture-goddess.
Nemausus	The god of Nemausus.
Nemesis	The Greek goddess of retribution.
Nemty	The Egyptian falcon-god.
Nenia	The goddess of funeral dirges.
Neper	The Egyptian god of grain.
Nepit	The Egyptian goddess of grain.
Neptunus	The Roman Poseidon.
Nereus	The god of the sea or ocean and fathering Nereids.
Nerio	The goddess of war and valor.
Nerthus	The German fertility goddess.
Nocturnus	The god of night.
Nodutus	The god of wheat, who brings the stem on as far as the joints or nodes.
Nona	The goddess of the ninth month of a woman's pregnancy.
Nortia	The goddess of destiny.
Nox	The goddess of night.
Nu	The Egyptian deity of formlessness.
Numeria	The goddess of the speedy delivery of mothers and childhood arithmetic.
Nut	The Egyptian goddess of the sky.

Nyx	The Greek goddess of night.
Obarator	The god of ploughing.
Occator	The god of harrowing.
Occupo	The god of opportunism.
Ops	The goddess of resources.
Orbona	The goddess of parents who have lost or might lose, a child.
Orcus	The god of punishing broken oaths.
Osiris	The Egyptian god of death.
Ourea	The Greek gods of mountains.
Paean	The Greek healing god.
Pakhet	An Egyptian lioness-goddess.
Palaepaphia	The goddess of Palaepaphos.
Palatua	The goddess of the Palatine hill.
Pales	The god and goddess of flocks and herds.
Pan	The god of shepherds and flocks.
Panda	The goddess of rustics.
Paniscus	The god of being a lesser version of Pan.
Paphie	The goddess of Paphia, Venus.
Parca	The goddess of birth.
Partula	The goddess of childbirth.
Patelana	The goddess of the opening of ears of grain.
Paventia	The goddess of terrifying children.
Pax	The goddess of peace.
Pecunia	The goddess of money.
Pellonia	The goddess of routing of an enemy.
Penates	The gods of the larder.
Pertunda	The goddess of hymen penetration.
Phanes	The Greek god of procreation.
Picumnus	The god of fertility, agriculture, marriage, infants and children.

Picus	The god of woodpeckers.
Pietas	The goddess of duty.
Pilumnus	The god of freshly born infants.
Pluto	Roman Hades.
Poena	The goddess of penalty.
Pomona	The goddess of fruit-trees, orchards and vineyards.
Pontus	The Greek god of the sea.
Portunus	The god of keys, doors, harbors and livestock.
Poseidon	The Greek Neptune.
Postverta	The goddess of breech births and the past.
Potina	The goddess of a weaned child's first drink.
Praestitia	The goddess of excellence.
Priapus	The god of fertility.
Primitia	The goddess of the first fruits.
Promitor	The god of bringing grain out of storage.
Prorsa	The goddess of children being born headfirst.
Proteus	The god of seal herding.
Providentia	The goddess of providence.
Ptah	The Egyptian god of craftsmen.
Pudicitia	The goddess of sexual purity, chastity, and virtue.
Punelope	The goddess of puns and childish humor.
Quies	The goddess of rest, relaxation and respite.
Quirinus	The god of being Romulus.
Ra	The Egyptian sun god.
Rediculus	The god of Hannibal losing.
Renenutet	The Egyptian goddess of agriculture.
Robigo	The goddess of rush-free crops.
Robigus	The god of rush-free crops.
Roma	The goddess of Roma.
Rumina	The goddess of suckling.

Sakhmet	The Egyptian goddess of leading Pharoahs to war.
Salacia	The goddess of sea-water.
Salus	The goddess of public welfare.
Sancus	The god of loyalty, honesty and oaths.
Saritor	The god of hoes.
Satet	The Egyptian goddess of the southern frontier of Aegyptus.
Saturnus	The god of harvest and agriculture.
Securitas	The goddess of security.
Segesta	The goddess of standing crops.
Seia	The goddess of sowing wheat.
Seker	The Egyptian falcon-god.
Semonia	The goddess of sowing.
Sentinus	The god that gives consciousness to a new-born child.
Sequana	The healing goddess of the river Sequana.
Serapis	The Egyptian god of abundance and resurrection.
Set	The Egyptian god of violence, chaos and strength.
Shu	The Egyptian god of wind.
Silvanus	The god of forests and uncultivated land.
Sobek	The Egyptian crocodile-god.
Sol	The god of the sun.
Somnus	The god of sleep.
Sopdu	The Egyptian god of the east of Aegyptus.
Sors	The god of luck.
Spes	The goddess of hope.
Stata	The goddess of fire protection.
Statanus	The god of wobbling toddlers.
Stercutus	The god of manure.
Suada	The goddess of persuasion.
Subigus	The god who subdues the bride to the husband's will.

Subruncinator	The god of weeding.
Summanus	The god of high places and nocturnal thunder.
Talassus	The Roman god of marriage.
Tartarus	The Greek god of the deepest depths of the Underworld.
Tatenen	The Egyptian deity of the primal earth.
Tefnut	The Egyptian goddess of moisture.
Tellumo	The god of the earth.
Tellus	The goddess of the earth.
Tempestas	The goddess of weather and storms.
Terminus	The god of boundaries.
Testimonius	The god of giving evidence.
Tethys	The goddess of the ocean.
Thalassa	The Greek goddess of the sea.
Thanatos	The Greek god of death.
Themis	The Greek goddess of order, and justice.
Thoth	The Egyptian god of writing and scribes.
Tiberinus	The god of the Tiber.
Tranquilitas	The goddess of tranquility.
Trivia	The goddess of crossroads and magic.
Tutilina	The goddess of harvested grain protection.
Uranus	The Greek personification of the Sky himself.
Vacuna	The goddess of sheep.
Vaticanus	The god of opening an infant's mouth for its first cry.
Venti	The gods of the winds and large coffees.
Venus	The Roman Aphrodite.
Veritas	The goddess of truth.
Verminus	The god of cattle worms.
Vertumnus	The god of seasons.
Vervactor	The god of fallow ploughing.
Vesta	The goddess of the domestic hearth.

Vica Pota	The goddess of victory and competitions.
Victoria	The goddess of victory.
Viduus	The god of separating the soul from the body.
Virbius	The god of forests.
Viriplaca	The goddess of helping wives to win back a husbands' favor after estrangement.
Virtus	The goddess of masculine virtue.
Vitula	The goddess of joy.
Vitumnus	The god that gives life to a new-born child.
Volcanus	The Roman Hephaestus.
Volturnus	The god of water.
Volumna	The god of childhood.
Volupia	The goddess of pleasure.
Volutina	The goddess of cereals at the stage when the ears are still enfolded by the upper leaves.
Wadjet	The Egyptian cobra-goddess.
Wadj-wer	The Egyptian god of the Nile delta and Mediterranean.
Yahweh	The Hebrew god.
Zalmoxis	The Greek god of the dead.
Zeus	The Greek Iupiter.

XIX Language

While there is no replacement for a Classical education, these phrases for Latin and Attic Greek might help you get by. You will need to practice to get a hang of the languages, but once you do it'll be smooth sailing. Be sure to smile and don't shout, no matter what language you speak, shouting it at them will not make it any clearer.

Latin

Latin words are pronounced very similar to most words in English, but with much more strict rules. It most cases with Latin or Latinised words, a letter makes one sound.

Consonants

B, D, F, H, L, M, N, P, Q, R, S, T are pronounced exactly as they are in modern usage. Ch is always a hard Ch like chemistry, not soft like cheese.

C and G are frequently interchangeable. C always makes the "Hard C" K sound. Later on the G takes on more of a personality of its own, but the names Gaius and Caius are pretty much alternate spellings, at least until Greek's gamma becomes popular.

The letters K, X, Y, Z are stolen from Greek and may not be in common usage depending on the time period you are in. X at first was sort of a placeholder when the right letter wasn't in Latin before becoming a standard equivalent for the Greek Ξ (Xi)[1].

Vowels

A is nearly always a long A sound, like in father.

E makes the short E sound, like hey.

I does double duty. It usually makes the sound of a double-e, like in machine. It is sometimes coupled with O to make the dipthong Io, which if you say a sliding ee-oh it sounds very much like "Yo". I also replaces J, which didn't really exist yet.[2]

---

[1] Not to be confused with the Greek X (Chi, pronounced Kai) which makes the K sound, but the Romans had one of those in C.

O is a long open O, like flow.

U makes the double-o sound, like crude. V and U are the same letter originally, the U being cross-polinated from Greek's υ (upsilon). At the beginning of a word, V makes something of a W sound, which is what you produce when you make a lazy sliding dipthong like "oo-ah". So words like *Vale* are pronounced Wall-eh, and *Veni, Vidi, Vici* is "Way-nee, Wee-dee, Wee-kee"

Y is used for "borrowed" Greek words, it's known to the Romans as *I Graeca*, the Greek I, seen mostly in words like *gymnasium*.

Dipthongs
Latin has a few dipthongs which is when letters combine to make slightly different sounds, and not small bathing suits used for quick swims.
ae   as in kite
au   as in ow
ei   as in hey
oe   as in oil
ui   as in Ooooooooey, y'll make some mighty fine gumbo!

There are rules on which syllable to place the emphasis, but they involve words like "antepaenultima". Suffice it to say that you'll pick it up pretty quickly from the locals. We'd recommend you pronounce everything flat and even until someone corrects you.

English	Latin	Pronunciation
Thank you	gratias tibi ago	gra-tea-as ti-bi ah-go
Please	amabo te	ah-mah-bo te
Hello (hello all)	salve/salvete	sall-way(-tay)
Goodbye (bye all)	vale/valete	wa-lay(-tay)
Yes	ita vero	ee-ta we-row
No	Non	non
I am	Sum	sum
Are you going to...?	isne...?	ees-nay
Where is...?	ubi est...	ooh-be est
The road to...	via ad...	wee-ah ad

---

[2] As remembered almost too late by one Dr. Jones, in the Latin alphabet, Jehovah starts with an I.

The latrine	latrina	la-tree-na
The tavern	taberna	ta-bear-na
The theater	theatrum	thay-ah-troom
The amphitheater	amphitheatrum	am-fee-thay-ah-troom
The baths	thermas	ther-mas
The circus	circus	kir-coos
I would like…	volo…	woah-low
to eat	esse, cenare	ehs-seh, ken-ar-eh
a room	cubiculum	coo-bi-coo-loom
How much?	quantum?	kwan-toom
When?	quando?	kwan-dough
Left	sinistrosum	si-nis-tro-soom
Right	dextrosum	dex-stro-soom
Straight ahead	prorsum	proar-soom
Yesterday	heri	Hay-ree
Today	hodie	ho-di-eh
Tomorrow	cras	cras
1	I unus, una, unum	oo-nus
2	II duo, duae, duo	doo-o, doo-eye
3	III tres, tria	trace, tree-ah
4	IV quattuor	kwat-tour
5	V quinque	kwin-kway
6	VI sex	sex…
7	VII septem	sep-tem
8	VIII octo	oc-toe
9	IV novem	no-wem
10	X decem	deh-kem
11	XI undecim	oon-deh-kim
12	XII duodecim	doo-o-deh-kim
13	XIII tredecim	tray-deh-kim
14	XIV quattuordecim	kwat-tour-deh-kim
15	XV quindecim	kwin-deh-kim
16	XVI sedecim	say-deh-kim
17	XVII septendecim	sep-ten-deh-kim
18	XVIII duodeviginti	doo-o-de-we-gin-tee
19	XIX undeviginit	oon-deh-we-gin-tee
20	XX viginti	we-gin-tee
30	XXX triginta	tree-gin-tah
40	XL quadraginta	kwah-drah-gin-tah
50	L quinquaginta	kwin-kwah-gin-tah

60	LX sexaginta	sec-sah-gin-tah
70	LXX septuaginta	sep-to-ah-gin-tah
80	LXXX octoginta	oc-toe-gin-tah
90	XC nonaginta	no-nah-gin-tah
100	C centum	ken-toom
1000	M mille	me-lay

Attic Greek

There are three primary kinds of Ancient Greek, the noble tongue of the Athenians, *Attic,* the exotic *Ionian,* and the country-bumpkin, *Doric.* The three are technically interchangeable, but unlike the Romans, the Greeks spelled their words based on how they were pronounced locally, and not how they were said in a central place like Roma. Their verbs also had six principle parts which charmingly follow no pattern whatsoever and really, it's no wonder why the Romans were able to overcome them, because the Greek sentries were probably spending 15-20 minutes arguing over which word they should use to tell people to flee.

Given that Greek used the Greek alphabet (for some reason), we've provided a brief explanation for how to pronounce the letters.

Consonants

β as in Beta
γ as in Gamma
δ as in Delta
ζ as in Zeta
θ as in Theta
κ as in Kappa
λ as in Lambda
μ as in Mu
ν as in Nu
ξ as in Xi
π as in Pi
ρ as in Rho
σ as in Sigma
τ as in Tau
φ as in Phi
χ as in Chi
ψ as in Psi

Vowels

α as in Alpha
ε as in Epsilon
η as in Eta
ι as in Iota (yota)
o as in Omnicron
υ as in Upsilon

ω as in Omega

Dipthongs
Greek also has dipthongs, namely:
αι as in high
αυ as in how
ευ Just pronounce them as one syllable
ηυ Also pronounce them as one syllable
οι as in foil
υι Bet you can't guess what to do here…

English	Attic Greek	Pronunciation
Thank you	χάριν ἀποδίδωμι	ka-rin ah-po-di-do-mee
Hello (hello all)	χαῖρε/χαίρετε	kai-re/kai-re-te
Goodbye	χαῖρε/χαίρετε	See above
No	μηδείς	may-deis
I am	εἰμί	eh-mee
Are you going to…?	βαίνεις ἐπί…;	bai-neis eh-pee
Where is…?	ποῦ ἐστί(ν)…;	poo ehs-te(n)
The road to…	ὁ ὁδός ἐπί…	ha ha-dos eh-pee
The tavern	τό οἰνοπώλιον	ta oi-no-po-lee-on
The theater	τό θέατρον	ta thay-ah-tron
The stadium	τό στάδιον	ta stay-dee-on
The hippodrome	ὁ ἱππόδρομος	ho hip-po-dro-mos
I would like…	βούλομαι…	boo-lo-mai
To eat	ἐσθίειν	es-thain
How much?	πόσος;	po-sos
When?	πότε;	po-te
Left	ἀριστερά	ah-ris-tay-rah
Right	δεξιά	deyk-si-ah
Yesterday	χθές	kthes
Today	σήμερον	se-mey-ron
Tomorrow	αὔριον	ow-ri-on
1	εἷς, μία, ἕν	ees, mee-a, ain
2	δύο	doo-oh
3	τρεῖς, τρία	trais, tree-ah
4	τέτταρες, τέτταρα	tet-tah-res
5	πέντε	pen-te
6	ἕξ	hex
7	ἑπτά	hep-ta
8	ὀκτώ	ahk-to

9	ἐννέα	en-nay-a
10	δέκα	de-ka
11	ἔνδεκα	en-de-ka
12	δώδεκα	do-de-ka
13	τρεῖς (τρία) καὶ δέκα	trais kai de-ka
14	τέτταρες (τέτταρα) καὶ δέκα	tet-tah-res kai de-ka
15	πεντεκαίδεκα	pen-te-kai-de-ka
16	ἑκκαίδεκα	hek-kai-de-ka
17	ἑπτακαίδεκα	hep-ta-kai-de-ka
18	ὀκτωκαίδεκα	ahk-to-kai-de-ka
19	ἐννεακαιδεκα	en-ne-a-kai-de-ka
20	εἴκοσι(ν)	ei-kow-se(n)
30	τριάκοντα	tree-a-kon-ta
40	τετταράκοντα	tet-ta-ra-kon-ta
50	πεντήκοντα	pen-tay-kon-ta
60	ἑξήκοντα	hex-eh-kon-ta
70	ἑβδομήκοντα	heb-do-me-kon-ta
80	ὀγδοήκοντα	og-do-eh-kon-ta
90	ἐνενήκοντα	en-en-eh-kon-ta
100	ἑκατόν	ek-a-ton
1000	χίλιοι	kee-lee-oy

Index

Here we list many prominent historical and mythical individuals, as well as the names of towns and landmarks listed in this book. Useful items like the *sarcina* are listed based off of where their usage is described.

You will not find the names of provinces or Rome listed here, for those you should see the table of contents. There are also far too many Gods and temples to list, as well as minor facilities such as baths and forums, so you should look to the list of gods for a more comprehensive list. We also do not list any person mentioned as Augustus, Iulius, or Caesar, because there are several. Find them listed in Chapter XVI- Who Rules When.

A note about accuracy

While this book is intended as a parody, and probably shouldn't be taken as a source for anything serious, we have done our best to deliver the most accurate information. Materials used include Perseus-Tufts list of Greek and Roman materials compiled by the Princeton Encyclopedia of Classical Sites, books used for the author's undergraduate degree, and bits and pieces of research about Roman culture compiled either as a student or as a teacher.

Some things, such as whether an individual city may have had a bath or not may still up for speculation, but we typically included whatever was mentioned by ancient sources or has been found through archaeology. We used online mapping tools to verify the locations of landmarks where possible, plotted every city mentioned in the book, and mapped the approximate boundaries of every province mentioned in order to calculate the square mileage.

From what can be determined, the boundaries of provinces, regions of Italy and regions of Rome itself are not super well-defined. We found ourselves agonizing back and forth about whether to include the northern Alps in Raetia or Italia, but Italia has over 200 cities mentioned, so it's not like they'll miss the few "given" to the province. If someone can give a definitive answer, we'll be happy to update in previous editions.

References to pop culture, film, textbooks, etc. will hopefully not be taken too seriously but only as the Easter eggs which they are intended to be.

About the Author

Colin John Parry is a middle school Latin teacher in Phoenix, Arizona. He lives with his wife Merissa, daughter Raelynn, hedgehog Willow and three dogs, Nox, Tiber and Kora. He obtained his bachelor's in Classical Languages from the University of Iowa. In his spare time he enjoys movies, books, writing, drawling comics, and reading Caesar's Gallic Wars to his daughter.

About the Editor

Clint Michael Parry decided to pursue a Bachelor of Arts in English from Cornell College in Mount Vernon, Iowa after reading an excerpt fom <u>Dave Barry Slept Here</u> in a Houghton-Mifflin reader. He also can thank Cornell's John Gruber-Miller for inciting an interest in the classics, though Clint has studied them nowhere near as diligently as his younger brother.
He lives near Detroit, Michigan with his wife Amanda. His day job is as the Master Builder at LEGOLAND Discovery Center Michigan.

71262770R00148